John Turner

John Turner
The Long Run

by Jack Cahill

McClelland and Stewart

McClelland and Stewart Limited
The Canadian Publishers
25 Hollinger Road
Toronto, Ontario
M4B 3G2

Canadian Cataloguing in Publication Data

Cahill, Jack
John Turner

ISBN 0-7710-1872-X

1. Turner, John N., 1929–   2. Politicians –
Canada – Biography. 3. Cabinet ministers –
Canada – Biography. 4. Canada – Politics and
government – 1963–   *I. Title

FC626.T87C32 1984   971.064′4′0924   C84-098993-8
F1034.3.T87C32 1984

Printed and bound in Canada

Contents

Introduction

The new information era we live in is a ghostly world of images rather than realities. Politicians are elected and prime ministers attain their tremendous power because they have nice blue eyes, or strong-looking chins, or are able to exude on the screen a charisma and confidence while reading a script somebody else wrote. Or they fail to gain power or lose it because they stutter or stammer, or can't kick a football, or walk unusually, or eat a banana when the cameras are watching.

In these strange and dangerous circumstances personalities have become more important in attaining and maintaining power than policies and philosophies, so that people are now likely to elect men and women to the most powerful positions in the world for the shallowest of reasons, often without really knowing anything about them. And they give to these unknown persons power to preserve peace, freedom, and dignity in the world or to preside over the end of it.

In these circumstances the duty of the print journalist is to try to find and explain the realities behind the images. This is why this biography of John Turner, which is also a story about power, has been written.

To most Canadians at the start of the recent Liberal leadership campaign, Turner was no more than an image, a good-looking man who seemed sincere on the screen, affable in public, skilled in politics, and who for some mysterious reason had been regarded as a future prime minister of Canada almost since the moment he entered Parliament in 1962. Remarkably, this image had persisted and even strengthened in the more than eight years since Turner officially abandoned politics in 1976, following a bitter argument with Prime Minister Pierre Trudeau, to become a private citizen and successful corporate lawyer in Toronto.

Yet at the beginning of 1984 few people really knew Turner and what he stood for. He was supposed to be somewhere right of centre of Liberal Party philosophy, but even his closest friends weren't quite sure why this was. He had been described by Canadian economic nationalists as a continentalist, overly anxious to co-operate with the United States in trade and business affairs and thus reduce Canada to the status of a puppet state or colony, but evidence to support this part of the image was also scarce.

Turner has purposely and carefully kept his family affairs separate from his public life, so that few know what kind of man he is personally.

I first met him in the early sixties when I was Ottawa bureau chief for the *Vancouver Sun*. He was a backbencher then, but it could not be said that he was an ordinary backbencher. Somehow, even then, there was this aura of prospective greatness about the handsome young man with the piercing blue eyes who sat in the third row of the Commons, four seats to the left of Prime Minister Lester Pearson. Everybody expected him to become a cabinet minister and almost everybody seemed to like him, even most opposition members, including John Diefenbaker, the acerbic Opposition Leader, who regarded all other Liberals as some lower form of life.

In the early 1970's, when I was Ottawa bureau chief for *The Toronto Star* and Turner was Justice Minister, I came to know him fairly well, as most senior journalists did, both as a contact and as a friendly acquaintance. Frequently, when other cabinet ministers were lunching in the opulent Parliamentary Restaurant or the expensive Chateau Grill, Turner and I would lunch at his favourite haunt, the old Belvedere Hotel on Albert Street, where the members of the Ottawa Rough Riders football team hung out and which turned itself into a cheap jazz joint at night.

Turner liked the jock atmosphere of this place and probably liked the bills, which we always shared, because he was not a rich man. Our lunch was usually a hamburger and a beer, which cost about $1.50 for each of us. He would talk political philosophy and personalities with a surprising frankness for a cabinet minister, but never once, as far as I can remember, did he tip me to an actual story, and certainly not to a cabinet secret.

He was still Justice Minister when I was posted by *The Toronto Star* in 1973 as foreign correspondent covering Asia. I was thus concerned with other affairs during the height of his political career as Finance Minister and his angry exit from the Ottawa scene.

But shortly before I left for my new base in Hong Kong I asked *The Star*'s Ottawa bureau staff to help put together a story that would show who held most power, political and otherwise, in Canada. To do this we simply asked selected groups of politicians to list in order the most powerful politicians, and civil servants to list the most powerful mandarins, and top businessmen to list the most powerful among them, and we also asked each group about the other groups. Then we awarded points according to the answers.

It was, of course, entirely unscientific, but nevertheless a valid indicator, and the results surprised us in the bureau and caused some raised eyebrows among our editors in Toronto. The poll showed, as expected, that Trudeau was the most powerful man in Canada. But John Turner, who was not then considered by us or the public as a very high-profile politician, was second and not all that far behind Trudeau in the point score.

None of us in the bureau could quite understand why this was. We would have chosen Allan MacEachen, or Mitchell Sharp, or Paul Martin, or one of the other old pros who had been around Ottawa much longer and knew the power game so intimately. But there was no doubt that Turner was the choice of his peers not just as the second most powerful politician in the land, but also the second most powerful person, and we had to go along with that in the story despite our journalistic scepticism.

Turner had been out of politics and was practising law profitably in Toronto when I came back to Canada in 1977. But for some mysterious reason there was still this aura of political power about him. People were still predicting, despite his public disclaimers, that he would one day be Canada's prime minister. His name still appeared occasionally in the public print. His advice was sought by many Liberals despite an antagonism among others because of his departure from the Trudeau government when it was suffering tough times. Much more scientific polls than the one we had taken in Ottawa in 1973 showed he was still a great power in the land and even a possible saviour of the ailing Liberal Party if he became leader. Almost any other politician who abandoned Ottawa to pursue a private career would have soon been forgotten. Turner wasn't.

Thus it was that I decided about two years ago to write this book. When I put the idea to Turner at the time, at one of our occasional lunches in Toronto, his reaction was at first startlingly but, I thought, genuinely modest. He asked: "Who, for God's sake, would want to read a book about me?"

This originally negative attitude to the idea changed gradually, however, under pressures from me and as the Canadian political situation changed, tempting Turner toward a return to public life. Finally he agreed to co-operate as fully as possible: by retrieving documents he had stored in the public archives, by helping with contacts and pictures, and by submitting himself to a series of tape recorded interviews which extended over twenty hours.

We agreed that the relationship in these interviews would be a normal one between politician and journalist, but that it would be necessary for me to ask questions of a more personal nature than usual. Turner did not object to this nor did he place any topics off limits. He did at times stress some facets of his life he wanted included, for instance his religious beliefs and love of the outdoors. But in general he allowed me to control the direction of our talks and he seemed to enjoy them.

I did not approach this book as an adversary or analyst or commentator, but rather as a reporter anxious to elicit facts so that readers could make their own assessments of John Turner, the man, rather than the image.

Jack Cahill
Toronto
July 1, 1984

1

Campaign '68:
The Start of Madness

T he ultimate power was up for grabs and there was a madness in Canadian politics.

Prime Minister Lester Bowles Pearson released his grip on the power on December 14, 1967, and went back to global affairs, his first love, as chairman of a World Bank commission on Third World problems. The little man with the lisp and perpetual bow tie had been Canada's most popular and best known civil servant, a Nobel Peace Prize winner and then Prime Minister for four tumultuous and difficult years.

His minority governments in the mid-1960's had brought a new national pride to the vast and diverse country, with a maple leaf flag its symbol and Montreal's Expo '67 a highly successful expression of hope for the future of the 100-year-old nation. The Pearson regime was beset by small scandals and constantly was in danger of falling. Nevertheless, it had begun to appease Quebec with a bilingual federal civil service and had transformed the country into a compassionate but costly welfare state.

Politically, Pearson's governments had been split internally between the forces of economic nationalism and continentalism. His casual cabinet was so leaky of its secrets that once when he sternly warned a cabinet meeting that no further leaks would be tolerated, the story of the warning appeared in the press within hours.

Canada was innocent then. It did not enter the harsh, real world until the Quebec Crisis of 1970, long after Pearson was gone, when suddenly armed soldiers were prowling the pavement under the Peace Tower and even in the corridors of Parliament, turning Ottawa, if only briefly, into a capital like too many others. But in those earlier good days, Pearson would invite reporters for a casual drink in the evenings on the back porch of 24 Sussex Drive and chat frankly and informally about such things as Canada's secret diplomatic peace moves in Hanoi, or he would show a set of pictures of proposed new Canadian flags to get a reaction before he made his own choice.

The prime ministerial mansion was a fairly simple place then, with homely furniture and no swimming pool, and Pearson, who was not a rich man, had to pay part of the costs of running his ordinary, and of course unarmoured, black Buick and for the uniform of his part-time chauffeur. The exercise of power was so casual that often in the evenings after dinner at 24 Sussex the Prime Minister would drive himself back to work in the Parliament Buildings in his wife's rusting and slightly battered 1962 Rambler, which frequently refused to start in the cold of the late winter evenings. When he wanted to go home again the Prime Minister would stand rather pathetically on Parliament Hill attempting to hitch a ride with anybody going his way, usually an executive assistant or journalist. Then in the driveway of his home he would apologize for not asking his benefactor in because of the late hour. But he would stand there chatting about baseball, or sometimes politics, fussing aloud and at length about whether he had taken the executive assistant or reporter out of his way and whether he knew his way home, quietly cursing all the time "that damn car of Maryon's."

Visiting American reporters, accustomed to the tight security around their leaders, would at first be appalled, then amazed, then delighted about this Canadian difference. Pearson handled the power in Canada in this casual way in these comparatively happy economic times and his rule was marked mainly by his good humour, enormous diplomatic skill, and love of a country that was changing.

But constantly in the Commons he had to face the shaking jowls and clever and constant vitriol of John G. Diefenbaker, an indecisive prime minister before Pearson but one of democratic history's great opposition leaders after his defeat in 1963. Diefenbaker was also one of the few Canadians who personally hated Pearson, and this hate had permeated Parliament, making it an unpleasant place.

So now the diplomatic and cheerful Pearson, with his inborn distaste of nastiness, was tired and, at seventy, growing old. He called a press conference at 12:30 p.m. in the National Press Building on a cold December 14 and stunned the national press corps with a quiet and unemotional reading of his letter of resignation to Liberal Party President Senator John Nichol.

Pearson chose that day in typical Pearsonian fashion. The previous day had been his wife Maryon's birthday and he wanted to give her the present she had wanted for years. Maryon had struggled to play her role well on the hustings and in the corridors of power, but she did not like politics at all and it showed. Once on a campaign tour involving the usual succession of coffee and donut parties in town after town Pearson asked at the end of a question period if there was anything else anybody wanted to bring up. Maryon, on the platform beside him, was heard by all to announce: "Yes, that last cup of coffee."

Pearson had held a small family party for Maryon's birthday the previous evening and made her happy with his news. And when he left the press conference after his public announcement, he raised his hands slightly and remarked with typical casualness: "Well, c'est la vie."

It was the signal for the start of the madness. Nine men, all able, most politically experienced and ambitious, grasped at the power like gymnasts jumping at once for the ring on which only one could eventually perform. They bumped and scratched and clawed and some fell badly and some were bruised. Within eight years all but two would be dead or out of politics.

Eric Kierans, erudite, forward-looking, and left-wing, was first to make the leap, declaring at a nationally televised press conference on January 9 that he was running because it was time for a new generation to guide Canada's destiny. Transport Minister Paul Hellyer, tall, young (forty-four), although silver-haired and experienced, was next on January 11, describing himself as one of the "genuine reformers of the Liberal Party." Allan MacEachen, left-leaning, quiet but politically brilliant, declared his candidacy the following day.

Then on January 17, Consumer and Corporate Affairs Minister John Turner, popular and pragmatic, a little to the left of the political spectrum, became the youngest candidate. He was thirty-eight and he apologized for his comparative youth by declaring that "the profession of politics has to recognize there are generation gaps today. Men of my age are being appointed to senior positions in business and labour. The men who appoint them are looking not at their age, but at their judgement and potential."

Two days later Paul Martin, the experienced, left-leaning old pro, Finance Minister Mitchell Sharp, right-wing continentalist, and Agriculture Minister Joe Greene, nationalist, who looked like young Abe Lincoln and spoke more eloquently, jumped for the ring.

The only surprise was that Minister of Trade and Commerce Robert Winters, the choice of far right-wing business, did not join them. Despite strong pressures from business circles he announced that he would not be a candidate and that he would resign his portfolio at the end of March. Winters didn't like the undignified nature of the campaign.

"In business when you want a man for an important job," he

said, "you turn to the man you want, not the job seekers. The job should seek the man, not vice versa . . . . I can't recall other leadership conventions in which the candidates have been called on to debate public issues during the course of the campaign. And I can't imagine any businessman accepting the chairmanship of a board that was so divided." But he did not rule out the possibility of a draft. Winters' worries about indignities and party problems were not unfounded. After all, this was not just a campaign for the party leadership but for the prime ministership, as the next campaign in 1984 was also to be. The seven early candidates, joined by Lloyd Henderson, a "nuisance candidate" with no chance at all, clashed on policy issues, indulged in angry exchanges at all-candidates meetings, and created an image of a party so seriously split it could not possibly govern. The situation prompted Mitchell Sharp to wonder aloud at one stage "whether we'll still have a party when this is over."

According to most political observers Sharp, Hellyer, and Martin were the frontrunners at this early stage of the campaign. But Dalton Camp, the politically astute national president of the Conservative Party, was giving even money on Turner and Sharp, five to one on Martin, ten to one on Hellyer, and thirty to one on Winters if he chose to run.

The candidates criss-crossed the country in begged, borrowed, and chartered planes, from sleek executive jets loaned by big corporations to unpressurized Cessnas and ancient pre-World War Two de Havilland Doves, which sometimes managed to fly hardly faster than the headwinds.

One day on the Hellyer campaign was typical of some. From five in the morning until after midnight he flew with his stately wife, Ellen, and three journalists in a borrowed four-seater Cessna across the vast Prairies, from Winnipeg to Edmonton, to Medicine Hat and little towns in between where there were only one or two delegates to influence, his face lighting with pleasure as he saw crowds at airstrips waving banners, then sometimes suddenly darkening in disappointment as he realized they were supporters of other candidates on the same campaign circuit.

The weather was terrible, forcing the tiny unpressurized plane to fly bumpily at cold, unsafe, and uncomfortable altitudes over 15,000 feet. There was no food on board and no time for meals on the ground. By about 8 p.m., when the Cessna was warming up at Medicine Hat for a final hopscotch flight to Ottawa, everybody, including Ellen Hellyer, was both ravenous and weary. Mercifully, Hellyer ordered a delay in the take-off while the pilot phoned a local motel for sandwiches, which were eventually delivered by a small, panting boy bearing a big cardboard carton packed with piles of plain cheese on brown bread, which looked delicious. But the boy was followed by the motel owner, who berated him loudly and angrily for preparing such plain fare for such Very Important People, one of whom might be the prime minister of the country within a few weeks, and he sent the boy back to the motel to do better.

The next delivery arrived on the boy's shoulders in a sealed cardboard carton and we took off hurriedly without opening it because the pilot was anxious about the weather and we had to immediately bump our way through awful, stomach-churning turbulence, with no oxygen, up to 15,000 feet again, where the bumps modified a bit.

Peter Thompson, the *Toronto Telegram*'s Ottawa bureau chief, who was occupying the co-pilot's seat in the four-seater, was sick on the instrument panel and both of his eardrums punctured, so that his face was covered in blood and vomit. Tony Westell, the *Globe and Mail*'s Ottawa bureau chief, and Ellen Hellyer had turned a pale shade of green. Hellyer didn't look well himself but still attempted to display his leadership qualities by cheerfully opening the box of sandwiches. They were fried oyster sandwiches, presumably because the unfortunate boy on the ground had observed Very Important People eating fried oysters. The oil had permeated the bread, making an ugly, soggy, and smelly mess, which began to spread over the cabin floor from the bottom of the box.

It was all too much, even for Hellyer. For the first time on the campaign, which he believed he was leading at that time, he became discouraged, even humble. He glanced lovingly at his airsick wife and asked the rest of us to try to stand in the centre of the cabin and shake his hand ceremoniously. "I want to solemnly swear to Ellen, with you gentlemen as witnesses, that if I do not become prime minister I will get out of politics immediately and forever," he said, holding our hands in his. "It's just not worthwhile."

But, of course, Hellyer didn't shake himself of the political disease. He started his own political movement and later became a Conservative. Sixteen years later he was tempted to run in the next Liberal leadership campaign.

Joe Greene's low point came when his chartered Beechcraft crashed on take-off from a rich farmer's private airstrip at Woodstock, Ontario, its wings weighed down by an unseasonable wet snowfall. The plane got fifty feet off the ground twice, then plunged to earth again, crashed through two fences, and hurtled across two farmers' fields, bumping against the grain of recently ploughed ruts until it tipped on its nose.

Greene, his campaign manager, Dan Murphy, and Ron Lowman,

a *Toronto Star* reporter, who were the plane's only passengers, made their way back to the farmer's mansion. Both Greene and Lowman had won the Distinguished Flying Cross and had been mentioned in dispatches in World War Two. They calmly played snooker in the farmer's basement until a car arrived to take them to Greene's next speaking engagement in Kitchener, where they arrived only a few minutes late.

But John Turner's campaign was uneventful. It was well organized by a group of young reformers, including campaign chairman Jerry Grafstein and David Smith from Ontario, Yves Fortier, Jim Robb, and John Claxton from Quebec, Lloyd Axworthy, aided by his brother Tom, from Manitoba, and Dick Hayes from British Columbia. They were backed by some old pros, including Senator Dan Lang of Toronto, John deB. Payne of Montreal, and Jimmy Sinclair of Vancouver, the former Fisheries Minister and father of Margaret Trudeau. There were only three sitting members on the Turner team, John Addison, Joe Macaluso, and Ron Basford.

"We were mostly young activists, long on policy and reforms, but we recognized that we also had to organize," says Grafstein, now a senator. "We decided it would be a classic campaign, but we would try to do it in a graceful way. We promised a 'new era' in Liberalism and aimed the campaign at the youth and minority groups. Turner told us right at the start that he would be sticking in to the very end, that he'd be going the full route, right to the end of the convention, and that we weren't on board for half a ride, that it would be a good, fair, all-the-way fight."

The campaign was, in fact, smoothly run by the young reformers and not costly in terms of the up to $1.6 million spent on similar campaigns in 1984. The entire budget for Turner's 1968 campaign was $128,000 and that was exactly what it cost. And it was one of the few campaigns in which the press was invited to cover talks with the delegates.

Turner did not disappoint his ideological young backers. He emerged in the campaign as a progressive, and an idealist. He eloquently explained his brand of liberalism in one of his speeches, which was condensed in his campaign book, *Politics of Purpose*: "Liberalism is not a dogma but an attitude of mind, and it is a state of mind that distinguishes the liberal from the conservative."

Then he quoted the English historian, Macaulay: " 'Everywhere there is a class of men who cling with fondness to whatever is ancient and who, even when convinced by overpowering reasons that innovation would be beneficial, consent to it with many misgivings and forebodings. We find also everywhere another class of man sanguine in hope, bold in speculation, always pressing forward, quick to discern the imperfection of whatever exists, disposed to think lightly of the risks and inconveniences which attend improvements, and disposed to give every change credit for being an improvement.'

"The former," Turner proclaimed, "are the conservatives; the latter are the liberals. What separates liberalism from conservatism is a difference in the flexibility of the human spirit. The conservative is suspicious of change; he adopts it reluctantly; he moves with an instinctive caution; and if he could, he would leave things the way they are – with improvements at times, perhaps, but basically the way they are.

"A liberal, on the other hand," said Turner, "is a reformer. He has the zeal of reform; he is impatient with the imperfections of today and looks forward – eagerly – to a better tomorrow. This being so, the liberal has an openness of mind, a willingness to experiment.

"And make no mistake about it," he told the 1968 campaign delegates, "this difference exists today in Canada between the Liberal Party and the Conservative Party. They can copy our program, but they can never steal our spirit."

Then he quoted Sir Wilfrid Laurier: " 'I am a Liberal. I am one of those who think that everywhere, in human beings, there are abuses to be reformed, new horizons to be opened up, and new forces to be developed.'

"A liberal is interested in people, not property," said Turner. "He is concerned with the personality of politics. He seeks the fulfilment of the aspirations of the individual in society . . . .

"A liberal must be tolerant, because liberalism rests on faith in man and on the recognition of the worth and dignity of every individual. Indeed, is not faith in one's fellow man the very basis of democracy? Unless we believe that in most circumstances, over a period of time, the people, in their good, collective common sense, usually arrive at the right conclusion – unless we believe that – we do not believe in democracy.

"But we, as liberals, must not consider ourselves wiser than the people, because we are not," he added. "The people are entitled to know what we mean . . . . The art of politics is, after all, the guiding, directing, and controlling of the aspirations of human nature. A political party must be willing to undertake the risk of leadership and thereby the risk of defeat. We must take our chances with the people."

He plugged, during his campaign, a need for the Liberal Party to seek a new approach, not only in policy but in method, and he urged that the priorities of this new approach be applied first to economic growth and full employment through new econo... ning, secondly to seeking a new freedom for the individual in society, and then to a new federalism and a new national unity.

By economic planning he said he did not mean socialist planning, whereby the instruments of production, investment, and distribution would be absorbed by the state. "I mean, rather, an economy whose direction is charted by government with the advice and with the free co-operation of management, labour, farmers, and other economic groups so that long-term and short-term goals can be set for this country.

"It's as simple as that," he told the delegates. "As a country we must decide where we want to go and what we want to accomplish. We set goals and we next decide how we are going to achieve them. We choose a method. Finally we decide what we need to use to get there. We find the resources, the material. This is planning."

In his call for new freedom he demanded better protection of the individual against bureaucracy, including appointment of an ombudsman, and reform of the structure of government to make it more responsive to the individual concerns of citizens. And in his call for a new federalism, he said: "Let us not underestimate the importance of language, the medium of personal communication. In order to bridge the psychological gap between the two elements in our country, we must overcome the problem of language and promote a true bilingualism at the federal level.

"I do not mean that we must achieve a bilingualism right across the country. That is obviously impractical. In Toronto, not everyone learns French, and if one does, it is not of necessity but as a cultural advantage. No Act of Parliament is going to change this.

"What I do mean is that wherever in Canada there are substantial numbers of French-speaking Canadians, the federal aspects of our national life ought to be open to them with all possible speed in their own language. Only in this way will French Canada turn back to Ottawa."

The young ideologues of his team loved him, and at this stage of the campaign they thought he could win. He was the candidate with the new ideas at a time when the country was optimistic and ready for adventure. He thought he could win himself, and as Jerry Grafstein put it, "he worked his butt off."

18

2

Enter Trudeau

The Liberals' concentration on the leadership campaign took its almost inevitable political toll on the evening of February 19. The House of Commons was half empty when Mitchell Sharp's important budget resolution imposing a 5 per cent surcharge on taxes was called for a third and final reading. Altogether forty-eight Liberals were absent from the House, mostly hustling delegates on the campaign trail. They included three leadership candidates, Paul Martin, Joe Greene, and John Turner, although Turner, unlike the other two, had arranged to be paired with a Conservative member so that his absence had no effect on the result. Prime Minister Pearson was holidaying in Jamaica. In these embarrassing circumstances the money bill was defeated by a vote of 84 to 82, a situation that would normally force a government to resign and call an election. The country was plunged into a major political crisis.

Pearson returned hurriedly to Ottawa the next day to try to salvage what he could from the wreckage of his government, stuttering and stammering his indignation. He immediately telephoned Opposition Leader Robert Stanfield and arranged for a twenty-four-hour adjournment of the House. And he met with a few selected cabinet ministers, including John Turner, in Allan MacEachen's West Block office to try to find a way out of the disastrous situation. Eventually the wily Maritimer MacEachen came up with a solution – to move a motion declaring that "this House does not regard its vote on February 19 in connection with the third reading of Bill C-193, which it carried in all previous stages, as a vote of non-confidence in the government."

This carefully worded motion offered the splinter Creditiste Party, which was desperately afraid it would be decimated in an election, a chance to reverse itself and vote with the government. Thus, on February 28 the period of acute political uncertainty was ended by a vote of 138 to 119 and the Pearson government survived.

But the political bill had been paid. In the heat of the argument on the validity of the government motion, New Democratic Party Leader Tommy Douglas summed up: "This government is like a ship without a compass, without a chart and without a rudder. And last Monday night it was without a skipper. As a matter of fact while the skipper was off the bridge the crew was shooting craps over who was going to wear the captain's hat."

Just before this drama, however, the whole nature of the leadership derby had changed with the entry on February 16 of an unusual, politically inexperienced, but colourful intellectual from Quebec named Pierre Elliott Trudeau. He was not well known outside Quebec and had no real roots in the Liberal Party although he had been an MP since 1965, when he arrived in the capital as one of the "three wise men" from Quebec along with Jean Marchand and Gerard Pelletier. He had been Justice Minister for almost a year.

Trudeau had attracted some attention in Ottawa, however, because of his dashing bachelor image, his love of fast sports cars and beautiful women, and his occasionally unusual attire. He had been criticized by Diefenbaker for wearing an ascot and sandals in the House and once he turned up at the Privy Council Office on a Saturday dressed in desert boots and a boiler suit – the commissionaire turned him away, convinced that he was a plumber at the wrong address.

He had made some impact as Justice Minister with progressive reforms of the Criminal Code, several impressive speeches in the Commons, and an aggressive defence of federalism at a constitutional conference, but still he was regarded as an eccentric intellectual. Suggestions early in the campaign that he might run for the country's top office were treated by long-time Liberals as a bit of a joke. Trudeau didn't want the job anyway. He was having enough trouble trying to make the difficult adjustment between the intellectual's search for truth and the politician's exercise of power.

But on the very day of his resignation Pearson had summoned Trudeau and Marchand, who was Pearson's Quebec lieutenant, to 24 Sussex Drive and insisted one of them must attempt to succeed him because of the tradition that English-speaking and French-speaking prime ministers alternated. "This is a tradition of the Liberal Party," Pearson told the two French Canadians. "And he may or may not win. But he must be a good candidate and get a lot of votes, and we must show that although the Tories can't, we can always come up with an alternative from Quebec."

Both Marchand and Trudeau promised to give the idea some serious consideration and Marchand went off to Miami to contemplate while Trudeau took a holiday in Tahiti. Marchand decided definitely against running, mainly because of his health, his poor English, the fact that his wife was reluctant to move to Ottawa, and a belief that his almost certain defeat would be a blow to national unity, and so on January 13 at a dinner attended by Marchand, Pelletier, and Trudeau in Montreal, Marchand told Trudeau it would have to be him.

According to Pelletier, Trudeau was startled. "He had always felt it should be Marchand . . . . There was silence," Pelletier recalled. "Then Trudeau said, 'I agree a French Canadian should run. And I won't say no. But I'll have to consider the thing.' " Five days later when the "three wise men" met again in Montreal, Trudeau still expressed reservations about his candidacy, including his lack of political experience, his reputation as an intransigent intellectual, and opposition to his constitutional ideas in Quebec.

In the meantime, however, "Trudeaumania" was sweeping across the country. It started at the annual meeting of the Ontario Liberal Party early in February when delegates carried him through the meeting hall on their shoulders and pretty young girls in mini-skirts squealed at the sight of him. Almost everywhere he went after that he was followed by television crews. Older women wanted to kiss or touch him and men wanted to shake his hand. Mostly he met this strange phenomenon with puzzlement and an embarrassed shrug.

Anecdotes about his interesting past circulated across the country: about his academic achievements at some of the world's best universities, his judo brown belt and acquaintance with yoga, his exploits as an underwater explorer and how he was once arrested by Arabs as an Israeli spy, his travels in China and the Soviet Union. And more important politically, how he had become the leading champion of federalism against nationalism in Quebec. Thus, to many English-speaking Canadians, he was a "tame" French Canadian who would "keep Quebec in its place" while fulfilling their image of the composite Canadian – a perfectly bilingual, charming, colourful, strong federalist who knew his way around the world, a Quebecer you could take a chance on at a time when, in all Waspish fairness, it was a Quebecer's turn at the top job.

Still Trudeau had not made up his mind and Pearson was worried that there would be no French Canadian in the campaign to succeed him. So in an attempt to bring matters to a head, Pearson called Marchand to his Centre Block office on February 12, listened sympathetically to the reasons for his decision not to run, and agreed that Trudeau would have to. He called Trudeau to 24 Sussex Drive the next day and told him of their decision. He said he believed Trudeau to be capable of the prime ministership, but he also warned that he was frankly sceptical about the depth and strength of "Trudeaumania."

Trudeau came to a decision on February 15. He told Marchand and Pelletier over breakfast in the Parliamentary Restaurant that he would run. The next day he explained his decision before a battery of television cameras, press photographers, and almost 100 reporters. It was an unusual explanation: "If I try to assess what happened in the past two months, I have a suspicion that you people [the media] had a lot to do with it," he said. "If anybody's to blame I suppose it's you collectively. To be quite frank, if I try to analyse it, well I think in the subconscious mind of the press I think it started out like a huge practical joke on the Liberal Party. I mean that because, in some sense, the decision that I made this morning and last night is in some ways similar to that I arrived at when I entered the Liberal Party.

"It seemed to me, reading the press in the early stages a couple of months ago, it seemed to me as though many of you were saying, you know, 'We dare the Liberal Party to choose a guy like Trudeau. Of course, we know they never will, but we'll just dare them to do it and we'll show that this is the man they could have had as leader if they had wanted. Here's how great he is.'

"But you wouldn't have said that if you'd known that the Liberal Party or myself would have taken up the challenge. I don't want to read interpretation into your minds, but this is the way I saw events in the past month or month and a half. It was a good joke on the Liberal Party, and after somebody else had won – it would be a good man because they are all good men in the field – the press would sit back and the public would sit back and say, 'Oh well, you know they didn't have the guts to choose a good guy because the good guy in your hypothesis really wouldn't be running . . . . And what happened, I think, is that the joke blew up in your faces and mine . . . , I think that what happened is that the joke became serious, and I tried to analyse it, and as I say, it looks a bit like when I tried to enter the party. I didn't think the Liberal Party would take me and suddenly they did. So I was stuck with it. Well, now you're stuck with me."

Trudeau's entry into the race affected two of the earlier candidates more than the others. Although he was from Windsor, Ontario, Paul Martin, the cagey, aging old pro, had ancestral links with French Canada, was bilingual, and fully expected to be regarded by both English and French-speaking Canadians as the next best thing to an actual French Canadian and therefore to win the support of delegates all over the country who were anxious to follow the tradition of alternation. John Turner was also perfectly bilingual and his comparative youth created expectations of rejuvenation and adventure at a time when Canadians were ready for that kind of thing. Trudeau was ten years older than Turner but appeared, oddly, to be also youthful, even somehow to be younger than Turner, and he created similar expectations.

Winters finally decided to run on February 29, bowing to the pressures of a draft-Winters committee that sprang up in his native Nova Scotia and quickly spread to include powerful businessmen in Toronto and Winnipeg, who were convinced that the country's economic uncertainties put a premium on his experience and managerial abilities. Though he was the last into the race he was immediately declared one of the favourites. And he stole support from most of the others. But he had to rent a huge DC-9 jet, the only aircraft available, in order to join the aerial circus.

Despite the hundreds of thousands of miles travelled by the candidates, the campaign speeches were thin. After the early lively arguments that threatened to split the party, the rules of cabinet solidarity, under pressure from Pearson, began to prevail, preventing much deviation from the party line. By March most of the weary candidates were repeating the same old speeches for the third or fourth time.

Although the major newspapers assigned a man continually to each of the campaigns, hard news was sometimes so sparse that even Trudeau's innocence about his age made headlines. He said he was born on October 18, 1921, his brother was sure it was 1920, while his sister said it was really 1919. Trudeau didn't help matters much by admitting "it's somewhere around there." Then *Time* magazine came up with the big scoop by checking court and baptismal records and revealing to the world that Trudeau was born on October 18, 1919.

Paul Martin also made headlines when a well-meaning but confused boyhood companion introduced him at a meeting by proclaiming, "You don't need brains to be a prime minister."

And Trudeau got a laugh at a meeting in Three Rivers when somebody asked him about changes in the criminal code he had advocated as Justice Minister, allowing homosexuality by consenting adults in private. He replied easily to the effect that Canada was becoming a pluralistic society. Then an apparently sensible, well-dressed man asked: "What about masturbation?"

The good, churchgoing French-Canadian audience gasped, but Trudeau was unperturbed. "Well," he shrugged, "I suppose everyone has his problems."

By the end of the long campaign it was as dull as that, but the convention itself in Ottawa's hockey rink on April 6 and the preceding week in the capital provided enough excitement and intrigue to offset all of this earlier dreariness. There was a sudden twist in the plot when Mitchell Sharp folded his campaign and declared his support for Trudeau. Sharp's chances had dropped with the defeat of the tax bill in February and Winters' entry into the race. His campaign funds had dried up and polls showed his support was wavering so badly that he was clearly not going to win or even become a kingmaker in the balloting. So in the week of the convention he quit. But he still had his aura of solidity and legitimacy and he also brought to Trudeau his credentials as an orthodox Liberal, quieting the fears of some delegates afraid to support such an unorthodox man.

There were only 2,396 delegates and 795 alternates, mostly elected by party riding associations across the country, but Ottawa was also crowded by almost as many wives, girl friends, and hangers-on, plus a press corps of more than 1,000. The city was a crush and the conversation about nothing but politics.

1

2

PHOTO 1: Turner's British paternal grandparents, Maxwell and Florence Turner. His grandmother's maiden name was Wahl.

PHOTO 2: Turner's maternal grandmother, Mary Margaret Macdonald, of Mulgrave, Nova Scotia, who married miner Jim Gregory of Stellarton, Nova Scotia. They moved to Rossland, British Columbia, in 1896.

3

4

PHOTO 3: Turner's mother, Phyllis Gregory, as a child in Rossland.

PHOTO 4: Turner's mysterious father, Leonard, a gunsmith, shortly before he died in London in 1932.

PHOTO 5: John and Brenda Turner, Ottawa, about 1934.

PHOTO 6: John Turner, aged about twelve months, in London. (Nancie Foster)

5

PHOTO 7: The Turner family, John, Phyllis, and Brenda. Ottawa, 1937. (Karsh)

PHOTO 8: John Turner, seventeen, of the University of British Columbia, winning the Canadian Junior 100-yard sprint championship in Edmonton, 1947. Wally Alexander, of UBC, was second. (Robert Steiner)

PHOTO 9: The sprinter, at a U.S. college track meet, 1948.

PHOTO 10: John Turner, UBC student, age eighteen.

PHOTO 11: The bachelor lawyer, Montreal, 1959.

8

9

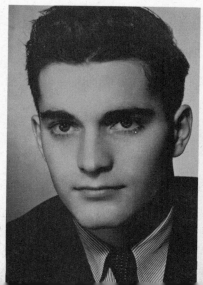

10

11

14

15

PHOTO 12: Turner's stepfather Frank Ross escorting Princess Margaret to ball at Vancouver's H.M.C.S. Discovery, July, 1958.

PHOTO 13: Turner's mother, Phyllis Turner Ross, Vancouver, 1970. (Gerald Campbell Studios)

PHOTO 14: The 1968 Liberal leadership convention. Geills and John Turner with son Michael. In the background, Phyllis Ross and Turner's sister, Brenda Norris.

PHOTO 15: The Turner family, on the Coppermine River, N.W.T., summer, 1982. (Geills M. Turner)

17

18

PHOTO 16: The canoeist, Burnside River, N.W.T., August, 1979. (Geills M. Turner)

PHOTO 17: The candidate, 1962 federal election. (O'Neil's Studios)

PHOTO 18: On the hustings with Lester B. Pearson, federal election, 1962. (Frank Tweel)

19

20

21

PHOTO 19: New Year's Eve, Tobago, 1963. Geills and John Turner, Olive, John, Elmer Diefenbaker. (Geills M. Turner)

PHOTO 20: On the beach at Tobago, January, 1964. The old pro and the young acolyte. (Geills M. Turner)

PHOTO 21: Prime Minister Lester B. Pearson welcomes new cabinet ministers Pierre Trudeau (Justice) and Jean Chretien (without Portfolio) after swearing in on April 4, 1967. John Turner was promoted from Minister without Portfolio to Registrar General.

PHOTO 22: The Turners, with Arthur Rubenstein, Montreal, 1967. (Allan R. Leishman)

PHOTO 23: Registrar General John Turner with Queen Elizabeth, July, 1967.

22

23

24

25

26

PHOTO 24: Awaiting the results of the final ballot. (Arnott Rogers)

PHOTO 25: Robert Winters pleads for Turner's support. The answer is "no." Turner remains in the race to the end. (Arnott Rogers)

PHOTO 26: The 1968 Liberal leadership convention. L to R: Brenda Norris, Phyllis Ross, Geills Turner, John Turner, Jerry Grafstein. (Arnott Rogers)

PHOTO 27: The Quebec Crisis, October, 1970. Turner introduces the War Measures Act in Ottawa. (Peter Bregg, Canadian Press)

28

29

Best Wishes John
Bill

30

31

32

33

34

35

PHOTO 28: With Indira Gandhi, Commonwealth Conference, New Delhi, January, 1971. (Canadian Press)

PHOTO 29: With Ontario Premier Bill Davis, the Winter Fair, Toronto, November, 1971.

PHOTO 30: With Alberta Premier Peter Lougheed, Federal-Provincial Conference, Ottawa, 1973. (*Calgary Herald*)

PHOTO 31: With Bobby Kennedy, New York City, 1968. (Henry Grossman)

PHOTO 32: With Prime Minister Pierre Trudeau, heading to the House of Commons to present his first budget on May 8, 1972. (Canadian Press)

PHOTO 33: With Deputy Finance Minister Simon Reisman, at a Parliamentary Committee on Finance, early 1970s.

PHOTO 34: With Queen Elizabeth, Ottawa, August, 1973. (Canadian Press)

PHOTO 35: With the Pope, Rome, January, 1971. (Pontifica Fotografia)

36

37

38

PHOTO 36: With Japanese Finance Minister (later Prime Minister) Masayoshi Ohira. International Monetary Fund meeting, Washington, 1974. (Canadian Press)

PHOTO 37: With U.S. Secretary of the Treasury William Simon, Washington, September, 1974.

PHOTO 38: Turner announces he won't run for the party leadership, Toronto, December 10, 1979. (*Toronto Star*)

PHOTO 39: Rusins cartoon, *Ottawa Citizen*, after Turner's resignation from the Commons in February, 1976.

PHOTO 40: Turner cleans out his office after resignation as Finance Minister in September, 1975. (Canadian Press)

40

I shall return

41

42

PHOTO 41: With German Chancellor Helmut Schmidt, Bonn, October, 1979.

PHOTO 42: With Australian Prime Minister Malcolm Fraser, Canberra, May, 1980.
(Geills M. Turner)

PHOTO 43: With Princess Margaret, Toronto, 1982. Twenty-four years after the first dance.

PHOTO 44: With Henry Kissinger, Montreal, May, 1983. (J.J. Randsepp)

43

45

47

48

49

PHOTO 45: Geills and John Turner arrive in Ottawa for the 1984 Liberal leadership convention. (Boris Spremo, *Toronto Star*)

PHOTO 46: The welcome at Ottawa Airport, 1984 convention. (Boris Spremo, *Toronto Star*)

PHOTO 47: Crisis as the convention. Don Johnston rejects Jean Chretien's plea for his support after the first ballot. (Doug Griffin, *Toronto Star*)

PHOTO 48: Mark MacGuigan brings his votes to Turner after the first ballot. (Boris Spremo, *Toronto Star*)

PHOTO 49: Turner and Chretien wish each other luck at the convention. (Boris Spremo, *Toronto Star*)

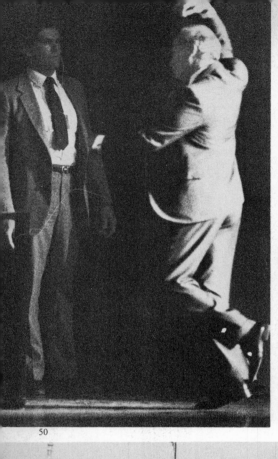

50

51

53

PHOTO 50: The final pirouette. Pierre Trudeau leaves the stage, and politics, after his convention farewell. (Ron Bell, *Toronto Star*)

PHOTO 51: The two different men. At the 1984 convention. (Murray Mosher, *Toronto Star*)

PHOTO 52: After the victory. The Turner family with Pierre Trudeau.

PHOTO 53: The moment of victory. John and Geills Turner. (Boris Spremo, *Toronto Star*)

PHOTO 54: Canada's seventeenth Prime Minister and the first lady acknowledge the cheers. (Boris Spremo, *Toronto Star*)

PHOTO 55: Two days after he becomes Prime Minister, John Turner is happy to be back in the House of Commons watching question period from the gallery. (Canadian Press)

54

55

3

The Club of 195

Ottawa was not big in 1968. There were only a few hotels. Hospitality suites were packed. So were policy workshops, which gave the candidates a chance to strut their serious stuff and show their differences.

The main workshop took place on the Thursday morning in three auditoriums so that the delegates could move from one to the other to hear the circulating candidates speak for twenty-five minutes on each of three subjects, "Our Life," "Our Country," and "Our Economy," a choice of topics that virtually allowed them to talk about anything at all.

The pundits said most of the candidates did well, but that John Turner was particularly good in the main auditorium. "Each of John Turner's sessions was packed with bright, eager, young supporters in their attractive pale yellow jackets and those strange white construction hats which made them look as if they were a huge construction crew come to look the property over," wrote Martin Sullivan in his book *Mandate '68*. "He did best in the main auditorium with a rock-jawed speech about Quebec, where the problems would not be solved by pure logic and intellect, 'but by the heart and gut – because that is what Canada is all about.' "

Trudeau also did well at these sessions, creeping into them, as Frank Walker, editor of the *Montreal Star*, put it, "like Jesus Christ." He was followed by large crowds wherever he went and he proposed, even then, policies that eventually came to pass, such as a Charter of Human Rights in Canada and recognition of Red China. He was still on a high roll, but his strategists admitted they were worried. Since Sharp's decision to go to Trudeau, they had detected a surging undercurrent for Turner and Winters.

Turner and his campaign chairman, Jerry Grafstein, were also concerned by deals aimed at stopping this anti-Trudeau surge. And Turner went on television to proclaim: "It disturbs me very much that what I hoped was going to be an open convention on Saturday is being taken away from many of us by deals that are being made behind closed doors." The outburst was criticized by some Liberals as cry-babyism, but there was also evidence that it helped polarize right-wing support for Turner and Winters against what many of the delegates regarded as a left-wing plot.

Lester Pearson made his farewell speech to the party on Thursday night and it was one of the best of his career, full of his usual wry wit, but also of pride in his achievements, especially in social welfare and the flag. He received thunderous applause from the sentimental crowd and a gift of a West Highland terrier puppy so that he could meet John Diefenbaker and his Labrador on equal terms as the two old adversaries strolled the streets of Ottawa's suburban Rockcliffe.

Then on the Friday night were the important wrap-up speeches, last chance for the candidates before the Saturday vote: the atmosphere in the hockey arena, packed with emotional, banner-waving supporters, was tense. Paul Martin was the first speaker, displaying no lack of confidence but full of clichés and partisan ploys. He was followed by Robert Winters, tall and distinguished. He delivered a speech that sounded like a board chairman's annual report. Then there was Joe Greene, tall and lanky, with an off-the-cuff speech full of sentimentality and humour, a wonderful performance that moistened the eyes of many and made all in the arena stand at the end and cheer themselves hoarse. It was easily the best speech of the evening and won Greene at least 100 extra votes in the first ballot next day, most of them Hellyer delegates.

Paul Hellyer made a dismal speech, written by two Toronto lawyers, which lost him support the next day, and Allan MacEachen, the authentic voice of the party's left wing, was eloquent, sincere, and ineffective. Eric Kierans followed, intelligent, impassioned, and courageous, but obviously not the choice of many.

Trudeau was next and the arena exploded with enthusiasm and forests of banners as he took the podium. His head was bowed humbly. He looked frail and shy. And the delegates listened in awed silence as he spoke softly and soberly, stressing mainly his passion for the rights of individuals: "For many years I have been fighting for the protection of individual freedoms against the tyranny of the group and for a just distribution of our national wealth," he said. "It was my concern with these values which led me to the Liberal Party. We are no longer satisfied with vague generalizations or adroit evasions. Those who resort to them betray a lack of confidence in democracy and in the judgement of the people."

And switching smoothly back and forth between flawless French and English, he gave glimpses of a basic attitude in the years to come. "For many of us the world today stands on the threshold of a golden age," he said. "Yet for many people the only reality is war and famine. We know that millions remain in poverty, in ignorance, in hunger and in sickness, and we know that even the most favoured people suffer from external conflict and internal division."

It was not a great speech, but the crowd loved it almost as much as they had Joe Greene's and it was a hard act to follow.

Unfortunately for him, John Turner had drawn this last spot, but he did well in the circumstances. Martin Sullivan reported: "To follow Joe Greene was hard enough. To follow Trudeau was impossible. And it was John Turner's luck to have that role. Under the circumstances he did extraordinarily well. Never before had Turner appeared to be so positive, so decisive, so gutsy, as he was that night."

Turner also displayed some amazing psychic ability by announcing the far-away year of the next convention in the most often reported paragraph of his speech. "I'm not just in this race so you will remember my name at some future date," Turner said. "I'm not here for some next time. I'm not bidding now for your consideration at some vague convention in 1984 when I've mellowed a bit. My time is now, and now is no time for mellow men."

Sullivan commented: "He bit into his monosyllabic words with an angry rhythm that evoked the Kennedies. And yet they were definitely his own, deeply felt, as if at last, after doing all the right things all his life, Turner was ripping apart the politician to expose the man he really is in private – a tough, sincere, honest fellow, who has a passion about Canada which demands and deserves respect.

"Whether he wants them to or not," Sullivan continued, "the delegates will remember John Turner warmly the next time around. And next time, who knows, it may be his turn. He emerged from that evening with new stature in the Liberal Party of Canada, and in Canada as a whole."

It was Saturday then and the Ottawa Civic Arena was jampacked with banner-waving supporters, the 2,396 registered voting delegates, and more than 1,000 newsmen. There was an exhilaration and excitement now, combined with the tenseness. People pushed and shoved. Security for the candidates was minimal and didn't work anyway as newsmen poked microphones into faces or hung boom mikes over candidates' boxes to pick up almost every word for a huge audience on national TV. Also, there was trouble with the counting of votes, causing long and dramatic delays.

The first ballot, the real nailbiter for the candidates because it would allow them to match their own estimates with reality, took more than an hour to count. There was an expectant silence in the big arena as Liberal Party President Senator John Nichol read the results alphabetically: Joe Greene, 169, proving that great oratory still had an effect on politics; Paul Hellyer, 330, way below what he had expected; Paul Henderson, the nuisance candidate, zero (because he wasn't a delegate he couldn't even vote for himself); Eric Kierans, 103, a bit better than most pundits had expected; Allan MacEachen, 165, a poor showing for someone supposed to have a firm base in the Maritimes; Paul Martin, 277, a disastrous disappointment for him; Pierre Elliott Trudeau, 752, the easy leader with almost exactly the result predicted by his strategists; John Turner, 277, tied with Martin, a decent result, but hardly enough to give him a chance of winning on succeeding ballots; and Robert Winters, 293, close to Hellyer but a long way behind Trudeau, with roughly what his advisers had anticipated.

The winner had to have the majority of the votes so the Trudeau lead could be surpassed by any number of votes transferred from the other candidates. Kierans withdrew first, leaving his bloc up for grabs, followed by Martin, who also endorsed none of the others. MacEachen withdrew, too, moving conspicuously to Trudeau's box preceded by two wailing bagpipers, but apparently bringing little delegate support with him. And his withdrawal was officially too late so that his name still appeared on the second ballot. Maurice Sauvé, husband of Canada's present Governor General and a key Martin supporter, also rushed to Trudeau's side, but only a few of Martin's men went with him. The second ballot took two hours to cast and count: Trudeau soared 212 votes to 964. Winters was in second place with 473. Hellyer was third with 465. Turner gained 70 votes to 347. Greene sank to 104, but refused to drop out. MacEachen had eleven votes because of his late withdrawal after the first ballot.

Now, obviously, a combination of Winters and Hellyer votes, with some small help from Greene and Turner supporters, could still beat Trudeau. Winters tried to talk Hellyer into joining him. Hellyer tried to talk Winters into joining him. At one stage Hellyer booster Joe Potts, now a judge of the Supreme Court of Ontario, suggested seriously that they flip a coin to see who would join whom.

Bill Lee, Hellyer's executive assistant, fought his way through the crowd to John Turner's box with Vancouver Liberal organizer George Van Roggen at his side, but Vic Chapman, the former B.C. Lions footballer and Turner aide, said his boss wasn't there and wouldn't say where he had gone. They ran instead to the box where Joe Greene was still holding 104 delegates, but Greene said he, too, was staying in the race for the next ballot. No deal. Then Lee bumped into Ron Basford, Turner's campaign manager, who said Turner had also decided to hang in. No deal again.

Lee returned to Hellyer's box and told him to withdraw from the ballot and support Turner. He was certain, he said, that Winters could not beat Trudeau on a final ballot, but that Turner might. Therefore Hellyer should now try to vault Turner over Winters into second place. Carol Wahood, a pretty Peterborough lawyer and one of Hellyer's trusted advisers, also pleaded with him to go for Turner. When he said he couldn't she walked out of the box and cried.

Judy LaMarsh, one of Hellyer's strongest supporters, tried to convince him he should join Winters. "You know him, Paul, and he knows you," she roared in a supposedly private conversation easily overheard by nearby reporters. "You're all right with him. It's tough, but what the hell's the point of going down and letting that bastard [Trudeau] be there. Come on, Paul, you're forty-four, and we've still got lots of time."

But Hellyer decided to stay in the ballot and he jumped to his feet shouting at his supporters: "Fight, fight, fight."

The third ballot did not take so long: Trudeau, 1,051, Winters, 621, Hellyer, 377, Turner 279, Greene, 29. Greene dropped out and joined Trudeau. Hellyer dropped out and joined Winters. So now the party was almost completely polarized between Trudeau on the left, Winters and Hellyer on the right, with Turner somewhere vaguely in the middle, and hanging in.

Turner's campaign chairman, Jerry Grafstein, remarked: "Our young people will not back either Mr. Hellyer or Mr. Winters, so that we cannot transfer mathematically our young support to either of them." But Winters and Hellyer were pressuring Turner in a joint appeal.

Winters: "We'd like you to join us, John."

Turner: "Gentlemen, I'm staying in the ballot."

Hellyer: "It's your decision, John."

Turner: "I respect yours."

Nichol announced the results of the fourth ballot shortly before 8 p.m. to an arena hushed in expectancy: "Trudeau, 1,203 . . ." The arena erupted so that it was almost impossible to hear the rest of the results. Winters had 954 votes, Turner, 195.

There was a new prime minister and he was to remain, except for a brief period, for sixteen years, surpassing the time in office of Sir Wilfrid Laurier to become the longest-serving French-Canadian prime minister in Canadian history. By the time Trudeau stepped down in the summer of 1984, he had been prime minister longer than anyone except Sir John A. Macdonald and William Lyon Mackenzie King.

Trudeau was a daunting intellectual. In the beginning he knew nothing about western Canada and the Maritimes; hence, the Canada he did know consisted mainly of an argument between Quebec and Ontario. He thought on a grand scale. He was statesmanlike, thoughtful, knowledgeable, and expert in foreign affairs and highly respected in rich and poor countries alike. He brought the Constitution home to Canada and changed the country with his Bill of Rights. He was tough, imposing the War Measures Act during the Quebec Crisis of 1970. He kept Quebec in confederation in face of massive separatist sentiment. He was different, daring, often exciting and outrageous, pirouetting in front of 10 Downing Street, dancing with sheiks in the desert and pretty women in Ottawa and New York, sliding down bannisters and diving athletically in swimming pools and deep in the oceans. He was also arrogant at times, telling the Opposition in the House to "fuck off," and occasionally sticking an obscene finger in the faces of the electorate.

The world economy was difficult during most of his regime and the Canadian economy faltered. Unemployment reached crisis proportions. Inflation continued and increased alarmingly. Trudeau was financially independent. He never had to meet a mortgage payment in his life and he did not seem to understand the ordinary man. Often he seemed impatient and out of touch with the middle class, where lay the power of the old Liberal Party. So, in his time, the power of the party ebbed.

But now, at the end of the 1968 leadership convention, he was the hugely popular, heroic, left-wing reformist victor over Robert Winters, the representative of Bay Street and big business. He was the adventurous hope for a different and better Canada. Another man, small and slightly hunched now, made his way quietly and almost unnoticed through the litter of the discarded placards to an arena exit. He waved to a reporter, smiled, and said casually, "See you around." Finally Mike Pearson was freed of the power.

Young John Turner sat, grim-faced, in his candidate's box. He had hung in to the end, refusing to give his support to anyone. He was still his own man. With his 195 votes he had kept his own power base within the Liberal Party. The power base was small then, and Turner's determined independence went almost unnoticed in the excitement of the start of the Trudeau era. But it was to prove crucial to Turner and the party in the years to come.

4

Roots and Beginnings

John Napier Turner was born on June 7, 1929, in a small nursing home in Richmond, Surrey, which is now part of London. He was the son of Leonard Turner, an Englishman with a mysterious and adventurous past who had spent some time in the wilds of Sumatra and was employed as a gunsmith at Ginnings, in London, when he met and married a brilliant and beautiful Canadian student, Phyllis Gregory. They had three children, John, the eldest, Michael, who died shortly after birth, and Brenda, now Mrs. John Norris of Montreal. Leonard Turner died from the effects of malaria and goitre shortly after Brenda was born, when John was three years old, leaving the family impoverished.

John Turner does not know much about his father. He does not even know why his father chose his middle name of Napier. But he keeps a photograph of Leonard Turner in a place of honour in his office, showing a tall man, almost the image of his son, dressed in tweeds, dashing looking, with a mischievous expression to his handsome face. He is standing in the picture next to his brother Will, John Turner's uncle, who is eighty-five now and living in the small village of Bexhill-on-Sea, in East Sussex. But Uncle Will has never told Turner much about his father, even though Turner has persistently questioned him and Will's sister Marjorie about his paternal background over the years.

"When I was at Oxford and the English bar in the late forties and early fifties, I used to have an annual Christmas party for Uncle Will and Aunt Marjorie at The Antelope, a pub on Sloane Square in London," Turner says. "It was run by a gal named Freda and she used to set up one of my favourite tables. Apparently I'm always having favourite tables. You could get a good meal there inexpensively and draft beer and Will and Marjorie liked that. But I really couldn't plumb too much from them about my father, for reasons I'll never understand."

He learned even less about his father from his mother, as she reared him first as a struggling widow and then as a highly successful civil servant in Ottawa. This gap had an obvious effect on the life of John Turner. "I have no idea whether my father was the black sheep of the family or what," Turner says, shaking his head in puzzlement. "Obviously when he died it was a great tragedy for my mother, and it was a great loss to my uncle and aunt. And I suppose they didn't want to relive those days. My mother certainly didn't. She didn't talk about my father at all. It was a part of her life she didn't discuss with me.

"You know, we were a close-knit trio, Mom, Brenda, and I," he says. "But Mom – my mother never revealed much of herself. There were unanswered secrets in her heart that she wasn't willing to share."

Still, Turner insists he was never conscious of not having a father, or of not having somebody in control.

"My mother was in control," he says, "and who knows whether being fatherless affected me. My wife feels that certain features about not having a father do show in me. I'm not handy with my hands, for instance. I'm not good at carpentry and fixing things around the house. My mother taught us how to play tennis, but she wasn't able to take us on fishing trips and that sort of thing, you know. We never had any of that. But we didn't miss it. I'm not conscious of missing anything.

"We didn't have much money but we were always well turned out, and we were well disciplined. Mother used to spank us with a hairbrush for the things that children do, disobedience and fighting and things like that. My sister and I used to have some dandy fights. But once the spanking was over there were no grudges. She was a very loving mother, but probably closer to us when we were children than when we were adults. And there were those unanswered secrets in her heart she was unwilling to share."

Turner was able to learn, mostly from his Uncle Will, that his grandfather was Maxwell Turner, who had an import-export business in France, and that his grandmother's maiden name was Florence Wahl. But there the paternal ancestry ends.

In the circumstances he seems to have turned some way toward his Uncle Will as a father figure. He speaks proudly of him, of how he worked for Brookes and Company, the tea importers, and fought in the King's Royal Rifle Corps, now known as the Royal Green Jackets, in World War One, and was gassed in the trenches; and how, in World War Two, Uncle Will was in the Home Guard, patrolling the tops of buildings in the blitz. "Uncle Will is an ordinary middle-class guy, but he was the kind of guy who kept Britain going," Turner says with pride. "I'm very close to him."

Turner's maternal background, however, is better known and cherished by him. His grandmother, Mary Margaret MacDonald, was the daughter of a rich captain and owner of clipper ships who sailed with cargoes of tea from his home port of Mulgrave, Nova Scotia. This well-to-do young woman, who lived in a house full of servants, married Jim Gregory, the hoist engineer at a Stellarton mine in Pictou County, and they had four children, Marcella, Gladys, Howard, and Phyllis.

Jim Gregory's job as a hoist engineer was not impressive. It meant that he operated the creaky old elevator that lowered the miners into their darkness at the beginning of a shift and hauled them, tired and dirty, to daylight at the shift's end. He was tough, with a ruddy complexion, full cheeks, and the same bright, blue, unblinking eyes that have become part of the image of his only grandson. He liked to drink and he could handle himself among the rough, uneducated miners of Stellarton.

Jim Gregory also liked politics. He was an ardent Conservative in those days when patronage in Nova Scotia was even more blatant than now and the rift between Tory and Grit wider and angrier. He made the mistake of campaigning for Conservative Sir Charles Tupper against Liberal Sir Wilfrid Laurier in the general election of 1896, while the boss of the mine supported Laurier. Laurier won and Jim Gregory was fired.

The vast Canadian federalism was being born then. The Canadian Pacific Railway had just been built. So Gregory packed his few possessions, his wife and the two children then born, Marcella and Gladys, onto the train to Montreal, then to Calgary. From there they took the old Kettle Valley line to Castlegar in British Columbia and then made their way by road to the booming gold-mining town of Rossland.

Rossland was a rough town of over 14,000 people, bigger than its neighbouring city of Trail in those days, its main street a row of saloons, its mostly immigrant people housed in shanties, tents, and small homes. Its mine, the Leroy, subsequently bought by the Consolidated Mining and Smelting Company (now Cominco), was taking more gold out of Rossland's mountain than was being taken from virtually any gold mine in the world.

Jim Gregory got a job at the mine, again as the hoist engineer, and he worked there for forty years, living in a little white house on Washington Street, which is still standing, and where his two other children, Howard and Phyllis, were born. He became one of Rossland's best-known characters.

Turner remembers him: "He was very popular in the town. But in the early days he was a tough liver, a hard drinker, but a good provider. My grandmother, of course, made sure she got the pay from Jim Gregory every Friday night because he would have blown it. He never got rich, of course. He was a miner, and the pay was very little. But when my grandparents eventually moved to Vancouver, to a little house on West 33rd, they were able to live on his pension. After all, he'd been at the mine from 1896 to 1936 and there was not much inflation in those days.

"I remember him in Rossland," Turner says, "putting an old rubber tire on the apple tree so I could swing in it when I was four or five, going with him to the barber shop and listening to him gossip. He was a rough man, but he was a gentleman. He was always well turned out. He loved wearing a sports jacket and pair of flannels and coloured weskit; always had his shoes shined, always kept his hair cut. Everybody knew him and everybody liked him. He was full of fun, always looking on the bright side of life, and he loved the companionship of men. His favourite day of the week when he retired to Vancouver was when he went down to one of his favourite pubs and whiled away the afternoon with the boys, sucking his pipe. He was a man's man."

Grandmother Mary Margaret held the family together. She was a staunch Catholic in the mining town where most of the other Catholics were immigrant Italians. Mary Margaret was organist at the church and sang in the choir. When the big flu epidemic of 1919 hit Rossland she took charge, organizing clinics and carrying hot soup from home to home. She knitted quilts and she sewed the children's clothes. Old-time residents of Rossland say she kept the city as well as her family together. She also made certain her children took their education seriously.

John Turner's aunts, Gladys and Marcella, both became school-teachers in the West Kootenays, and Gladys married Michael Gillespie, who was with the North American Life Insurance Company and became the first insurance salesman in the Yukon, helping set up the firm of Howard and Frith, which is still in business on the main street of Whitehorse. He moved to Dawson City in 1902, where he became a close friend of Frank Berton, the mining recorder, who was the father of author Pierre Berton.

Marcella married an American, Charles Mulch, a locomotive engineer on the Great Northern Railway who drove the great eight-wheelers from St. Paul, Minnesota, to Seattle, Washington. They lived in Spokane, and Turner remembers regarding Mulch with awe, particularly on the few occasions he was allowed to drive part of the route in the cab with him. Marcella became a master bridge player in the United States and made her living as a professional player after her husband died. Neither Marcella nor Gladys had any children.

Turner describes his Uncle Howard, who was also childless, as "a bit of a roustabout." He was a good athlete, who played hockey for the Trail Smoke Eaters at a time when they were one of Canada's best hockey teams, and he played semipro baseball in the United States.

"He wasn't a very big man, but he was beautifully co-ordinated," Turner says. "I remember throwing a baseball around with him when I was a kid. But he sacrificed his education, much to the disappointment of my grandfather and grandmother. He never lived up to their expectations of what he might have done in life. I guess it was seeing the bright lights and all that athletic ability he had. He ended up in a series of odd jobs all over the western United States and Canada and he finally settled in Vancouver where he worked at a steel foundry until he died in the fifties."

But Phyllis, the youngest of the four Gregory children, was far from a disappointment.

5

The Early Years

By the time Phyllis Gregory met and married Leonard Turner in London she was as well educated as any Canadian woman of the time. She had been first in her class in every grade at the Rossland Public School. She played the piano and sang well, and her childhood in the little, white house on Washington Street was happy and full of friends. Her favourite fun was riding a toboggan from mile-high Rossland to Trail, six miles below, then taking the train home.

In 1921, when she was seventeen, she enrolled at the University of British Columbia. She was the only one of the four Gregory children to get to university and she studied economics and political science, a strange choice of subjects for a woman in those days. She graduated with honours in both subjects in 1925 and won the Susan B. Anthony Scholarship, named after the great suffragette, to Bryn Mawr University near Philadelphia. Academic standards were high but she breezed through her M.A. in economics, writing a thesis on the Doukhobors of British Columbia. She also started her Ph.D. at Bryn Mawr but transferred to the London School of Economics, intending to return eventually to complete it.

She never did. She met Leonard Turner and had her three children. When he died she was twenty-nine and destitute. Phyllis Turner packed her possessions in a few suitcases and came home to Canada with her two small surviving children. They crossed the Atlantic by ship and then travelled across Canada to Rossland in trains John Turner remembers although he was not four years old at the time.

"I can hardly remember the ship, but I can remember the train ride," Turner says. "I got to know the conductors and porters and I remember the meals on the train. Everything was done in great style in those days – linen on the tables. The service was excellent and they were very good to children. I remember staying out in

36

the observation car in a tunnel and almost choking on the smoke and getting hell from the conductor for being out there. I remember the mountains and the tunnels and the flat prairies, and the conductor and everybody waving good-bye to us at Calgary when we changed to the Kettle Valley train. Those are my first memories of Canada."

This was the time of the Great Depression and the Turners lived for a short period in the little Rossland home where Phyllis had grown up, supported by the meagre earnings of miner Jim Gregory. Then in the winter of 1933-34 the young economist received a reply to a job application from the Tariff Board in Ottawa, which had just been set up by Prime Minister R.B. Bennett. She was told to travel to Ottawa for an interview, but not to bring her children because the job was by no means certain.

Phyllis knew she could not afford the fare back to Rossland so she gambled. Once again she packed the few suitcases, bundled up the children, and this time took them across the country to Ottawa, where she knew no one except Norman Robertson, who had studied with her at UBC. He was a very junior official in External Affairs then but was to become the country's most powerful mandarin as Clerk of the Privy Council and Undersecretary of State for External Affairs in the fifties and sixties.

"That was a high-risk operation for her," Turner says. "It sure was. But she had confidence and talent and she was good-looking. I'd say she was spectacular."

Phyllis Turner got the job as an economist with the Tariff Board, but it did not pay well. She lived with the children in a tiny walk-up apartment on Sparks Street, now the site of Ottawa's downtown mall. There was a small kitchen, a room for Phyllis, and a cupboard-sized room for John and Brenda. The bathroom was down the hall and the heating didn't work well.

"The place was freezing and everything was freezing in Ottawa that winter," Turner recalls. "It was the coldest winter in Ottawa for years. And I didn't have any friends. Brenda and I just played with each other until we moved, after about six months, to a rented duplex at 132 Daly Avenue in Sandy Hill, and were old enough to go to school."

He went to the Normal Model School in Ottawa when he was five and a half years old, a school so named because student teachers were brought in for a week every month to take over classes from some of the best teachers in Ottawa. Like his mother, young Turner did well at school, always at the top of his class. He was so good he skipped grade four, which meant he was younger than most of his classmates throughout the rest of his education.

He was a wiry kid and he could run, not with a lot of style, but fast. He was mainly a sprinter. In May, 1938, he entered four events in the junior school track and field championships, the 100-yard dash, the 220, the 440, and the broad jump. He won them all and, of course, the junior boys all-round cup for athletics. "I remember winning all of those fairly convincingly," Turner says. "I could move."

Phyllis Turner progressed rapidly up the civil service ladder. She moved the family to a bigger duplex, still on Daly Avenue, on the corner of Chapel, where John and Brenda had their own rooms, and then to a single, but still-rented, three-bedroom house at 434 Daly, just behind the Soviet Embassy.

Then tragedy struck the fatherless family. Brenda, a beautiful, lively youngster, was stricken by polio when she was four. "I woke up one morning and I walked into Mommy's room and she saw my legs were swollen to about four times their normal size," Brenda says. "But fortunately we had a very good doctor in Ottawa named Dr. Campbell, who had heard of the Sister Kenny method of treating polio by massage, by not letting the muscles die. Mommy didn't go to work for a week. She massaged me every hour on the hour. It went on and on. And every two days they'd measure my legs and the muscles didn't die. She massaged, massaged, massaged, through the days and nights. It's an extraordinary story and I completely recovered but only due to her. Now, occasionally when I'm tired, one leg hurts a bit."

By 1937 Phyllis Turner was able to buy a Plymouth car with a rumble seat so she could take the children on picnics to Dunrobin and sometimes Kingsmere, and in her work she met important people, the Walter Gordons, the Graham Towers, and the Hugh Keenleysides. Norman Robertson introduced her to another up and comer in External Affairs named Mike Pearson and they became friends. As she rose up the social ladder the two Turner children would be invited by Lord Tweedsmuir to Government House for children's parties.

Brenda remembers: "In those days they used to have Walt Disney movies, can you believe it, it was so thrilling! And Mommy used to know the aides, so we were invited, and everybody else there had a nanny standing behind their chair and we were the only two who went on our own. She'd drop us off and then she'd go back to work, then come and pick us up. So we were the only ones there without nannies."

Eventually Phyllis became chief economist to the Tariff Board, the most senior woman in Canada's public service, but she was paid only two-thirds of the salary of male civil servants of equal rank because she was a woman. John Turner still mentions this with some anger.

She liked playing the piano in her little house, especially when Donald Gordon, who was to become president of the CNR, brought his accordion. She was an attractive widow, clever and talented, and she became very much a part of the Ottawa scene. "She was quite beautiful," says Walter Gordon, "very bright, extremely capable, and everybody liked her."

The bachelor Prime Minister, R.B. Bennett, fell in love with her. "At one stage R.B. Bennett sent her a dozen roses every day," Brenda remembers. "I used to come home from school and arrange them. He was courting her very seriously and I know he asked her to marry him."

In the summers she would rent a cottage at Kirk's Ferry on the Gatineau, near Wakefield, next to a cottage the Pearsons rented, and John and Brenda played and swam there with the Pearson children, Patricia and Geoffrey. John fought frequently with Geoff Pearson then and again later when they were both at the same private school, causing some physical damage to each other, but they have managed to remain friends over the years as Pearson rose to be a top-ranking Canadian diplomat.

Barbara Ann Scott, the world and Olympic figure-skating champion in 1948, lived around the corner from the Turners in Sandy Hill and was a playmate of Brenda and John's. "John was a year younger than me but he was always the leader when we went on bicycle rides and played together," recalls Barbara Ann, who is now Mrs. Thomas King of Chicago. "But he was a leader without being bossy. His mother was quite a disciplinarian, but she was nice, and such a beautiful woman. Brenda was beautiful, too. We other kids were all a bit in awe of them.

"John had to learn figure skating," she adds, "but he didn't take it too seriously. He didn't like playing bit parts at the annual Minto Follies ice show, getting all gussied up as a chocolate soldier or a candle. But he suffered through it because the boys were allowed to play broomball after the practices and that's what he liked. He was the leader there, too."

Barbara Ann and John also took piano lessons together from Mrs. Gladys Barnes. "Barbara Ann wasn't much better than I was at the piano," Turner says. "In fact, we were easily at the bottom of Gladys Barnes' class. Barbara Ann was too busy skating and I was busting my knuckles playing football and every other damn thing and not really practising that much. But we had to go in the annual recitals that were held down at the Rideau Street Common, with all the parents there. And, boy, that was nerve-shattering. I did those recitals, I guess, for about five years. I played the "Moonlight Sonata" one time, and some Mozart and one of Schumann's sonatas and a Chopin sonata, but not very well, I want to tell you. But Barbara Ann was almost as bad."

Despite her occasional lack of success with some, Gladys Barnes was obviously a great teacher and influence on her students. Once she took some of them to hear Rachmaninoff play at Ottawa's Capitol Theatre. "And you know," Turner says today with some awe, "he came around the next afternoon to have tea with Miss Barnes. God knows how she knew Rachmaninoff. You know he was the greatest pianist of his day. And I remember being in Miss Barnes' house in a little street off Sussex, right opposite the National Research Council, and she had Rachmaninoff in for tea and he played for us. I mean to hear Rachmaninoff play like that and to meet him, that was really something." Turner believes his interest in music, which is passionate, goes back to that day.

When he was eleven, John Turner was sent to Ashbury College in Rockcliffe, an exclusive private school, and there he was second in most of his classes to Michael Shenstone, later Canadian ambassador to Saudi Arabia and now a deputy minister in External Affairs. Shenstone remembers Turner as being "very bright, very athletic, and very good-looking, but there was no rivalry between us in the classroom. We both just did our best. It was a terrible pity that he had to leave Ashbury. His mother was a widow, you know, and she couldn't afford it."

Turner won the junior debating cup at Ashbury, played soccer for the junior school, cricket, and left wing and sometimes defence in hockey. And he continued to run fast. When he was twelve years old he was running the 100 yards in just over eleven seconds and he also won the junior school's 220-yard, 440-yard, and hurdles championships. He was the first recipient of the Woods Trophy, named after a master of the school who was killed in the early years of World War Two and presented to the best all-round student in the junior school.

Turner remembers one race particularly well. It was by no means the most important race in his life, but he still repeats the story with glee and pride, and the experience of this race has obviously had a lasting effect on him. In his first two years at Ashbury he had run in the junior cross-country race and finished in the top ten, although he had skipped another grade and was now two years younger than most of the other competitors. He was a sprinter and the cross countries were tough. In the third year the favourites were boys named Sy Thompson, Jeff Caldwell, and Ted Pilgrim, who were distance runners and, Turner says, ran as a team, using tactics to beat back any upstart threatening to take the race away from any one of them. The course was about two and a half miles around MacKay Lake, now a plush residential area but then a mosquito-infested marsh.

"Those three boys and maybe one other were ahead of me, but I was holding on like crazy," Turner recalls. "They didn't think I could win it and they stopped to share an orange. But I kept moving. I got by them. I must have had fifty to seventy-five yards on them when they came after me. They caught up a lot, too. But I held on and they couldn't quite catch me. So I won the race by about fifteen yards, just staggering over the finish line in the end. Those fellows were too confident and they allowed me to get too far ahead. That was a good lesson to them, that you never stop midway in anything."

When Ted ("Pill") Pilgrim, who went on to become the school's senior cross-country champion, run the Boston Marathon, and become headmaster of Ridley College, was reminded of this race recently, he refused at first to believe that Turner had ever beaten him. "Turner was a great athlete, a great sprinter," Pilgrim said. "But he never beat me in the cross country at Ashbury. Nobody ever beat me."

However, when he was told it was a junior championship race and the details as Turner recalled them, Pilgrim reacted with amazement. "My goodness," he said, "he could be right, you know. Maybe he did beat me once in junior race. What a memory he must have? It must have been important to him."

Turner spent three years at Ashbury and was then sent to St. Patrick's College, both because of the expense and because his mother felt he should go to a Catholic school. It was a tough school, a real melting pot with boys from all economic and social backgrounds who did not take kindly at first to a snobby youngster "coming down" from a posh private school.

"I used to go to school in a sports jacket, while most of the guys just wore sweaters," Turner recalls. "I used to get the jacket torn off me. I had a lot of fights. I'd come home all bloody, but my mother didn't say much. She took a hands-off view."

Turner loved the Oblate Fathers who ran St. Pat's, although they were tough disciplinarians. "Oh, they'd whack you," he says. "We had a couple of them who could twirl and throw a chalk right by your ear. They could really let it go. It was a rough, disciplined school, well run, good standards, and it really represented that Irish Catholic community in the Ottawa Valley.

"There were some great priests there," Turner says. "For instance there was Father Thomas Mitchell, who taught us English.

He was an Englishman, a small guy with the movements of a bird, glasses, a great wit. He could recite Shakespeare by the yard. I remember him once telling Eddie McCabe [now sports editor of the *Ottawa Citizen*], 'Take that gum out of your mouth, Eddie, throw it out the window and hold onto it.' And there was Father Harold Conway, who later became principal of the school, Canadian head of the Oblate order, president of the Ontario Teachers' Federation, and then president of the Canadian Teachers' Federation. He nearly became president of the World Teachers' Federation, but he lost by a few votes."

Father Conway remembers Turner: "He was a brilliant student, always at the top of his class and by a long way. His average marks were 91 or 92 and those were days when exams were marked hard. The next best average would be 81 or 82.

"It was a bit tough for him because he was two years younger than the rest of his class, but he was on the debating team and the junior football team and co-editor, with John Grace of the school paper [later editor of the *Ottawa Journal*, and now Privacy Commissioner], and, of course, he was a good athlete. He was a very sincere young fellow, a good leader, always gung ho, you know. And there was no doubt about his Catholicism and practice of it. He thought very seriously about becoming a priest, joining the Oblate order. Even after he left St. Pat's he kept in touch with Father Mitchell and he wrote from university telling him he still had the priesthood in mind.

"We've been in close touch over the years," Father Conway adds. "Sometimes he just wants to talk religion and sometimes we talk about all sorts of things. He didn't run for the Liberal Party leadership when Trudeau resigned temporarily in 1979, you know, because he is very committed to his family. People and the press were saying the main reason he would run was just because he was ambitious and he told me he didn't want his children to have to put up with that sort of thing. 'There's no way I'm going to subject my children to that sort of stuff,' he told me. He's a good family man, very committed to his children, possibly partly because he had no father himself. And he's actually a very dedicated man, you know. He feels he has a lot to offer and that he has to give something back to his country. He's a very sincere, concerned sort of person with a strong sense of duty and he was like that as a young fellow at St. Pat's."

Phyllis Turner was at 9 a.m. mass every Sunday with her two children at St. Joseph's in Sandy Hill and the Oblate Fathers nurtured the religion in John. He was an altar boy in Ottawa and when he was older at the parish church in St. Andrews, New Brunswick, where his family took holidays.

"At St. Andrews I was the only guy who knew how to handle the incense and all that stuff that goes with it," Turner boasts. "As a matter of fact I could twirl that stuff. Most of the other guys could just swing it like that, but I could twirl it. I could really get it going red hot. One time when the Bishop was there in the old church in St. Andrews I lost my touch and a couple of pieces of charcoal went right down the centre aisle. Nearly set the place on fire."

Once, when he was serving at a funeral from the small church at Rolling Dam, near St. Andrews, he stepped forward to sprinkle holy water on the coffin, tripped in some wreaths, and fell into the grave. "Hell of a thing to happen," Turner says.

Later, Turner was closely involved with the Newman Association of McGill University, a member of the board of Newman House for Catholic students, where Emmett Carter, now Archbishop of Toronto, was chaplain. They are still firm friends.

For thirty years he has attended and helped organize a conference of Catholic laymen who meet annually in residence at St. Michael's College in Toronto. There, for four days each year, he participates in theological discussions at the leading edge of Catholic thought on subjects ranging from the liturgy to abortion and euthanasia.

Turner carries a small Bible with him when he travels – the King James version – and he reads a chapter every day. On his holiday in Jamaica in March, 1984, shortly before announcing his intention to run for the Liberal Party leadership, he relaxed by reading theology. "I've been influenced," he says, "by the encyclicals of Pope Leo XIII, which favour the working man, one's duty to one's employee, and one's duty to the weaker elements of society, so my religion has a lot to do with my liberalism. The social conscience inside me comes from a lot of those theological writings. I have an intellectual conviction to Catholicism and certainly all the habits of my life are Catholic, so the intellectual commitment accords with the emotional commitment."

St. Pat's also produced great hockey and football teams and Turner can still rattle off the names of alumni who made it to the National Hockey League or the Canadian Football League. He played football on the junior team, mostly on defence, and not spectacularly. Leo Seguin, who played for the Ottawa Rough Riders and was later Ottawa's police chief, was the coach, and Turner could never understand why he was made to play defence.

"Leo didn't take advantage of my speed," Turner says. "I should have been in the backfield but he made me play on the line. I had this speed, but I played on the line, for God's sake. And I wasn't very big. Boy, I used to take a tremendous beating with those guys coming through the line from Ottawa Tech and Glebe and Nepean and Lister and those other high schools. I really got rocked up. But looking back on it I suppose it was a good experience."

St. Pat's emphasized team sports and showed little interest in individual sports like track and field, but the priests did put together a sports day in May, 1945, in Turner's second year, when he was fifteen. Turner was competing against seventeen- and eighteen-year-olds, but he entered the 100-yard dash and won it, the 220 and won that. Then he won both the 440 and the 880, and most of these races had heats and finals. Then he won the broad jump. When the start of the mile was called he collapsed on the way to the starting line. He was presented with the Governor General's Cup for all-round excellence at the school.

Also in 1945, Phyllis Turner married Frank Mackenzie Ross, a roly-poly millionaire industrialist and entrepreneur, who had been a dollar-a-year man in Ottawa – one of the many Canadian industrialists and experts who worked for nothing in the war effort – and they moved to Vancouver. She cut a swath through Vancouver society. She became president of the University Women's Club and the Georgian Club and worked on the committee of St. Paul's Hospital.

"Mom was still handsome, she had proved herself, and now she was enjoying a side of life she had never had," Turner says. "Mom and the Old Man were really part of the scene. They were friends with all the movers and shakers in Vancouver."

Phyllis and Frank Ross, and her children John and Brenda, were also well known in St. Andrews, New Brunswick, in those years. Ross owned a farm at Bayfield, about halfway between St. Andrews and St. Stephens, and the family spent its summers there. The farm, overlooking the St. Croix River flowing into Passamaquoddy Bay, carried about 150 head of Hereford cattle, some Welsh ponies, and a few dozen pigs. It has an old house of thick stone walls that was built about 1784 by a character named Hurricane Jack Mowat, who was a sea captain and smuggler. John Turner loved the place as a youngster and still does.

Sir James Dunn, C.D. Howe, and E.P. Taylor also had holiday places near St. Andrews and Sir William Van Horne, who built the Canadian Pacific Railway across the Rockies, once owned a tidal island there. "Bobby Cochrane ran a damn good drug store in St. Andrews," John Turner remembers, "and C.D. Howe and E.P. Taylor and Frank Ross and all the boys would meet in the back room over pipes and cigars and a cup of coffee and talk about the affairs of the world. And as a boy I'd sit around with them and listen in."

In 1955 C.D. Howe, the businessman-cabinet minister, recommended Ross for Lieutenant-Governor of British Columbia and Prime Minister Louis St. Laurent appointed him. He was one of B.C.'s most popular lieutenant-governors and Phyllis a much beloved First Lady from 1955 to 1960. Subsequently, she was elected Chancellor of the University of British Columbia, the first female university chancellor in the Commonwealth.

Phyllis Gregory Turner Ross is eighty now and living at the Lady Minto Hospital on Saltspring Island. She has Alzheimer's disease. John and Brenda see that she is well cared for. But when they visit her they are not sure if she recognizes them.

In the years when he had neither father nor stepfather, young Turner turned to substitute father figures, the priests at St. Pat's, later to a booze-besotted but kind and clever athletic coach, and in his adolescence in Ottawa to a grizzled old outdoorsman named A.L. Cochrane, who ran a summer camp, called Cochrane's Camp or Camp Timagami, in the Upper Ottawa River area. Phyllis Turner sent John there every summer because she could not give him the outdoors experiences a father could.

Turner still describes A.L. Cochrane with awe and a respect verging on love. "He was as straight as a die," he says. "Any transgression and you'd get sent right out of the camp. He was a strict disciplinarian. But, you know, he could still do a soldier dive off the three-metre board and all the difficult lifesaving manoeuvres when he was well into his seventies. He was a great swimmer and a very strong influence on my life."

Turner went to Cochrane's Camp almost every summer from the ages of seven to twenty-four, first as an inexperienced kid, then as a counsellor, teaching youngsters canoeing and swimming and how to recognize trees and birds. Often he'd take the younger boys on week-long or two-week-long trips into the wilderness. He even tried to buy the camp on behalf of a board when Cochrane finally became too old to run it, but the old man couldn't bear to sell it, and it faded away in the fifties.

Turner had some adventures at Camp Timagami. He was in charge of a canoe trip, four days out in wild country on the upper Nipissing, when one of his group, Charles Taylor, the son of industrialist E.P. Taylor, was stricken with a painful earache. Turner thought he had mastoids and he had been taught in first-aid classes not to touch eyes or ears but to get the patient to a doctor quickly. He and another youth paddled Taylor over sixty miles back to the camp in a day and a night without stopping to rest. Taylor's ear was infected, but it was found to be not serious.

On another trip one of the younger boys contracted polio. He was canoed out and rushed to Toronto while the group he had been with was isolated on a small island well away from the main group. Turner and another counsellor, Don Wright, volunteered to stay with the isolated group for ten days until the quarantine period expired. They had to paddle to a rock, far from the island, where food was left for them. "It was like a leper colony," Turner says. "It was scary, like a death watch." But the polio didn't spread.

One time, Turner had a fishing plug deeply imbedded in his backside while trying to grab a pike he had pulled into his canoe. All normal attempts to remove the hook failed. So a medical student, Alex Bryan, heated a knife to disinfect it, had eight youths pin Turner to a rock, cut a deep triangle in his rump, removed the hook, and flooded the wound with iodine. Turner still has the scar on his backside.

The most lasting effects Cochrane had on Turner's life were to teach him to canoe, to draw and follow maps, to challenge the white-river waters, and to survive in the wilderness. And despite his track and field successes, these are the recreations Turner loved best, and still does. Turner's usually clipped and pragmatic phrases become poetic as he talks, even today, of the Canadian wilderness, as if he believes there must be a mystic bond between a true Canadian and the land itself; that he must be able to respect and challenge its rivers and mountains and lonely wildlands in order to be a real part of it, and to understand it.

As his own family has grown he has taken them annually on hazardous trips down Arctic rivers – the Hanbury, the Thelon, the lower Lockhart, and others – where they have been alone for weeks at a time, surviving the shallows and rapids, the long portages, the grizzlies and the loneliness.

His one entry into popular journalism in his later years was a graphic description in *Toronto Life* in August, 1981, of his family's journey down the white water of the Burnside River, across the Arctic Circle, dropping 1,300 feet over about 180 miles into Bathurst Inlet on the Arctic Ocean.

"We could see no one else," he wrote. "Our company would be the sky, the river, the birds, the caribou. The terrain was rugged: hills dotted with boulders, large areas of massive rocks and muskeg. There were strands of dwarf birch and scrub willow bushes, but no real trees; we were above the treeline, which has come to be accepted as the southern limit of the Arctic. . . . Even in the barrens, however, there is stubborn life. And not only the scrub willow and the birch; everywhere there were Arctic flowers of extraordinary brilliance and delicacy."

He ended this story of the family voyage down the Burnside: "Once again we had survived the test of the north. We had shared another unique family experience. Together we had escaped into our northern frontier – and we had survived. Before us had been a big, unspoiled, majestic country of treeless land and water, game, and birds in their undisturbed habitat. Wildlife bloomed everywhere. Many times on our trip I wondered how long this river would remain untouched and unspoiled. How much longer would this solitude last? What a privilege to have run these waters so much alone. We had travelled one of the last frontiers of the world. Because we love the country, we were careful to leave it as we found it, with no signs of our passing. And, like my family, I have never felt more Canadian than when alone with my thoughts in the remote northern vastness."

And again, at a dinner for the great Canadian Arctic canoeist Eric Morse, in Toronto in 1983, the man noted for his jock talk and practical political speeches had this to say: "Only those of us who have paddled the wilderness waters of North America can truly understand why we are here. Can we evoke for ourselves tonight the memories of a silent paddle on still waters, the slowly evolving landscape of tree and rock and tundra, the easy rhythm of our thought as the paddle cleaves the water, the exhilaration of running rapids, the pain of the portage and, above all, the companionship at the campsite." Then he quoted from Sigurd Olson's *The Lonely Land*:

The movement of a canoe is like a reed in the wind. Silence is part of it, and the sounds of lapping water, bird songs, and wind in the trees. It is part of the medium through which it floats, the sky, the water, and the shores. A man is part of his canoe and therefore part of all it knows. The instant he dips his paddle, he flows as it flows, the canoe yielding to his slightest touch and responsive to his every whim and thought. . . . There is magic in the feel of a paddle and the movement of a canoe, a magic compounded of distance, adventure, solitude and peace. The way of the canoe is the way of the wilderness and of a freedom almost forgotten, and the open door to waterways of ages past and a way of life with profound and abiding satisfactions.

Turner's lyrical speech, full of feeling and emotion, brought tears to the eyes of an audience who understood him.

But he was thinking about an old man, A.L. Cochrane of Timagami, who taught him about the wilderness and thus about Canada, and who was like a father to him.

6

Golden Boy

The Rosses' house at 4899 Belmont Avenue in Vancouver's posh West Point Grey area overlooked Spanish Banks and the Pacific Ocean. Garfield Weston, the billionaire businessman, lived on one side and Lawren Harris, the artist, across the street. The house was a mansion and to John Turner, who was now sixteen, it was a long way from the little white miner's house in Rossland and the tiny, cold, walk-up apartment on Ottawa's Sparks Street and the three-bedroom house in Sandy Hill. He had a room of his own, which was more like a suite, above the garage, and the living room was as big as a ballroom. Young Turner, just graduated from tough, middle-class and working-class St. Pat's in Ottawa, was at first embarrassed by the affluence.

Frank Ross was very rich then and he lived hard and well. Phyllis was a sophisticated and gracious hostess, experienced and knowledgeable about the intricacies of the far-away government in Ottawa, and they entertained often and lavishly in this big and beautiful home.

Frank Mackenzie Ross had come a long way. He was a chubby little man who emigrated to Canada from Scotland in 1910 without a penny in his pocket. He got a job with the Canadian Bank of Commerce in Montreal and served overseas with the Winnipeg Rifles in World War One. He was wounded twice, rose in the ranks to regimental sergeant major, was promoted to major in the field, and won the Military Cross and Bar in 1918.

But when he was demobilized in Canada, he found that he was still a junior in the Bank of Commerce while men who had not gone overseas had been promoted, so he quit the bank and took a job as nightwatchman at the Saint John Drydock in New Brunswick. Six months later he was made general manager and in 1926 he borrowed from the bank and bought the company.

He became an entrepreneur of consequence, with diversified roles including the chairmanship of Western Bridge and Steel Fabricators Ltd., International Paints (Canada), and the Canadian Dredge and Dock Co. He was president of West Coast Shipbuilders, vice-president of Hamilton Bridge Western Ltd. and the Douglas Lake Cattle Co., and during World War Two director-general of naval armaments and equipment in the Department of Munitions and Supply in Ottawa, where he met and married Phyllis Turner, and subsequently he was Lieutenant-Governor of British Columbia.

John Turner remembers him as a caring man, "a great guy," but also a strong disciplinarian, and "not really a father to me."

"There is always that resistance between stepson and stepfather," Turner says. "He was a very strong-minded, straight guy and he had a temper. Sometimes he lost it with me, usually because of my independence of views. We'd argue at the dinner table and sometimes I'd be asked to leave. He expected you to dress properly for dinner and he expected you to be on time. Once I was to go fishing with the Old Man and some of his friends, and I was supposed to meet him at the Vancouver Club at twelve noon and I arrived five minutes late and he was gone.

"Oh, yes, he was tough," Turner says. "He was down at the office at seven in the morning virtually until the last few years of his life. He was a hard worker. And then he would be at the club for lunch and have a few drinks with the boys and go back to the office and sign some mail. By four o'clock he'd have some of his cronies in his den at Point Grey and they'd be killing a bottle of Scotch. The old man could come close to killing a bottle of Scotch a day by himself.

"But he never drank after dinner. He always claimed the food would absorb it. And he never drank wine, so he didn't mix it. He just loved a good Dewar's Scotch."

Ross arranged a few odd summer jobs at West Coast Shipbuilders for Turner in his late high school and early university years, once as a "gofer" in the blueprint department and once as a rivet catcher in the shipyard. Turner becomes animated and paces his plush law office high in the Royal Bank Tower in Toronto as he describes the rivet-catching job with dramatic gestures.

"They were building these big ships," he says, "and I remember holding that can there and the boys were throwing those red-hot rivets. The boys would take them out of the fire. They throw the rivets. You catch the rivet and then you take it out of the can and hand it to the guy who was drilling it in. Of course, when the boys knew my old man owned the place, those guys were throwing the rivets pretty hard at me. And I could see some of those guys with scars in their cheeks and I was scared shitless."

According to Turner, Ross lost a lot of money in the late years of his life, partly from repaying debts for which he was not technically liable, but for which he felt personally responsible. Still, there was enough money in the end to keep his widow in reasonable comfort. But he left nothing to his stepson. "I don't have any complaint about that," Turner says. "I believe every generation looks after itself."

Turner went to the University of British Columbia from the big house in Point Grey. He was just sixteen then and once more he was thrown together with people much older than he was, because it was 1945 and his was the first post-war class, packed with veterans just back from the European theatre.

Again he was brilliant academically. He had done part of his grade thirteen at St. Pat's, particularly algebra and geometry, but the university insisted he do those subjects again in his first university year. He went to see Professor Walter Gage, who was in charge of mathematics, and Gage said: "Look, it's a few months to Christmas. If you can get 100 on either of those subjects at Christmas I'll give you a credit." Turner got marks of 100 in both algebra and geometry at Christmas and was given both credits.

He studied for his Bachelor of Arts, intending to make a career eventually in physics or chemistry, but decided in his second year to move into political science, economics, and English. His deskmate in French 100 and also his lockermate in the gym was Peter Worthington, who was to become a foreign correspondent for the *Toronto Telegram*, right-wing editor of the *Toronto Sun*, and maverick Conservative candidate in the Toronto riding of Broadview-Greenwood.

"Turner really had everything in those days," Worthington says. "He was young. He was good looking. He was terribly clever. He was a great athlete. And he was nice. You could always tell the popular guys because they went out with the cheerleaders. Turner always went out with the prettiest cheerleader.

"And he didn't seem to have to work hard to achieve all these things. The strange thing was he managed to beat everyone else at all of them and seem to have everything going for him, with rich parents and a big home, and still be considered a good guy. That took some doing at that university in those days. But he got away with it because he was just a genuinely nice person.

"I think he'll make a good prime minister. He's not a power-mad sort of a guy. He's the sort of guy who has old-fashioned standards and feels it's his duty to serve his country and I think there are still a lot of people around who appreciate that. He could beat [Conservative Party Leader] Brian Mulroney in an election, you know."

Turner did his honours B.A. in political science under the renowned Professor Henry Angus, who had taught the same subjects to his mother in the twenties, and he wrote his thesis on the Senate of Canada. The thesis is still on file in the university archives and was published in a book of scholarly work done by former students of Professor Angus. It reads in part:

What useful purpose does the Senate have today? Neither in its federal nor legislative aspects has the Senate accomplished its purpose. If this is so, there can be no logical impediment to its reform or abolition. The argument, however, is more severe. The waste of talent in the Senate of recent administrations has made that chamber a functionless oddity; but it has been the abuse in the method of appointments which has bankrupted its reputation in the country.

It was originally hoped that the Senate would be an impartial and reflective body. The Fathers of Confederation were not unaware of the partisan use to which the appointment procedure could be put, but they hardly foresaw the proportions it would reach. They expected that the legislature would have some control over the appointments and thereby limit the extent to which political patronage could be pushed; but two developments in the post-Confederation era completely dashed any such hopes. The first was the gradual dominance of the Prime Minister over the Commons and later over his cabinet – a development which had not been foreseen in 1864. Consequently appointments to the Senate have become his virtual preserve as his personal patronage. It is not surprising, therefore, that they have been made on the basis of partisanship . . . .

Because of the partisan source of the appointments, the nominations have fallen largely in three categories: Cabinet ministers who are weary of the burdens of office [or who have become burdens themselves]; old political war horses who have lost their seats or who are tired of running elections; and what the Americans call "fat cats," meaning rich men who have become generous subscribers to the campaign funds of the party. Party affiliation does not always mean the best appointment. Despite the fact that most of the ex-ministers are very useful senators and that some of the wealthy appointees bring to the debates an informed understanding of financial prob-

51

lems, the general standard of contribution to the debates by most of the senators is paltry . . . .

Why is it that the discussion [of reform] never ripens into action? There are a number of very good reasons. Undoubtedly, from a realistic point of view, the strongest is that power corrupts. A prime minister once in office is loath to foment any agitation which might result finally in his being deprived of a very convenient source of patronage with which to humour his party followers . . . .

Essentially, Turner, who was not yet twenty, argued that while the Senate had been useful in some areas, particularly the committee system, it had not fulfilled its purpose because it was non-elected. He concluded, in general terms, that the Senate served no useful purpose in Canada, but that there was no way to get rid of it.

Turner was known as "Chick" at UBC, a nickname given to him by Francis Percival ("Bun") Highley when they played neighbourhood hockey together in Ottawa. Worthington, Turner's desk and lockermate at UBC, didn't even know his name was John until he met him years later when he was a foreign correspondent in Russia and Turner was a parliamentary assistant on a tour of the Soviet Union with Northern Affairs Minister Arthur Laing.

Chick Turner wrote a sports column for the student newspaper, *Ubyssey*, called "Chalk Talk, by Chick," and later became the paper's sports editor. A poll of students at the time showed that "Chalk Talk" had the second widest readership on the campus after a humour column by Eric Nicol.

Ron Haggart, producer of the CBC's *The Fifth Estate*, was editor of the paper and on the student council with Turner. He describes his writing style as a mystic code language, which was popular with some sports writers of the time. "For instance," says Haggart, "a basketball to Chick Turner would be a 'sphere' and basketball teams 'copped the gonfalon on the maple boards' or something like that."

Haggart recalls that Turner once wrote in his sports column: "This corner bills Doug Whittle's UBC mermen as odds-on favourites to edge out the College of Puget Sound, Willamette and Lewis and Clark entries and to latch on to the first conference seaweed crown put on the velvet." As the newspaper's editor, Haggart says, he interpreted this to mean that Turner expected UBC's swimming team to win something.

He can also recall Turner actually talking in the same sort of complicated jive-code style of address considered hip at the time, including asking one friend: "Hey, snappy pair of kicks, who ya featuring tonight," which Haggart says he found understandable but difficult to render in a literal translation. He also remembers Turner as a hard worker on the paper and a social animal on the campus, involved in everything and extremely popular with everybody.

Turner's hero then was Pierre Berton, who had worked on the *Ubyssey* and had become a reporter on the *Vancouver Sun*, and there were times when he considered a career in journalism: "I always had a respect for that profession," he says. "You know, I appreciate the homework that has to go into it if you are to do it well, the ability to get at the facts, the art of getting balanced opinions . . . ."

He joined the Beta Theta Pi fraternity, one of the international fraternities, which has continued to play a role in his life with its ideals of cultivation of the intellect, unsullied friendship, and un-altering fidelity, along with a reputation for good singing and sportsmanship. Turner was the main speaker at the seventy-fifth anniversary of Beta Theta Pi at the Royal York Hotel in Toronto in October, 1981, quoting in his speech an earlier Beta: "Thus it is that Beta can be eternal. It is an ageless idea, and within ideas lie enshrined the spirits of men . . . . It is by this spirit that we shall continue to live, not simply by the love of brother for brother, but by the idea of love, the conception that love is possible and usable. It is this idea that is eternal! As long as we dare to believe in love, Beta Theta Pi will grow from more to more."

The fraternity met frequently in Turner's big home in Point Grey, lifting the rafters, he remembers, with their songs although drinking was taboo at all Beta gatherings. "For me," he said in his Toronto speech, "I cannot reminisce about my college days without reviving the bond of Beta Theta Pi: my fraternity – our fraternity. The fraternity was so much of my life at the University of British Columbia that I cannot reflect upon those days without reliving those fireside chats, the mystique of the ritual, the bonds of friendship and, of course, the singing."

He did not run in his first year at the university, choosing instead to swim for the fraternity and winning a few intramural races, but he was never in championship class. And he took no interest at all in politics except at the campus level as co-ordinator of activities of the student council, supervising the activities of the various clubs on the campus and arranging for visiting speakers.

"I don't think I had any political leanings at that time," he says. "Probably I was Liberal if anything, due to my stepfather, who was an old-fashioned Liberal and friend of people like Mackenzie King and C.D. Howe. But possibly my mother was a Conservative. She'd been a great friend of R.B. Bennett during those days in Ottawa. I just don't know."

In his second year, in 1947, he went back to track and field, training daily in the old UBC stadium under the renowned coach, Johnny Owen. Within weeks he was running the 100 yards in 10 seconds flat and the 220 yards in 22 flat, and he became the sprint star of the track and field team, competing in the Pacific Northwest Conference against smaller American colleges like Whitman, Walla Walla, the University of Oregon, and Washington State Teacher's College.

Late in that same summer the B.C. government provided a few hundred dollars to send a team of twelve young men and women to the Canadian track and field championships at Edmonton. Turner was appointed captain. It was a ragtag team competing against other provinces heavily sponsored by their governments, particularly Ontario, which sent a team of over sixty athletes, coached by the famous physical fitness expert, Lloyd H. Percival, who had additional sponsorship from the Canadian Broadcasting Corporation.

But the B.C. team did well. Its members won the mile, the half-mile, and the high jump. Chick Turner won the 100-yard dash, crossing the tape a whisker ahead of Wally Alexander, also from Vancouver. He also won the 220 junior championship and entered himself in the 440, but Percival talked him out of running the longer distance, claiming he would be overexerting himself. "I could have won it," Turner says, "but I let Percival talk me out of it. We had no coach, just me as captain, and I was seventeen, and we had no training, nothing compared to those guys from Ontario, but we cleaned up anyway and the Vancouver papers loved that."

Turner's athletic ability soon came to the attention of a remarkable character named Major H.B. Morris Kinley, who probably left as lasting an impression on Turner as anybody from his youthful days except his mother, stepfather, and A.L. Cochrane, his mentor at Camp Timagami. The Major – and nobody was sure that he really was a major – was a disinherited Irishman who claimed to have come from one of the great Irish families, a family so rich and superior it owned racehorses he used to train prior to whatever dark event occurred that caused his banishment to the colonies.

The Major had no visible means of support. He had once been a political organizer for Gordon Wismer, who was B.C.'s attorney general, but that was all over and by the time Turner knew him his full-time occupation appeared to be the training of amateur athletes. He was a small, dapper man with a ruddy complexion. He wore a bowler hat, spats, and a coloured vest. There was a perpetual cigar in his mouth and a constantly depleting mickey of cheap rye on his hip in a classy silver flask, which Turner would occasionally polish for him.

The Major trained athletes the same way he had trained racehorses. He believed if a horse had to run a six-furlong race, it had to be trained to sprint over four furlongs and also over a greater distance of eight furlongs. Then it would run the middle distance fast in the race. That's the way he trained Chick Turner, sprinting him repeatedly over 50 yards and then over 220 yards to prepare him for the 100, and over 100 yards and 440 yards for a 220 event. It may not have been scientific, but it worked. Turner began to run the sprint events in world-class times, about 9.7 seconds for the 100, and he travelled to university and other major meets throughout the Pacific Northwest with a group of about twelve other top athletes in the Major's care. They called themselves the Owls' Club. They had to pay their own expenses and chip in for the Major's, including the cost of a constant refilling of the silver flask. And they won constantly.

Turner was favoured to win the Canadian 100-yard dash at the Canadian track and field championships in Vancouver that year, but he decided to run for his parish, Our Lady of Perpetual Help in Point Grey, in a Catholic Youth Organization meet two days before the big championship race. He wanted to show that the small suburban parish could beat the big downtown Cathedral Parish and he took advantage of a rule allowing each team four athletes who were not actually parish members. Turner brought in four "ringers" from the University of Washington, the University of Oregon, and the Owls' Club, all capable of running world-class times, and the tiny parish won the meet easily. But there were angry allegations of crookery. Turner won the 100 at the CYO meet, coasting past the tape in 9.9 seconds, but he broke the Major's training schedule and the Major was furious with him for running without his permission, in what he called "that two-bit meet, two days before the Canadian championships."

The Major was right, as usual. Turner had a slow start in the 100-yard dash and was beaten by Roger Wellman in the slow time of 10 seconds flat. But he started well in the 220 final later in the day, pounded around the turn with the long stride his colleagues described as powerful but not graceful, arms pumping awkwardly, running with his shoulders, and he held on to win in 22.5 seconds.

His main ambition was to run for Canada in the 1948 Olympic Games, but in February, four months before the trials in Vancouver, he drove to a party in New Westminster with a girl friend and another young couple. A heavy fog enveloped them on the way home. A train hit the car at the Arbutus Street level crossing, which had no gates. It swept the car about 100 feet along the track and wrecked it. They all suffered minor injuries. Turner's left knee was smashed and his left leg muscles shrank away.

Turner never ran as well again. Doctors fixed up his knee and he trained hard for the Olympic trials. But his left leg gave way after 70 yards in the 100-yard final. He fell to the ground writhing in pain, and weeping in disappointment.

Later in his life, when he was a prospering young lawyer in Montreal, Turner would call on the Major during visits to his family in Vancouver. "I was very close to the Major," Turner says today. "He was one of my heroes and I loved him." The Major was living then in a shabby, dirty room on Vancouver's Skid Road, and Turner would bring him a bottle of Scotch and slip him a few hundred dollars. When Major H.B. Morris Kinley died in the fifties, Chick Turner flew to Vancouver and paid for his pauper's funeral. Only twelve people – a few bums, a few former athletes, and two sportswriters – showed up.

Somehow Turner also managed to study at UBC. He was, according to Professor Henry Angus, who is now ninety-three and living in Vancouver, "a particularly good student, with the right approach to work. He had a good general attitude, intellectual ability, skill in sports, a sense of public service, and a commitment to his fellows. His mother, Phyllis, had the same attitude."

In his fourth year at UBC, Turner applied to Dalhousie Law School, because his mother wanted him to go there, and also to Harvard, where he wanted to go. But Dr. Angus suggested he might like to stand for a Rhodes Scholarship. "I really didn't know what I wanted to do," Turner says, "but I guess I had a feeling law wasn't a bad thing to do. It was a good education, whether or not one became a lawyer. And, frankly, on the Rhodes Scholarship application I had to put down something, so I put down what they call jurisprudence over there."

There was one scholarship for each of the provinces except Ontario and Quebec, where there were two, and there were more than fifty applications in British Columbia that year. Turner won, after beating out an old friend and fraternity brother, David Williams, now a leading barrister in Duncan, B.C., in the final interviews.

As he left for Oxford, the university newspaper voted him the most popular student on the campus. He was a golden boy.

56

7

The Oxford Years

In the beginning, even in the end, Oxford was a humbling experience for the Canadian golden boy. There were young men there who could think and talk better than he could, get better marks and prettier girls, even run faster and further.

"I remember," Turner says, "being overwhelmed by the ability of the English and Scottish student to talk – to make an after-dinner speech. We couldn't touch them, you know. They just had the skill and the literary training and training in the English language that we didn't have. I felt a bit inferior."

He applied to Magdalen College, where his Canadian mentor, Henry Angus, had been the first student in almost a century to get straight A's in law, and he lived in the college for the first two years, studying jurisprudence under tutors Dr. J.H.C. Morris, who subsequently edited several classic textbooks on the conflict of law, and Rupert Cross, who was blind and who became one of the great British experts on criminal law. Sometimes Turner didn't study very hard, failed to complete a written essay for Cross, and tried to fake the finish of it when reading to the blind tutor, but Cross always caught him out.

"God, that got a little shoddy at the end, didn't it, John?" Cross would say.

And Turner would admit: "Well, to tell you the truth, Rupert, I was winging it."

But he got along well with Cross, taking him often on his arm to pubs for extracurricular conviviality. His other tutor, Morris, was somewhat more fearsome and sometimes criticized his student for a lack of effort. "I used to tell Dr. Morris that I hadn't come 6,000 miles just to study, that I was looking for the whole experience, and I didn't have much time to study on vacations because I travelled. But I had a great respect for him," Turner says.

He had a good time. One of his best friends was Malcolm Fraser, who became Prime Minister of Australia from 1975 to 1983, although he was considered by his contemporaries at Oxford, Turner says, as the student least likely to succeed. Turner was also an acquaintance of Bob Hawke, the present Australian Prime Minister, who also was a Rhodes Scholar.

Fraser, whose way through Oxford was paid by rich Australian parents, owned a hot Aston Martin car and Turner was his co-driver in many weekend automobile rallies around Britain and Scotland. They even set off for the Monte Carlo rally once, but didn't get to the start. "I don't think we ever even finished a race," Turner reminisces. "We'd meet a couple of gals somewhere, and you know . . . ."

Turner liked the girls. He wrote to his sister at McGill University:

Dearest Brenda,

. . . I received a long letter from Gay the other day: She is enthusiastically happy with nursing and with most other things; as you say, of course, I know nothing of her social life in Toronto. Why should I? Let the competition kill itself off, say I with a smug shrug of self-confidence. . . .

I am happy to hear that you are still the social centre of the metropolis and also that you are stopping (or coming up) for air long enough to absorb a little passive culture. . . . I continue to pound the books during the vacation in a rough 6-8 hour day. The rest of the time I chew the fat with the international set up here or read a little outside the law. I've told you what a jealous mistress the law is; lawyers are so apt to get chained to the legal tomes that they forget about the beauties of the outside world, especially philosophy and literature; uncultured parasites!

My social life, which never fails to interest you – loyal sister that you are – progresses aimlessly. I crashed a few of the "smahter" parties of Oxford undergraduate life during the last week of term – just for the gusto and grins. My coup was "kidnapping" – by charm alone, my dear – the leading actress of the university. Good company! . . .

Blair, Frank and I decided to pass up the Blackheath ball and settled instead for a quiet evening in the girls' flat in Earl's Court. Six – and I repeat, six – girls made dinner for the three of us: We played parlor games and bridge and thereby saw out the evening. . . .

I am spending Christmas in Rouen, or Paris – I haven't quite decided – with a French family; they are students I met during my travels this summer. Agnes and Annie are their names.

Some other jokers are being invited so it should be good for grins. I am working on an invite with Helene for Christmas, but I can't be too blatant about it. I might have to settle for New Year's; but that again, say I licking my fangs, wouldn't be at all a disaster. My excuse to the outside world, including the family, is that I am there to learn French. It will be a necessary byproduct.

Jean Pierre and I saw the Spanish Ballet in London the night before the Twickenham game. It was unconscious. . . . Those lovely girls just exploded into passion and frenzy as the heat of the dances enveloped them. The technique was perfectionist; but it was difficult indeed to restrict one's gaze to the artistic strands of the dance: I have never seen such beautiful and tempting women on the stage; and they had poise and that certain fetching aloofness which is the challenge of every red-corpuscled Canadian youth. Even after a year and a half of English fare, I was able to respond to treatment. . . .

Merry Christmas,

John.

PS: Tell Semple that I appreciate her approval.

And he ran. Roger Bannister, the first four-minute miler, was captain of the track and field team in Turner's first year and Chris Chataway, the other great distance runner, was captain in his third year and they were firm friends of Turner's, especially Chataway, who still visits him frequently in Toronto. Turner sprinted for Oxford and England, winning some races, and he was told, along with another Canadian athlete, Jack Burney, that there would be a place for him on the 1952 Canadian Olympic team, based on his British times, without his having to travel home to participate in the Olympic trials at Hamilton. But whoever made that decision was overruled and neither he nor Burney was allowed to run.

Turner went to the Olympics at Helsinki anyway and watched his friend Bannister finish fourth in the 1,500 metres and Chataway, in one of the Olympics' great races, challenge the great Emil Zatopek for the lead on the home turn of the 5,000 metres, only to trip on the concrete lining of the track, pick himself up, and finish a close fifth. Turner and Chataway went out on the town in Helsinki with two Finnish girls that night and they had a party they both recall with considerable awe.

But Turner's twenty-first birthday party at Oxford was even more memorable. His friends booked former Magdalen man Oscar Wilde's rooms, overlooking the Char River, which had been turned into a private dining room, for the birthday celebration. It was an all-male party and guests were required to wear black tie.

Wilde's rooms were packed with celebrants drinking wine and beer in considerable quantities. Some of them eventually became influential and important people. Turner lists a few he can remember. Malcolm Fraser was there, of course, and Chris Chataway, and Bill Forbes, who was to become the United Kingdom's Law Reform Commissioner; and Nick Browne-Wilkinson, now a judge of the British Court of Appeal; Tim Everard, now a high-ranking British diplomat; Alex Morrison, who runs the J. Walter Thompson advertising company in the United Kingdom; and Jeremy Thorpe, who became leader of the British Liberal Party. They were just a few.

Late in the evening the entire party jumped from Oscar Wilde's windows into the Char River in their dinner suits and swam about a quarter of a mile, under the Magdalen Bridge, to St. Hilda's, the ladies' college, where they staggered ashore to a giggly and friendly welcome. Turner and his yet-to-become-important friends were all in serious trouble with the university proctors next day.

At about this time he wrote to his mother:

Dearest Mom,

Another two weeks have slipped past. The amount of work declined but I guess it's a natural relapse after nine weeks of pounding. It's the end of term next Saturday, and everyone gets those end-of-term lapses. . . .

I am running in the relays against Cambridge again this year, in the 4 × 110 yards and the 4 × 220 yards. It is being run in Oxford this year and is the occasion of the opening of a new track by the vice-chancellor, Dr. Lowe. We should win this year; last year, you may remember, we lost 4-3. Prediction this year: Oxford by 5-2. I am not running especially well as old standards go, but in the trial I was only a foot behind the captain who won and beat Wilkinson and Pinnington, two English internationals; a bit of luck!

I am in the throes of writing Christmas cards: I'll have to get them off by next week. I think the final count will be around 160, a large number despite the shearing I've done off last year's list.

Last night was one of the greatest. After a tough afternoon of baton practice for the relays, I flopped down for some tea and wrote cards. Then about 6:30 I put on my suit and went over to Tim's and there he was doling out free sherry to a few of the "boys." Then I went to Charles Richeson's cocktail party. Charles was a good friend of Joe McKnight and comes from Oklahoma: good friend of lame-duck Senator Elmer Thomas and of Perle Mesta. At any rate it was a "smaht" party and since I didn't know a soul when I entered the room I'll call it bizarre too. However champagne cocktails soon breached the gap caused by lack of acquaintance. There were some interesting characters among an overwhelming majority of dross. Charles was proud of the aggregation assembled, however, winking at me and telling me there were two marquis and an earl present. Among the guests was a girl, Kim Sutherland, from Flint, Michigan, who knew Pierre Thurber, my great pal at Camp Timagami. I kidnapped her from the party in great style and we wandered into another "smaht" party in University College to which she had been invited. There again, I hardly knew a soul, but found a couple of golfing blues whom I met in Vincent and who had secreted away a few bottles of champagne, so we enjoyed ourselves. By this time, Kim was off on her own – since she had been invited by some sod – so I stumbled into a lovely little blonde, who had spent seven months in Duncan, B.C. You could hardly call that Canadianization, but I used it as sufficient excuse to wrap the mantle of common nationality around us. That solved the evening there. I took leave of her – not knowing the hosts or even what they looked like – and got into college by 12:00. Interesting evening, for one night, but on the whole not my type of people. The party in Univ. must have cost somebody 150 quid.

I'm on my way to mass now.

You could send some boxes of chocolate, if you want, for Christmas. A cheque would be best: skip the presents – the British government would do too well. Also a lot of Kraft Velveeta cheese would be good: I love the stuff.

Give my regards to Mr. Ross.

Love and kisses,

John.

PS: Excellent sermon at mass this morning on the "Attributes of God." Heard an excellent performance of Handel's *Messiah* in the Oxford Town Hall this afternoon.

The college's dining room steward, a Mr. Bond, who didn't seem to have a first name, took a liking to Turner, occasionally honouring him with an invitation for a drink in his office after dinner. "Bond was only the steward of the college," Turner says, "but you never went into that office for a drink or a port after dinner unless Bond invited you. You were brought in first as a guest, and unless Bond said to you as you left the room that first time, 'Mr. Turner, I enjoyed having you here. I hope to see you again,' you never showed up there again. If Bond liked you, you were in, and if he didn't like you you weren't in. There was no fooling around."

Bond liked Turner and Turner became a member of the college's wine committee, which meant he had to go to London twice a year with Bond and another student to taste and order the wines for the college. "That was a hell of a time," says Turner. "We used to taste all the good wines and have a hell of a dinner, all paid for by the Junior Common Room."

Turner loved London and still regards it as his favourite city. Twelve times a year, because he wanted to be called to the English bar, he had to "eat dinners" at Gray's Inn, one of London's four Inns of Court, so that the barristers could pass judgement on whether he was a gentleman, as well as a scholar, and thus suitable eventually to wear the robe.

On at least one occasion, his colonial exuberance was too much for the barristers. He was accused of disturbing the dignity of the place by loudly conversing with Joe Potts, now a judge of the Supreme Court of Ontario, who is still renowned for his bullhorn voice at Liberal gatherings, and both were summoned by the treasurer of the Inn and ordered to pay for their crime by singing for the Inn from the head table. Turner and Potts did a duet of "Annie Laurie" and then "Alouette" for an encore and brought the house down. They were not only pardoned for their boisterous behaviour but given a decanter of port to oil their throats for a continuation of their loud, colonial conversation.

"These dinners were a legitimate reason to get out of Oxford," Turner says. "It was a perfect cover and we could have a hell of a good time in London. I used to love going to a place called The Players' Theatre, which was almost vaudevillian. Unemployed actors, amateur actors, actors in between engagements would perform there. I tell you, for two shillings and sixpence you could get in there on a Sunday evening, grab a chair and drink a beer and watch this stuff – pantomimes, music hall stuff, outrageously corny, most of it. It was a lot of fun."

Of course, there was also serious work at Oxford, and Turner did not do badly at it. He represented Oxford against Cambridge at the Moot Court, appearing before some of the great judges of the era in mock trials, and was secretary of the Oxford Law Society.

In October, 1950, he wrote his mother:

I brought my working week up to 51 solid hours last week

before my collections. My results were adequate, but not outstanding, considering that I knew nothing about Roman Law aside from the texts and messed the Real Property paper up because of bad planning of time; and a law exam is a new experience for me.

This week I started my Criminal Law and it is the most interesting subject yet: this week: Homicide – murder and manslaughter, with suicide and infanticide thrown in for color.

I have a fairly heavy lecture schedule, but will soon discontinue Goodhart on Jurisprudence and Waldock on International Law so soon as I see that the notes I have of Joe McKnight's on them are good (and it appears that they are).

However, I must attend Nickolas on the Roman Law of Delict, Fifoot on the Sale of Goods Act, 1893, Cross on Possession, and Treitel on Roman Law of Contract, still. However that schedule won't be so heavy as far as lectures are concerned. . . .

I have been elected to two fairly "smaht" clubs. The first is the Raleigh Club which discusses political affairs relating to the Commonwealth and is open to 36 members therefrom. The speakers are always outstanding. The second is the renowned Vincent's Club, home of the Blues. I secured election on first ballot and so may eat with the great and near-great in the club. It is a club primarily for sportsmen so I consider myself lucky to be in it. With an Achilles and a Vincent's tie one is awfully "smaht."

He passed his B.A. in Jurisprudence in two years, then had the scholarship extended a year to pass his Bachelor of Civil Law (B.C.L.). But almost for the first time in his life he was not head of his class. His marks were second class, though high in the second-class range mainly because of his skill in oral exams.

"Yeah, so Oxford cut me down to size," Turner says. "The university set a standard of excellence that could never be reached, but I built up life-long friendships at Oxford, broadened my view of the world, and although some of my friends mightn't conceive this, it gave me intellectual humility. I learned where my place was in the cerebral spectrum.

"You learn all sorts of things at Oxford apart from having to write those essays," Turner says. "You learn that while the North American undergraduate takes courses, at Oxford a man studies a subject, and questions it. You learn the development of the powers of thought, the capacity for independent work, the studied nonchalance of the British, the sheer excellence of conversation, the

63

coherent, disciplined use of the English language, the gift of understatement, and the joy of the playing field, where sport is played for the love of sport."

He sometimes quotes Donald Gordon, the former president of the CNR: "A Rhodes Scholar is a young man with his future behind him," but Cecil Rhodes, who made the scholarships possible, is still one of his great heroes. Turner has collected a library on his life and describes the much criticized multimillionaire, who made his fortune in South Africa and Rhodesia, as a gigantic figure, a genius with a vision and a man of tremendous mental and physical courage.

"Nobody who ever got the scholarship has yet measured up to Rhodes," Turner says. "He was not an imperialist and mercantilist as his critics claim. He wanted South Africa and Rhodesia to stand on their own two feet, not just to funnel their wealth back to Britain. He opposed Downing Street and was one of the first advocates of what we call dominion status."

Turner's eyes shine and he bubbles with enthusiasm when he talks of Rhodes: "He was a multimillionaire at twenty-four and then he sent himself back to Oxford on the money he'd earned himself because he wanted to get an education," he enthuses. "He believed with Aristotle that the definition of happiness is activity in excellence, and he set forth in his final will the main characteristics he wanted in his scholars – moral character, leadership, and interest in one's fellows."

Turner says Rhodes' vision of an Anglo-Saxon elitist power block has never been realized, nor should it be, and until lately his scholarship winners had not achieved the eminence in public life he had hoped for. "But lately in Canada, you know, we had four members of the federal cabinet at one time who were Rhodes Scholars: Jack Davis, from British Columbia, Otto Lang, from Saskatchewan, Alastair Gillespie, from Ontario, and me from B.C. And Premier Allan Blakeney of Saskatchewan was a Rhodes Scholar. Now we've got a lot of deputy ministers and hundreds of men who have influenced education and the professions in this country," he says. "Rhodes is a hero and I think he has been painted unfairly by the modern writer because he was a free enterpriser."

When he came down to London from Oxford in the fall of 1952 to study for his bar examinations he shared a rented house on Gilson Road, off Old Bromley, with a group of other colonials, including Chester Butterfield, who is now practising law in Bermuda, Ron Barnard, who became Bermuda's Crown Prosecutor, and John Horsman, who ran the half-mile for Oxford and is now a gentleman farmer in Australia.

"There would be a number of people who might stay with us for a week or two," Turner says. "We used to cook our own meals. We had a perpetual stew going and we'd just add stuff to it, scrape off the fungus and keep the thing moving. All of us had come down from Oxford and were studying for our bar exams and it was boring work, just working on those damn papers. But we knew a lot of girls around London, and the parties were all-night killers."

Turner moved to Paris in the spring of 1953, while awaiting the results of his bar examinations, and enrolled at the University of Paris to study for a doctorate of law, taking some courses under Henri Battifol, one of the world's leading authorities on private international law. He lived in a pension owned by a Madame De Labauchere on the Right Bank, not far from the Arc de Triomphe.

Theatre was thriving then in the City of Light and student tickets were inexpensive. He spent many nights in the balconies, particularly at Le Grand Guignol, which was a kind of horror theatre, performing Draculian types of plays, which fascinated him. And he attended the opera often. It was a great time and place for students, and Turner whiled away some afternoons and evenings in the bistros, particularly Brassarie Litps, on St. Germaine, a haunt of intellectual socialists, arguing about what was wrong with the world. He also travelled extensively in France, to the homes of French friends he'd made, and in the summer of 1953, with his sister Brenda, around the borders of France and the adjoining countries in a rented car.

Turner has always kept in touch with his friends from his year in Paris, as he has with the friends of his life, creating a wide network of them. Diana Gill, who got him his room at Madame De Labauchere's and is now the wife of David Kirkwood, a deputy minister in Ottawa, remembers him in Paris as "just wonderful, very excited about life and busy all the time. He was also very religious," she says. "He went to mass every morning and then took some lovely girl out every night. They seemed to be mostly English girls, people he'd met at Oxford. He knew an awful lot of people, a lot of beautiful girls.

"But the people we stayed with at the pension were middle-class people, awfully nice people, and they provided an entrée into the French world for him too. None of us spoke good French, including John. He spoke French very rapidly and very badly, but he was very personable in the language and he improved," she says.

He played squash in Paris with Paul Crepeau, now a member of the Faculty of Law at McGill University, who is revising Quebec's Civil Code, and Crepeau remembers: "He was a very good squash player, very quick, but not the sort who tried to get the better of you all the time. He used to beat me just the same. But he was a good sportsman and it was enjoyable playing with him. In those days he was very candid, brilliant, witty and sharp, a social animal, who loved people and put them at ease, often by poking fun at himself. I always thought then he'd eventually go into politics. I remember telling friends he was going to end up prime minister one day."

When he visits Paris, Turner still drops in on the family of Madame De Labauchere, who is dead now, to reminisce on the good meals she served and the wine she watered down a bit, and how she tried to teach him Moral Disarmament and kept him out of trouble with her motherly advice.

He returned to England late in the summer of 1953 to be called to the bar at Gray's Inn, intending to go back to Paris to complete his doctorate. But his stepfather Frank Ross wrote to him: "You've had a good run, you know. When are you going to come back and get to work?" So Turner flew home to Canada, intending to start a law practice in Vancouver.

8

The Young
Montreal Lawyer

Turner returned to Vancouver only briefly to study for his Canadian bar exams, and his thoughts at the time were mainly back at Oxford because he had received a wire from his friend Chris Chataway, urging him to fly back to England because something special was going to happen at the annual meeting between the Amateur Athletic Union of the United Kingdom and Oxford at Oxford's old Iffley Road athletic grounds.

"Chataway didn't say, but I knew they were going to have a crack at the four-minute mile," Turner says. "I couldn't study very well. I kept thinking of my friends and that Iffley Road track, where I'd run so often with Chataway and Bannister. There were no showers there, just those little half-assed tubs they used to get in, and the water was usually cold anyway. There was just the most elementary type of changing room. In Canada, high schools had better facilities, and this was Oxford University, for God's sake, and they were going to do the impossible there."

Turner decided to stick with his studies in Vancouver, but he remembers waiting anxiously for the *Vancouver Sun* to drop on his doorstep and reading the big headline: BRITON RUNS FOUR-MINUTE MILE. "I don't think I've ever been so excited in my life," Turner says. "I ran into the house to show Frank Ross the headline, nearly tripping over everything. But I've regretted all my life not going back to see it happen."

Chataway phoned him that night anyway to tell him all about it, and Turner can still describe the race in minute detail, how Chataway took over the pace for Bannister on the third lap, and how Bannister collapsed over the finish line into the arms of Guy MacLean, a Canadian Rhodes Scholar who is now president of Mount Allison University.

Turner stayed only a short time in Vancouver because he had stopped over in Montreal on his way home from England to visit some friends, and he had fallen in love with the place. Montreal was a lively and beautiful city in that summer of 1953, a little like Paris. Place Ville Marie was being built, and Dorchester Boulevarde, and the Queen Elizabeth Hotel. Jean Drapeau was not elected mayor until the following summer, but his optimistic enthusiasm was spreading infectiously. And no movement for extreme nationalism had yet emerged, so that English and French were spoken almost equally on Montreal's streets and nobody felt uncomfortable in the great restaurants, thriving stores, and government offices.

There was some dissatisfaction behind the scenes, however, mostly in union and intellectual circles, and mostly with the conservative, autocratic rule of Premier Maurice Duplessis. The "three wise men" who later came to Ottawa, Pierre Trudeau, Jean Marchand, and Gerard Pelletier, were plotting against the Duplessis regime, to the extent even of considering entering politics themselves. In the first volume of his memoirs, *The Impatient Years: 1950-1960*, Pelletier wrote:

> To be honest we had no desire to 'get involved in politics,' but we were dissatisfied with life in a society that had come to a standstill. In the early 1950s it was becoming obvious that every segment of Quebec society was ripe for change – except the political.
>
> There was no swallow in sight to announce even the most tentative political springtime. On the contrary, the Duplessis government was hardening its opposition to any change, backed up by nonstop praise for all our traditions, the worst along with the best, but particularly the worst. They kept finding new ways to tell us we had the best education system in the world, that social peace held sway in Quebec as it did nowhere else in the universe, that we were exempt from the ills of which the United States and France were dying, that we alone still possessed the Christian values that elsewhere were being held up to ridicule.
>
> We were thoroughly sick of it all. But a question was starting to be asked that couldn't be ignored: how would we ever arrive at vital social transformations if Maurice Duplessis remained riveted to power? For he was the one who was blocking the horizon. And his regime showed no signs of weakening . . . .

But all of this was below the surface of Quebec at the time, and Montreal was a bustling, gay, and lively city, which John Turner loved. He wasn't interested in politics anyway, and eventually he was to become a friend and admirer of Maurice Duplessis.

Turner rented a room in a big house on Mountain Street behind the Museum of Fine Arts for $50 a month while he sought job interviews with the senior partners of Montreal law firms and finally accepted an offer of about $100 a week to become the first student-lawyer of what was then the small, new firm of Stikeman and Elliott.

"Frank Ross, who was a friend of mine, asked me to look this young fellow over and see if I could get him through the Quebec bar," says Heward Stikeman, who is still head of the firm in Montreal. "But he wasn't sure he wanted to go into law. He'd come down from Oxford with all those degrees and he wanted to be a priest. He was really serious about it, and he talked to me about it as if I was his father. He seemed to be in need of a father figure, always did, and I guess I was one of them. So one day I took him to the Mount Royal Club and we went through a bottle of Burgundy and I talked him out of the priesthood. And then he became such a good lawyer and we eventually fought so many great cases together, some of them important precedents.

"He was a great guy, a self-starter, and he worked very hard," says Stikeman. "His main ability was to analyse a situation, spend the necessary time on research, and then come up with the right solution. If he had an Achilles' heel it was that he was used to adulation and he wanted to be loved. Because of this, I didn't know if he would be tough enough to make it in politics, but eventually when he was Finance Minister he was faced with some tough situations and did some tough things, so maybe I was wrong."

"He was a delightful young fellow when he came to us," says the other senior partner, Fraser Elliott, who now runs Stikeman and Elliott's major Toronto law business. "But he didn't know whether to go into law or into religion. He would talk very seriously to Stike and me about that and get our advice. But he turned out to be an excellent lawyer, absolutely first class, and he worked hard. He was a coats-off sort of young fellow, right down to business. There are some lawyers with academic qualifications like he had who aren't any good because they are too academic, but Turner wasn't like that. His main attribute was just plain common sense. When he had a problem, he analysed it, thought it through and got to the bottom of it. He was a pragmatist. And he was full of fun and enthusiasm."

Elliott recalls Turner being upset only once, when he sent him on a lowly errand for something he can't remember, either his laundry or some coffee. "John flared up and asked me why I didn't send my secretary on a job like that," Elliott says. "And I told him: 'Because her time is more valuable than yours.' Turner thought about that for a while, then told me what I'd said was true. I don't think he was making $100 a week then, more like $50 or $75."

Turner was in serious trouble at the beginning of his law career, however, because none of his law degrees or his call to the English bar qualified him to practise under the Civil Code in Quebec. He went to night school at McGill, taking courses in the Civil Code, hoping to memorize it and be allowed to sit for the Quebec bar examinations with others who had spent three or four years on the Code at university, but the task was almost impossible.

Turner decided to do something about what he regarded as this injustice. He'd heard of another young lawyer who had come down from Cambridge and been called to the English bar, then been refused admittance to the Quebec bar without three more years of study, and who had managed to have a private bill passed by the Quebec legislature to overcome the situation. Turner borrowed a copy of this precedent bill, drafted an exact copy, and asked a backbencher named Daniel Johnson, whom he didn't know but who was eventually to become Premier of Quebec, if he would sponsor the private bill.

Johnson agreed and Turner travelled to Quebec City to appear before the Private Bills Committee of the Quebec legislature. This is the way he tells the story:

"So I went up to the legislature and I looked in and there was the committee sitting at a long table, and at the head of the committee was Antoine Rivard, who was then the Attorney General of Quebec, and sitting at his right was Premier Maurice Duplessis. I tell you, I was just a young fellow and I was a little nervous about how all of this was going to come out.

"But I went to the cloakroom where the lawyers were all getting gowned and I ran into this fellow, Camile Noel. He introduced himself, said he was a lawyer. I guess he must have been in his forties then. He said. 'Who are you representing?' and I said, 'I'm representing myself, Mr. Noel.' And I said, 'Who are you representing?' and he said, 'I'm representing the City of Hull, and we want to get an amendment to the charter, so we have to appear before this committee.'

"So I told him about my bill, and he said, 'It makes a lot of sense, but how are you going to handle it in there?'

" 'Well,' I said, 'I'll plead my own case.'

"And he said, 'Are you going to do it in French or English?'

"And I said, 'Well, in order to be precise, I think I had better do this in English.'

"And he said: 'Do it in French.'

"So," Turner says, continuing his story, "I go in there and I listen to Noel get his bill through. He was a well-known Conservative and he got along well with Duplessis. You could see that. And then my bill is called, and I get up and start talking in French, which wasn't all that good, although it was improving.

"And I was describing the bill and where I'd come from and why I needed the bill, and Maurice Duplessis interrupted, in French, of course, and he said: 'Mr. Chairman, I'd like to ask the petitioner how it is that coming from British Columbia he speaks such good French.'

"So I described how I felt that anybody who lives in this country ought to be able to handle both languages and this set Duplessis off on one of his favourite speeches, which must have lasted ten minutes. He went on and on about the necessity for two languages in this great country called Canada, etc., etc. Duplessis was a good Canadian, you know, a strong nationalist, but a good Canadian. And during this whole oration, I just stood there, with my hands behind my back, just listening and wondering, for God's sake, how was I going to get out of this.

"Then at the end of his speech, Duplessis said: 'I don't see any objections to this bill,' and he looked at the chairman and said, 'Are there any objections?' and Antoine Rivard said, 'I don't see any objections. Are there any objections?' And, of course, if Mr. Duplessis saw no objections, there were no objections. So the bill was passed.

"Later on Camile Noel was appointed by Diefenbaker to the Exchequer Court, and then when I was Minister of Justice I re-constituted the court, making it the Federal Court, and I made him Associate Chief Justice – my friend Noel. That's the way life works, you know. It's not just that I owed him one. He was an excellent judge, and I remained friends with him over the years."

Turner also remained friends with Johnson and Duplessis over the years. After the hearing he sent Johnson a forty-ounce bottle of Dewar's Scotch as his fee for sponsoring the bill, and Johnson approached him in the legislature corridors and told him the Premier would like both of them to join him in his office for a sherry before lunch.

"Then when he used to come to the hockey games to see the Montreal Canadiens play on Saturday nights, he would have a couple of extra tickets," Turner says. "And there'd be a message at the law office saying the Premier would like to have me join him either at Drury's or Café Matin and then go to the hockey game. He sort of took me under his wing. I was one of the people he could talk to frankly about what was going on in the province. I wasn't a member of his party. I wasn't a member of any party. I was just a junior lawyer in Montreal.

"I liked Duplessis," Turner says, "and I think there is a revival of thought in Duplessis's favour now. He was a strong nationalist. He ran a very personalized type of government. He used to spend every morning, you know, in his room at the Chateau Frontenac phoning all over the province. He was very much like Willy King in that way. The fact that he was sitting on that Private Bills Committee showed he supervised every aspect of the legislature. He was a great parliamentarian, very much involved, and a first-rate orator. He understood the rules and had respect for the Assembly, but I tell you it was hands-on government, really hands-on. But then a few of the premiers of that day were like that. "Wacky" Bennett was a hands-on premier in B.C., and Manning in Alberta.

"Of course, he was a strong nationalist," Turner continues. "And there have been two strains of Quebec life which have been legitimate right from Confederation. You have had the Cartiers on the one hand and the Bourassas and the Papineaus on the other. So Duplessis was a legitimate provincial rightist fellow although I guess that under him the alliance with the Church and with business was never out in the open, and of course labour resented that.

"The intellectuals resented that," Turner says. "And largely through the influence of Georges Levesque at Laval and his famous students Jean Marchand, Gerard Pelletier, and Pierre Trudeau – largely through the influence of these fellows – the memory of Duplessis has been put out of kilter. But I think it is coming back.

"I think the explosion in Quebec after his death and the Quiet Revolution of Jean Lesage was a natural aftermath of Duplessis's type of paternalistic government. But I think one has to concede that he ran a good government. This is not to say that there wasn't a share of influence peddling – although no one has ever attached any corruption to Duplessis himself. I think he was frugal – he was a bachelor, as you know, and his only indulgence was the Krieghoff paintings businessmen used to give him. But there was never any insinuation that the Premier himself was corrupt."

Turner practised law in Montreal for eleven years. In the beginning he was involved in a few criminal cases and a lot of matrimonial law and later mainly in corporate and tax litigation, including many cases against the federal Department of Revenue, and he appeared often before the Board of Transport Commissioners in Ottawa. He helped unionize the doctors and nurses in Quebec, did some of C.D. Howe's personal legal work, and prospered as Stikeman and Elliott's specialist in litigation.

He was a well-known figure in the Quebec courts, pleading cases in both languages against such contemporaries as Jerome Choquette, who became Quebec's Minister of Justice, Claude Wagner, who became a judge and then a federal politician, Philip Casgrain, and other well-known barristers. In 1960 he followed Casgrain and Choquette as president of the Montreal Junior Bar and played a major role in organizing and instituting Quebec's legal aid system.

"Every third year there was an English-speaking president of the Junior Bar," Turner says in a reference that could be transposed to the traditional alternation of French and English-speaking leaders of the Liberal Party. "The other two years there would be French-speaking presidents, and that was the way it worked. It still works that way. Frankly, it was useful for the English-speaking bar, as we called ourselves, because if we didn't have that arrangement we would never have gotten the presidency because we were such a minority."

As his law practice progressed he moved from his original rented room to a basement apartment at 1536 Summerhill, which had a small kitchen, a single room with a pull-out bed, and a bathroom painted mauve, and finally to a new, more opulent penthouse apartment at 1520 McGregor, near McGill University. They were all a short walk to the centre of the city and he never owned a car.

He was a rarity in the community as an English-speaking Quebecer who had not grown up in the province, but in two other provinces, so he was not caught up in the rigidities of the old population of Westmount, and he engaged constantly in dialogue on the French-English question and the future of Quebec with contemporaries at the bar, two-thirds of whom were French-speaking.

"There developed among my contemporaries the feelings of very strong nationalism – of wanting to be masters in their own house – and I have always felt at home with that movement," Turner says. "When you get six or seven million people living in a territory where they form a majority, where they've had a connection with the geography for almost four centuries, where they've got their own language, where in those days they had a common religion, where they have their own system of law, which is quite distinct in many areas, quite different from the Common Law tradition, where they have their own sense of humour, where television arrived and gave them a collective identity, because they're a great verbal people: when you get this group of people in these circumstances with a common history and common feeling of purpose, then it is inevitable that the heart is going to struggle with the reason.

"They had to ask should they move towards their own independent state, or should they move towards more autonomy within confederation? On the other hand they have a 33 per cent interest in the second largest country in the world with good government and protection within that confederation against the tremendous population and land mass of the United States. You know that is the question and that is the struggle that will never be won one way or the other, I don't think.

"I can understand the psychology of the French-speaking Quebecer," Turner says. "During my years at the bar I had great friendships. I understand them. They are the most sociable, hospitable, humorous people around. I don't think I'll ever lose that affection and feeling for the province."

Early in his years at the bar, following his talk with Stikeman, he appears to have put aside completely his ambition to become a priest, although he still says today: "I think the priesthood is the highest vocation, the highest call – to serve God directly. I think the family is also a vocation, a high calling if you do it properly. I think that public office in a society where there is government by the governed, that's also a high calling, a very high calling. It disturbs me that public office is in such current disrepute. I mean, look at all the mudslinging these days in the House of Commons."

As a highly eligible bachelor in Montreal, he played squash at the Montreal Badminton and Squash Club and tennis at the Mount Royal Club. He skied in the Laurentians. He was, according to Christina McCall-Newman, in her book *Grits*, "the sexiest thing on the squash courts, the handsomest man at the balls, escorting the prettiest and most eligible girls."

"Oh, yeah," Turner reminisces now with a twinkle in his eyes, "I had a lot of action there, mostly French-speaking girls. And I knew all the jocks, too. I got to know all of our Davis Cup players at the tennis club, and I've always known the leading squash players in the country. Our law firm used to do work for the Montreal Alouettes, so I knew the football players and I knew the hockey players from going to the games with Duplessis."

In late July and early August of 1958, Britain's Princess Margaret visited Canada. She was a beautiful twenty-seven-year-old woman and her much publicized romance with Peter Townsend had just been officially broken because he was a divorced man and could not marry her under the rules of royalty and the Anglican Church.

The Rosses were her hosts for the B.C. section of the tour in the last week of July and Phyllis Ross suggested John should fly from Montreal to help entertain her. He declined, however, stating he was too busy. Then he received a wire from Vancouver, addressed to the office of Stikeman and Elliott, which read:

74

He also had a phone call from his sister Brenda and her husband,
John Norris, who were staying with the Rosses at their home in
Vancouver's Point Grey and were entertaining Britain's Princess
Margaret there because a fire had destroyed Government House in
Victoria.

"My husband and I were staying there in the same house as
Princess Margaret and we, of course, fell in love with her," Brenda
says. "She was most entertaining and appealing and in those days
she was perfectly gorgeous, lots of fun, and we liked her tremendously. But John didn't seem to want to come to Vancouver and
Mommy was so upset that he wasn't going to meet her. So finally on
the night before the ball John Norris and I got on the phone and said,
'John, look, we're having this big ball tomorrow night and Mommy
would just adore it if you could come, and she's worked so hard, so
you've just got to come. And besides, trust me, you'll like her.'

"So he arrived. He flew out the day of the ball. And there was
an instant attraction. We had a dinner party at our place first for
about twelve people and you could see that he thought she was
pretty attractive. And then when we got to the ball at *HMCS
Discovery* they were sitting at first at the head table, but they left
and sat at a table for two. She spent the whole night with him,
didn't want to dance with anybody else. She sent the aides away
and she wouldn't let anybody else come to the table and it was sort
of fairy tale stuff. The press was right in what they wrote about
that evening."

The press wrote a lot about it, especially the British tabloids.
Dorothy Howarth and Andrew MacFarlane wrote under a huge
front-page headline in the *Toronto Telegram*:

VANCOUVER – Princess Margaret sat in the moonlight last
night in an intimate tete-a-tete with a young bachelor-lawyer.

For an hour and 10 minutes, while officials and aides at the
Lieutenant Governor's Ball waited for her to join her party for
supper, she stayed with John Turner, the Lieutenant Governor's 29-year-old stepson at a secluded table on the lawn of
HMCS Discovery naval base.

Hardly anyone noticed the young couple as they chatted, laughed, sipped drinks and smoked cigarettes.

Four times Lieutenant Governor Frank Ross or one of his aides walked over to the table to remind Margaret and her escort that the Royal party was taking supper on the dais of the flower-decked ballroom.

And four times the Princess waved them away.

This was the first time in the tour to date that Margaret has had a chance to talk at length with someone her own age.

And she obviously welcomed the change.

She sparkled and bubbled with gay conversation and obviously enjoyed herself immensely . . . .

And MacFarlane reported from Banff a few days later:

Johnny Turner, the young Montreal bachelor who sat in the moonlight with Princess Margaret is almost certain to be seeing her again before she leaves Canada.

The 29-year-old John, who squired Margaret at the gala ball given by his stepfather, the Lieutenant Governor of British Columbia, made a definite hit with Margaret.

This was confirmed today by an official attached to the Royal household.

He told The Telegram: "It's a very good bet indeed that they will be seeing each other in Montreal" – where Margaret will be on August 5-6.

John – who danced and laughed and chatted with Margaret while a coterie of selected partners cooled their heels in front of the Royal dais – was revealed today as a reluctant (at first) Prince Charming.

While everyone else who could was busy preening and scheming for the ball – biggest party of the Canadian tour – John was lukewarm about leaving his Montreal law practice to join the fun . . . .

Turner and the Princess danced together again at an Ottawa ball on August 3, sending the British tabloid press into a greater tizzy and creating more headlines from New York to Rhodesia. 3,000 MILES TO DANCE AGAIN WITH PRINCESS, headlined the *Rhodesia Herald*, then stated: "The man who charmed Princess Margaret so much in Vancouver, 29-year-old Montreal bachelor lawyer John Turner, travelled 3,000 miles from Vancouver to Ottawa to meet her again during the weekend. Once again he monopolized her attention at the dance on Saturday evening in Government House, Ottawa."

But the Princess skipped the ball in Montreal, claiming tiredness and creating a banner headline in *The Toronto Star*: MARGARET MISSES BALL. BLAME PALACE ORDER. The story said she had received a royal command from Buckingham Palace to halt any possibility of a romance with Turner. The law offices of Stikeman and Elliott in Montreal had to put on two additional switchboard operators to handle calls from all parts of the world. "What a to-do all that was," says Heward Stikeman, "but John assured me there was nothing to it, absolutely nothing."

"Oh, there was no doubt there was a definite attraction between them," Brenda Norris says. "But I didn't think anything would ever come of it. John would never want to be in minor orbit with the royals and besides there was religion. John was a very strong Catholic. But it was a very definite thing and she still speaks very fondly of him, always asks after him.

"I'm very fond of her and she's a very loyal friend and every time I go to England we still have a drink together or dinner," Mrs. Norris says. "We had dinner at Kensington Palace just a few months ago, and she asked after John. She always asks after John."

Turner was a "secret" guest of Princess Margaret's at Clarence House in London almost exactly a year after her Canadian visit and when the tabloids learned of this – long after he had returned to Canada – there were more screaming headlines and stories that "his friendship with Princess Margaret has reached the stage where the Princess has discussed the matter with the Queen."

Papers in Turner's archives include twenty receipts dated between April 16, 1959, and August 3, 1960, for registered air mail letters addressed to Princess Margaret at Clarence House or Balmoral Castle, two addressed to Queen Elizabeth at Windsor Castle, one to the Queen Mother at Clarence House, and one to Princess Alexandria at Kensington Palace. Princess Margaret announced her engagement to photographer Anthony Armstrong-Jones on February 26, 1960, and Turner was the only unofficial guest from outside Britain at their summer wedding.

Turner, however, dismisses speculation that his friendship with the Princess involved serious romance. "She was staying at our house in Vancouver and we had a lot of laughs together and she enjoys a martini – as her mother does. We hit it off and we had a lot of fun," he says. But the friendship has continued over the years and Turner has been a fairly frequent guest at Windsor Lodge and has come to know the whole royal family well. "Yet, in all those years there's never been any publicity about my comings and goings," he says. "And Geills has got to know the Princess well, too."

The Turners entertained Princess Margaret when she visited Toronto in 1982. "She had two free nights," says Turner, "so I threw a party for her at home – which nobody ever heard about – and she wanted to do a return party. So I said, 'Who would you like to come?' and she said, 'Well, I don't know. Invite some different people and it will be my party.' So I invited some other people I thought she would enjoy and we had it at Winston's. That was only discovered by *The Toronto Star* at the end as we were coming out, and Zena Cherry (the *Globe and Mail* gossip columnist) was sore as hell at me, and I said, 'Zena, these were not public events and when I have private parties they are private parties.' That's the way I've operated. I've never had anything in Zena Cherry's in my life. Mind you, I like Zena. Geills and I see her all over the place. But nobody ever got the lists. There were rumours, but nobody ever got the lists. That's the way I've played it over the years, quietly and diplomatically.

"I've got a great admiration for Princess Margaret," Turner says. "She's one of the brightest, wittiest women I know. She has unfortunately got a bad press because of her situations and because she doesn't cultivate her public relations well. But she's been a great servant of the Crown. She has taken a big load off her sister in public engagements and so on. She's got panache. She's got a great sense of humour. She's great on the piano, a great limericist. And she's a great mimic. She's got talent to burn. If she hadn't been the sister of the Queen she might well have been in vaudeville. Yes, she's good. So, she's full value and I'm sorry that life hasn't gone happier for her."

From his bachelor days in Montreal Turner recalls, with less embarrassment than the Princess Margaret interlude, the weekend train trips he used to organize from Montreal to his stepfather's farm in St. Andrews, New Brunswick, which became regular and notorious. "I used to rent a whole Canadian Pacific railway car," he recalls, "with those twelve or fourteen little bedrooms and I'd knock two of them off for a bar and my pals would come down and we'd take guys and gals from Montreal and we'd spend the long weekends down at St. Andrews. I used to phone the railway and say 'I'll take that car again' and they liked to sell a whole car, and we'd decorate the thing with bunting. I'd organize it, but the guys who went down would reimburse me.

"Oh, we'd have a party all night on that train, for God's sake, and the car would be shunted onto the little St. Andrews train which took a couple of passenger cars and freight cars from Macadam right to St. Andrews, and we'd get there about ten-thirty or eleven in the morning.

"Then we'd go to the farm," Turner says. "The Old Man was in British Columbia and couldn't get down to the place and I was running it. And I'm sure there were a lot of eyebrows raised in the summer colony of St. Andrews about these wild parties going on at my place. You know, we had motorboats out there and we'd water ski; we had a tennis court in those days; and great swimming; and lobster broils. It was great lobster country and we had a couple of lobster pots ourselves right out in the river. I suppose there were a few games played between the guys and gals. You know, we were all single and in our mid-twenties, all young working guys and gals. But it was mostly just good fun, just a great time. Those were convivial good days. Then on the Sunday or Monday night we'd all load back on the same railway car, be all hitched up, and away we'd go for another party."

But life was not all fun. In Montreal he was on the executive of the Quebec Red Cross and he was secretary and then president of Harterre House, an organization caring for mentally and emotionally troubled children. Gertrude Harterre, who is seventy-five now and living in Waterloo, Ontario, says: "John Turner was my lawyer when I was with the Montreal Protestant School Board and I opened a little school in a small house for children with learning disabilities, and he decided to help. He was so very kind, and he loved the children and they loved him.

"In the beginning," she says, "we had only four children and this little house and in the end we had four buildings, 127 children, and a staff of eighty-seven. I always gave John Turner the credit for that because I couldn't have done it without his guidance. He was always there when I needed him, always available when I had any troubles. He always thought before he spoke and knew what he was doing and he was terribly kind. He seemed to be particularly interested in children who needed help.

"And, you know, so many of those children eventually achieved their goals and went to university," she says.

Turner was also a member of the junior committee of the Montreal Symphony and its president in 1956 and 1957, mobilizing many young people to support the orchestra, and he came to know many of the leading musicians and conductors of the day who came to Montreal: Pierre Monteux, the great French conductor; Charles Munch of the Boston Symphony; George Soltie; Igor Markevitch; Thomas Beecham; and, of course, Pierre Beique, who was general manager of the Montreal Symphony for thirty-five years. Turner is a particularly close friend of Zubin Mehta, whom Beique discovered and who is now musical director of the New York Philharmonic.

Beique says this of Turner: "He loved music, really loved it. He played amateur piano, not very well, but he knew the notes. He is a very intelligent person, very knowledgeable, and he has a fine memory. On the committees he expressed great qualities of leadership. There are not many people who could do what he did. He was a leader but he was also a plodder. He thought about things before acting and then when he did act he was a good communicator. And he was humane. When a musician had a union problem or an immigration problem, he used his legal knowledge to help him out. You know, in my experience there have only been two federal politicians really interested in Canadian cultural affairs, really interested deep down in their hearts, and they are Mitchell Sharp and John Turner.

"One of the odd things about him is the way he keeps his friends despite the huge number of people he knows. His friends know he's just a big teddy bear. He's wide open. He's transparent. You can always see through John and that's very revealing. He's so different to Trudeau in this way. He's just a very straightforward person and maybe that's why he keeps so many friends.

"You know, I've known him for twenty-five years. To me personally, he's been proven. He's a man worthy of friendship, who can be trusted. Of course, I like him very much. I'm a Frenchman, but I like the way he understands the broadness of this country. I travel a lot and in Paris and California people ask me when is their friend Turner going to be prime minister and I tell them, 'Well, it may be. It depends on whether his time has come.' "

Turner built up a huge symphonic repertoire of his own, but his taste in music was catholic. He would sit fascinated for hours in the Alberta Lounge, opposite the Windsor Station, listening to Oscar Peterson, or in the Café St. Michel, the great jazz haunt in Montreal's black section.

His major coup as president of the symphony's junior committee was the organization, with socialite Nellie Burke as his co-chairman, of the first ball ever held on a ship tied up at the Montreal docks. They borrowed the huge Greek liner *Homeric*, festooned it with lights, and attracted all of Montreal society to what many still describe as the most successful ball in the city's history.

"It was sensational, I tell you," Turner says. "We had Drapeau there and I was dancing a waltz with Madame Drapeau, twirling her around, and we lost our balance and fell right into the kettle drum. Drapeau wasn't too pleased about that.

"Gee, that party was a great success," he says. "I didn't bring anybody because I was going to be pretty busy as host, and I went down to get some food about three a.m. after everyone was clearing off and I crawled into one of the bunks and flaked out. And the next thing I knew the ship was heading for Quebec City. So here I was in my white tie, for God's sake, and I got off the ship in Quebec City and had to take the train back to Montreal. I ran into a lot of flak. I mean, there were a lot of lawyers on that train and here I was unshaved, in my white tie, going back to Montreal.

"It was a dumb move. I should have rented a car and played it quietly."

9

Getting into Politics

J ohn Turner wasn't interested in politics. His stepfather told him it was "a mug's game." His mother had no political ambitions for him. His boss, Heward Stikeman, thought that under the handsome facade and the confidence he exuded in court and Montreal society circles was an insecurity, a softness, that made him unsuitable for the rough and tumble of the political arena, despite his many other attributes.

"The insecurity showed in the way he tried to please everybody," Stikeman says. "It showed in the way he talked jock talk to jocks and ordinary talk to ordinary people, whereas in fact he was a highly intellectual young man. I doubted if he would be able to take tough decisions that would displease people, as he would have to do in politics. But he eventually showed I was wrong."

C.D. Howe did encourage him sometimes to give some thought to a political career, but he was the only one, and Howe's papers and letters made public after his death show that Turner was the only person he ever tried to entice into politics. Howe also asked Turner to help organize the 1957 election campaign of Wes Stuart, in Charlotte County, New Brunswick, which includes St. Andrews, and Turner agreed, mainly for a lark. Stuart, the sitting Member of Parliament, was also a member of the Quoddy Poker Club, named after Passamaquoddy Bay, which met four times a year in Mayor Fraser Keay's cottage on Chamcook Lake, near the Ross farm, and Turner was co-chairman of the poker club. So he knew Stuart and liked him.

Most Liberals were in trouble in that 1957 election, but Stuart, a fisherman in a riding divided almost equally between fishermen and farmers, was in particular trouble. He was supposed to have been promoted to parliamentary secretary to the Minister of Fisheries but he had a few drinks before a session of the Commons in which somebody accused him of smuggling. "Sure I smuggle," Stuart replied. "Everybody in my constituency smuggles."

Some of his constituents were upset about this and he was known in the Commons forever after as "Smuggler Jack." He was also not promoted to parliamentary secretary, and he was in grave danger of losing his riding, which regularly swung between the two major parties.

"I'd go around with Wes to some of the islands," Turner says, "and I'd say to the fishermen, 'Forget the issues, forget the pipeline and all those things. The real issue is that Wes was a lobster fisherman and he went up to Parliament and he's the only professional fisherman who ever got elected for a hell of a long time. He's one of yours and if you elect him this third time he gets a pension.' So I said: 'Let's give Wes his pension,' and all the fishermen said, 'That makes sense.' So all the fishermen voted for him. All the farmers voted against him and we won the thing by under 100 votes."

C.D. Howe was pleased with Turner's efforts in that campaign and Turner remained close to him until he died in 1960, and then he helped W.J. Bennett, who later became president of Eldorado and the Iron Ore Company, organize Howe's funeral.

"All the young professional and business men were fans of Mr. Howe," Turner says. "He symbolized, of course, the close working relationship between government and business, and he'd had a lot to do with transforming Canada from an agricultural to an industrial nation during the war. But organizing that funeral was a major undertaking. It was eighteen hours a day for three days, phoning across the country to see who was coming and arranging the protocol. Then I had to organize the reception with the family afterwards, decide who was coming back to the apartment for a drink, who was going to be looked after the night before and all that sort of thing. Everybody was there, Mr. St. Laurent, Mr. Diefenbaker, Mr. Pearson, and the Governor General, Mr. Vanier. It was a big deal and a lot of work."

In 1960, Turner was invited, as president of the Montreal Junior Bar, to attend the Liberal Party's Kingston Conference, chaired by Mitchell Sharp, which was an attempt to rebuild party policy by inviting outsiders to present papers and ideas. Turner delivered a short paper on legal aid, spent three days at the conference, and found it fascinating. Then the following year he was invited as an observer to the big Liberal rally in Ottawa, chaired by Walter Gordon, and he delivered a five-minute paper on medicare, comparing it with legal aid.

"Our view in the Junior Bar then was that legal aid was something that had to come, and that if we were smart we'd institute the plan and run it ourselves rather than have the government run it," he says. "And, of course, the lawyers got ahead of the doctors on that. We got a pretty good system of legal aid across the country run by the various provinces and professions, but we haven't got the government all over us."

Turner was impressive at these meetings. So, in late 1961, Paul Martin travelled to Montreal, took him to dinner at the Mount Stephen Club, and suggested he consider a career in politics. Then Allan MacEachen, who was executive assistant to Opposition Leader Mike Pearson, took him to dinner at Chez Stein, one of his favourite haunts just off Sherbrooke, and put more direct pressure on him to run in the riding of St. Lawrence-St. George in the election expected in 1962. It was his first meeting with MacEachen and they decided they liked each other.

Keith Davey also talked to Turner about politics, but that was after he became a candidate. "The first time I ever met Davey was at my bachelor penthouse apartment. Talk about Bay Street! That apartment was more of a [political] liability than Bay Street has ever been. We threw some of the best parties in town at that place. At any rate I must have had about twelve people there that night, John Claxton, Emmet Kierans, Dino Constantino, Jim Robb, Ken Mackay – a lot of lawyers – and Keith came in to tell us how to run an election. They listened to him for about ten minutes, then, it was Emmet Kierans, I think, said, 'Come on Keith, that may work in Toronto but that's bullshit. We know more about running a campaign than you guys with your little candidate's manuals. Why don't you stick to your little books and toys because we know how to run a campaign in Montreal.' I mean, a lot of my guys were pros and the boys gave Keith a rough time. But that's the first time I met Keith. I think we went out to dinner afterwards. I liked him."

Diefenbaker called the election in April, 1962, with a June 18 polling date, and Turner had to make up his mind in a hurry. He would have to compete for the nomination against at least four other candidates, including Claude Richardson, who had previously held the St. Lawrence-St. George seat for the Liberals but was undecided about running again. And the sitting Conservative member was Egan Chambers, a war hero and parliamentary secretary to Minister of Defence Douglas Harkness, a former national president of the Conservative Party who had helped René Lévesque solve the CBC strike the previous year and was extremely well connected in Montreal. Turner didn't have much chance in the circumstances. But he calculated that the Montreal Junior Bar, a highly organized political machine with a membership of about 3,500 lawyers, would back him, along with many young businessmen, and he consulted with his law partners.

"I was fully supportive of him running," says Fraser Elliott, the senior partner. "It was obvious he would make a good politician and I told him it would not affect his status in the firm. But I was worried about his finances. He was making good money then as a lawyer, considerably more than he would make as a Member of Parliament, but, of course, like everybody else on a salary, he was spending it. It was going to be a sacrifice for him and I told him that."

In the end, when Turner declared his intention to seek the nomination, Richardson decided not to run and three others dropped out, leaving the contest between Turner and Dr. William H. Pugsley, a professor of management and marketing at McGill, who was also secretary of the riding's Liberal association.

Turner told the convention, chaired by publicist John deB. Payne, in the High School of Montreal on May 1 that the real question of the election was whether the country could survive another four years of Diefenbaker. "The present government," he told the delegates, "although it was elected with the largest majority since Confederation, has become one of inertia, indecision, and confusion. It has puzzled every friend Canada ever had. There is no doubt Mr. Diefenbaker has lost control of the country. He is just like a weather vane, blowing one way, then the other," he said.

Turner won the nomination by an undisclosed number of votes and immediately launched a razzle-dazzle campaign backed by many of Montreal's young lawyers and many of its prettiest and smartest young women. They "blitzed" apartment buildings and held lobby meetings in them. They threw classy cocktail parties in the plusher apartment blocks, mostly hosted and paid for by friends of Turner's sister, Brenda Norris. They put up a gaily decorated "Vote for Turner" marquee at the corner of Sherbrooke and Peel, which included a section called the Chamber of Errors, after conservative opponent Egan Chambers, and released a blimp balloon over Sherbrooke Street bearing Turner's name and colours.

One of the pretty young campaign workers, Geills Kilgour, daughter of David Kilgour, president of the Great-West Life Assurance Company in Winnipeg, introduced computers into the campaign, possibly for the first time in Canadian political history. She'd been to McGill, then Radcliffe and the Harvard Business School, and was a systems engineer with IBM, helping install computers at the head office of the Bank of Montreal. Together with another computer expert, Dino Constantino, she set up a system that broke down previous election results poll by poll to show where the party's strengths and weaknesses were so that Turner could concentrate in areas where there was strength or some hope and not waste time on hopeless polls. Turner fell in love with Geills Kilgour during the campaign and married her the following year.

Turner persistently challenged a reluctant Chambers to debate the issues and aimed his campaign at Montreal's new population and youth. "Canadians have been relying too heavily in recent years on seniority as a qualification for political office," thirty-two-year-old Turner told one important election rally. "I certainly would not deny that politics needs the wisdom and guidance of older men, but it also needs the vigour and impatience of younger men."

He recalled that Sir John A. Macdonald was elected to public office at the age of twenty-nine and Sir Wilfrid Laurier at thirty, and that Mackenzie King was an MP at thirty-four and a cabinet minister at thirty-five. The result of the current tendency not to make full use of youth in politics was "the tendency in Canadian government to postpone or avoid making decisions on many vital matters of national policy," he declared. And the young people and the new people of Montreal listened so that the riding of St. Lawrence-St. George had a horse race. A few weeks before the election the pundits couldn't pick the winner between the upstart young Liberal and the experienced, old-pro Conservative.

St. Lawrence-St. George was an interesting riding. It literally covered the waterfront and also the old mansions and big apartments overlooking Sherbrooke Street, where the rich English lived. It included Chinatown and the red-light district. The population was about 12 per cent Jewish, and overall about a third ethnic, a third French, and a third English.

Turner and his young team worked all bases, including the red-light district. "I got to know all the madams in the riding," Turner recalls. "I mean there must have been 500 prostitutes there. I used to call it the horizontal vote. Liberal morally, Liberal politically."

The big boost to his campaign came when party leader Pearson came to town a week before the election day to a tumultuous welcome organized in good part by the young Turner team, and which Turner remembers now mainly because of a picture that appeared on the front page of the *Montreal Star* showing Pearson, former Transport Minister Lionel Chevrier, Liberal candidate C.M. ("Bud") Drury, and Turner chatting together while an unknown woman peered over their shoulders. Turner points out with glee that the "unknown" woman in the picture, which hangs in a place of honour in his Toronto law office, is Pam Ambrose, one of the local madams.

Peter Desbarats described that rally in the *Montreal Star*:

> They filled open convertibles with pretty girls. They filled open-air tourist buses with ragtime bands. They filled the streets with people, the air with cheers and the Show Mart with a standing-room-only audience that topped the prime minister's Monday night crowd by at least 1,000 people.
>
> They borrowed tricks from U.S. presidential elections. They brought placards to the Show Mart in trucks. They hammered on bass drums while crowds chanted, "We Want Mike." They even managed to smile through the aftermath of two mighty "stinkbomb" explosions in the Show Mart during the Pearson speech. . . .
>
> Newsmen who have travelled across the nation with both Liberal and Conservative leaders gave Montreal the crown for the best meeting of the campaign to date. It was smaller than West Coast rallies staged for both leaders. But Montrealers were far ahead of Vancouverites in the noise, hoopla and heck-raising departments.
>
> Rarely has the city seen the likes of the parade that left John Turner's "campground" at Peel and Sherbrooke at 8:30 p.m.
>
> Standing outside his circus tent, the young Liberal candidate for St. Lawrence-St. George proclaimed: "We've expropriated this city. The Liberal Party is moving on to victory."
>
> Several hundred shouting camp-followers immediately expropriated the Peel-Sherbrooke intersection and about a mile of Montreal's stately boulevard. It was young Westmount's night to howl. Clean-cut junior executives dove into convertibles and came up cheering. Pretty girls waved banners from open cars and shouted, "We Want Pearson."
>
> Beatniks tumbled down the steps of greystone houses, waving their hands in the air and wondering if the world had suddenly gone sane.

Tactics on polling day were tough in Turner's riding, as they were throughout Quebec in those days, but the Turner team was ready for them. Turner had 150 lawyers working for him, at least one manning every poll, each with a walkie-talkie and pockets full of signed but otherwise blank warrants of arrest. When Frank Hanley, an organizer for Chambers, was suspected of bringing in phoney voters to stuff the ballot boxes, the young lawyers used the walkie-talkies to call police, issued the arrest warrants, and had the police drag them away. They had fifty derelicts arrested in the first hour of the election.

"They were bringing in phonies and voting for dead people and

all of the old Quebec game," Turner says, "and we just kept ar-
resting them. So Frank got hold of me about noon when I was at
Pam Ambrose's place. She ran a certain type of place. She'd always
say it was a rooming house, but I mean, come on! She'd always
throw a lunch on election day and she had a lot of booze going,
and, of course, you couldn't get a drink anywhere in town on
election day. So the hoods we hadn't had arrested we'd invited
down to Pam's place. So Frank got me there and said: 'Hey, what
are you doing to my boys?'

"And I said, 'Frank, draw them off, boy, because I'm going to
get anybody I can all day.'

"And he said, 'When are you going to let them out?'

"And I told him: 'After the polls close.' Frank and I got to be
very good friends later on."

Turner won by 2,214 votes, overcoming a 2,570 plurality for
Chambers in the previous election, and he headed for Ottawa.

10

A Rising
Political Star

He was young and inexperienced and at first the "Old Guard" Members of Parliament treated him with an avuncular attitude, especially Prime Minister Pearson, who had known him as a small child. In his maiden speech, usually used in praise of a member's riding, he demanded that the government reveal how much the Bank of Canada was spending to prop the dollar at the "Diefenbuck" level of 92.51 cents and urged new parliamentary rules, which was a little brash for a new boy. Then, in the few months he served in opposition, he asked about eight questions, none of them particularly brilliant or incisive.

But by the time the Liberals defeated the Diefenbaker government in April, 1963, and started their series of shaky minority regimes, Turner felt he had played his part for the party by dramatically doubling his plurality over Egan Chambers in St. Lawrence-St. George. He thought he had performed reasonably well in the few months in opposition. And the press, even then, was describing him as a "glamour boy." He thought he had a chance for a cabinet post, but instead Pearson appointed him parliamentary secretary to the Minister of Northern Affairs and National Resources, Arthur Laing.

"Mr. Pearson said that I needed to understand the administrative process, to be in 'the kitchen' of government for a while," Turner says. "He thought I was impatient, especially when I saw some of the klunks he was promoting, and he advised me to be patient. It was good advice and I have no quarrel with not getting a ministry in 1963. It turned out to be a big plus in the long run."

In fact, Turner wasn't very patient. He was a leading member of the "Young Turks," which *Maclean's* magazine described then as "probably the brightest group of MPs ever to appear simultaneously in a Canadian Parliament." *Maclean's* reported: "This elite includes Richard Cashin, Jack Davis, Herb Gray, David Hahn,

Harry Harley, Pauline Jewett, Don Macdonald, John Munro, Jean-Luc Pepin, Gerald Regan, Maurice Sauve and John Turner. And what sets the group apart is that, unlike some cabinet members, these MPs don't subscribe to the theory of Liberal rule by divine right. They believe their party must *earn* its mandate, and that it has not yet done so."

Following the notorious but in some areas fruitful "100 days of Decision" in 1963, which included Walter Gordon's first and highly controversial budget, these Young Turks were angry and frustrated. They thought their careers were being endangered by policies they had no hand in making and they impudently demanded that the caucus be consulted in advance on plans for legislation. When Old Guard members tried to explain at stormy caucus meetings that it was constitutionally impossible for cabinet to consult backbenchers ahead of Parliament, the Young Turks jeered them into silence. Then, in order to pacify this irreverent block, Turner was appointed chairman of a caucus subcommittee on the role of the MP and he took to the road, urging, at service club luncheons and wherever he could get a hearing, a drastic overhaul of House of Commons procedures to take the power away from political organizations and give it back to individual MPs. In one nationally reported speech to the Kiwanis Club in his Montreal riding, Turner said:

A century ago the private member was genuinely free to defy the party Whip, or the discipline of his party. It was the independence of the ordinary MP that gave the House of Commons its importance and was the best check upon the government of the day.

But now, as Richard Crossman, an English Labour MP writes, 'the prime responsibility of the member is no longer to his conscience or to the elector, but to his party. Without accepting the discipline of the party he cannot be elected, and if he defies that discipline, he risks political death.'

What does this mean? It means, first of all, that the debates in the House of Commons, which used to make it the forum of the people, have become mere sounding boards. It means that there are no surprises. It means that the cabinet, through the party, controls the private members who support it but who no longer can control it.

The real struggles for power today are not fought on the floor of the House of Commons; they are fought inside the party councils. The caucuses of the government party and of the chief opposition party have become the real battlefields of politics. Democracy has become invisible.

There is in the conscience of every Member of Parliament a point where principle would dictate that he must rebel against his party. This still happens, but it doesn't happen as much as it used to, and it is becoming harder each passing year. As the political party becomes more organized and more disciplined, the scope of the backbencher becomes more restricted.

There are other forces that restrict him. I want to mention the power of the civil service, the bureaucracy, what has been called the mandarin class – that race of faceless experts, protected by the anonymity of a government department, operating beyond the range of the people's control.

The average MP, who comes from a background like yours and mine, is faced with a monopoly of information and technical competence which he cannot match. As governments increase their intervention in our society, and as the technical background needed for intelligent criticism becomes more complicated, a Member of Parliament fights a losing battle with the civil service.

We have a concentration of power in the cabinet and the Prime Minister, accompanied outside Parliament by a growth in bigness of finance, industry and labour. . . . Television has added a new factor: The leadership cult. Because of television we now have really a presidential-type government in Canada.

Insofar as the member relationship with his own party is concerned, it would be my suggestion that the government stop treating every vote as a vote of confidence. Naturally most votes have to be treated as confidence votes, but it would bring enormous life back into the House of Commons if the members occasionally could follow their own consciences which are often against their vote. In such circumstances, if the government were defeated, it would not necessarily mean a loss of prestige.

Turner then advocated publicly paid research assistants for backbench MPs and a much greater use of committees in which individual members could express their own personal opinions free from the party whips. It was all fairly revolutionary stuff, hardly aimed at pleasing people like Pearson and his chief political and policy adviser, Walter Gordon, and it continued to upset the Old Guard traditionalists. But an undaunted Turner subsequently expanded his reform campaign and strengthened his burgeoning rebel image by calling for a "streamlining" of all parliamentary procedure to eliminate unnecessary duplication.

Asked by a reporter at one stage of his campaign if he was, in fact, a rebel backbencher, Turner replied: "If I'm a rebel backbencher, there are thirty more like me in the backbenches who feel the same way." In any event, what appeared to be a Turner-led revolt was successful.

"What is remarkable is not that Mr. Turner and the Liberal Young Turks felt this way," Christopher Young, editor of the *Ottawa Citizen*, commented in November, 1963. "What is remarkable is that the party leaders listened and acted. Today, nine committees of the Liberal caucus are working on future legislation, and any back-bench member who is not making a contribution should be.

"If this system can be made to work effectively, the future of the Liberal Party glows bright. There is every reason to think that a similar system would be just as valuable for the Conservative Party, whether in government or opposition."

Turner was also chairman of the "bachelor caucus" of the party, which met for a monthly dinner to talk politics and complain about the activities of the Old Guard. Herb Gray was secretary-treasurer of the fifteen-member group and on one particularly raucous evening Turner consecrated Judy LaMarsh as the Official Den Mother. But his bachelor days did not last long. He married Geills Kilgour at St. Ignatius Church in Winnipeg in May, 1963, after some trouble with the Jesuits because Geills was, and still is, an Anglican. John Grace, then associate editor of the *Ottawa Journal*, was best man. Prime Minister Pearson gave Turner five days off for a honeymoon at the Coral Beach Club in Bermuda and the marriage was to produce four children in fairly rapid succession, Elizabeth, Michael, David, and Andrew.

"You know," Turner says, "despite the Diefenbaker-Pearson mutual antipathy the House was still a fun place to be in those days. The mood was good for most of the years I was there. The boys tell me today that there is no fraternization across the aisle at all; that there's a siege mentality in the House. Well, we didn't have that. We had a lot of cross-fraternization and friendships. I always felt at home in the House of Commons, you know. I don't know what it will be like if I get back there. And to get back on top is not the same, of course. Just as I had to take some time to get adjusted to this [lawyer's] life I'm going to have to get adjusted to the House again. The mood has changed. It will take me a little time. But I consider the House of Commons to be the forum of the nation and the single most important aspect of our parliamentary and democratic life. I have respect for it – for the rules. And I always welcomed anyone who was elected. Anyone sitting there, no matter what you might think of him or her personally, was elected by 80,000 or 100,000 people and therefore had the same rights, whether in government or opposition. Somebody put them there. That gave them their status and distinction. I had respect for them all. I don't think there were more than two or three I didn't like or who really disliked me. When you like a guy he usually likes you and I was close friends with all sorts of Conservatives and New Democrats. They're not a bunch of nobodies. Nobody in the House of Commons is a nobody."

Turner was noted for this apolitical attitude between elections. He played squash with opposition members, particularly Conservative Pat Nowlan. When respected NDP member Frank Howard admitted a serious criminal record in his youth, Turner was first to walk the Commons aisle and put an arm around him. Then he took Howard to lunch. When former Conservative Finance Minister Donald Fleming's son was involved in a shooting incident, Turner consoled Fleming in his office all night. The son had been a student at Harterre House in Montreal, which Turner had helped establish. Afterwards, Fleming and Turner became firm friends. When he became a minister his office door was always open to MPs of any party, without appointment if the matter was urgent, and at between-election ceremonies he always insisted that the local member join him on the speakers' platform or at the ribbon-cutting without regard to political affiliation. "That's not only the right thing to do," Turner says. "The right thing is usually also the right political thing to do."

The press gallery understood why many opposition members liked him, but could never fathom why he was also singled out for special, almost fatherlike fondness and respect by the otherwise scathingly partisan Opposition Leader John Diefenbaker. After all, Turner had won his first election on a platform of bitter criticism of the Diefenbaker government. He had gone on TV in a series of advertisements, holding up a Canadian dollar to the cameras and blaming Diefenbaker personally for reducing its value to 92.5 cents. Across the country and in the Commons he had accused the Old Man of "committing a fraud on the Canadian people."

The answer is here: both Diefenbaker and Turner took their holidays in the Caribbean. They first met, by coincidence, at a little resort in Tobago in the winter of 1963. Geills Turner was there with John, and Olive Diefenbaker was with her husband and Diefenbaker's brother, Elmer. The recently married Turners were at first embarrassed by being together with the distinguished Diefenbakers at the isolated resort and tried not to bother them, but the Old Man approached Turner one day and invited him to dinner. They decided the two families should spend the New Year's Eve together. And then Diefenbaker and Turner began to spend their days sunning together on the beach while the Chief related his life story to the young man. "It was fascinating," says Turner. "We had a hell of a time."

Two years later, again by coincidence, both families found themselves together at the Sandy Lane Hotel in Barbados and Turner and Diefenbaker often shared the beach, although now, with Turner a cabinet minister and Diefenbaker in trouble with his caucus, they usually sat separately, each trying not to disturb the other.

One morning when the surf was very angry Turner looked up from a book he was reading and noticed that Diefenbaker had disappeared, although his towel was still on the beach. He searched the white-capped water and saw, about seventy yards out to sea, a head bobbing and an arm waving. Diefenbaker was being swept away by a strong undercurrent and was drowning. Turner was not the fastest of swimmers in his UBC days but he was a strong one. He dived into the rough ocean and swam easily with the undertow to where the Chief was disappearing regularly under the waves. Turner used the lifesaving techniques taught to him by A.L. Cochrane at Camp Timagami. It was a long, hard swim against the undertow back to the beach, but the two men made it. Turner laid Diefenbaker stomach-down on the sand and watched the water pour from his mouth. He was convulsing and Turner was scared; people gathered around and said they thought he was going to suffer a heart attack. Turner was about to begin artificial respiration when the Old Man suddenly sat up. "Thanks, John," he said. He never mentioned the incident again.

They were both House of Commons men who enjoyed the game of politics and they remained friends and rivals, runners in a tough race who respected each other.

Sometimes it's best to let Turner talk for himself: "So we were down in Barbados a couple of times when he (Diefenbaker) was there. He loved Sandy Lane," Turner says. "And he called me up one day and says, 'Do you like fishing, John?' and I said, 'Oh, yeah, sure.' We'd gone fishing a couple of times before. 'Well,' he said, 'I've got a boat,' and I said, 'Where'd you get the boat, sir?' He said, 'It's the Barbados Fisheries Boat.' You could trust Dief to do something like that. He says, 'I want to bring somebody who may not be a friend of yours but I think you should get to know better – Ross Thatcher.' Well now, in the 1968 leadership, Ross Thatcher thought I was a Communist, for God's sake, and he had supported Bob Winters. So Ross came up and we got to know each other pretty well, through this introduction by Diefenbaker. Of course, Ross didn't like Trudeau, so later I used to go out to Saskatchewan every five or six weeks and do all the deals with Saskatchewan. I used to do the deals here in Ontario with Robarts, too, and Wishart when he was Attorney General and Charlie McNaughton when he was Treasurer because Robarts didn't go for Trudeau – and I did a lot of this when I was Attorney General and Minister of Finance. And so Ross and I and Dief were out in this boat, and it got too rough and they wouldn't let us fish. So we just drank rum."

Question: "Dief did? But he always insisted he was a teetotaller."

Answer: "You're goddamn right. He was with us glass for glass."

Question: "Was he really?"

Answer: "Oh, sure. He could hold it. Oh, yeah. And oh, the stories and bullshit. And then when I was on that exercise prior to the [1971] Victoria Conference – you know, trying to get the new charter and the new constitution – Ross invited me to speak from the well of the legislature. So I spoke from the well of the legislature in Saskatchewan – and in Alberta and in British Columbia. I got back from that particular trip and Dief comes across and says, 'John, that was quite an honour they paid you in Saskatchewan. I've never been down there, you know.' He was envious. And I said, 'Well, sir, I think it was unique and I very much appreciated it.'

"And there was one time when I was Attorney General and Dief found out that I was a member of the Barbados bar," Turner continues. "And the Dief says, 'You know my connection with Barbados. I'd love to be called to the bar down there.' I said, 'Sir, the reason I was called to the bar there was that I was a member of Gray's Inn and I got automatic certification before independence.' Well, I called Frederick ("Sleepy") Smith, who was the Attorney General of Barbados and a good friend of mine, and I said, 'Sleepy, I've got a problem and when you hear my problem it's going to become your problem.' So I told him, and he says, 'I don't know how we can do that.' 'Well,' I said, 'talk it over with the Prime Minister and the Chief Justice.' So Sleepy called me in about ten days and says, 'We can't do it, John, there's no way.' So I said, 'Why don't you make him an honorary member, and ship the brute a certificate and keep the "honorary" so small, right at the bottom, so that he'll never see it.' Sleepy says, 'Fine.' So, we go down there and there's a big ceremony welcoming Dief to the bar. He never knew till he died it was only an honorary degree and he couldn't practise law down there."

Turner was an honorary pallbearer at Olive Diefenbaker's funeral and when Diefenbaker died in August, 1979, he was the only Liberal appointed a pallbearer, but he couldn't get to the funeral because he was canoeing in the Arctic.

"I thought Diefenbaker must have been a great defence lawyer, although he didn't know much about the law," Turner says. "He was a great parliamentarian. I mean the guy made the greatest speeches I ever heard in the House of Commons and that was when he was past his prime. But I tell you, he was sensational. The only man who could approach him, in my view, was Tommy Douglas, and Allan MacEachen, at his best, could be pretty good. But Dief really could be electrifying. His phrases were evocative. He'd operate off strings of ideas and phrases and kind of leap up to the punch lines, you know. As a performer in the House he was magnificent. Of course, he dusted me off a couple of times so I knew what it was like to be on the receiving end of his abilities."

So Turner got along well with his political peers and he learned early on to cultivate contacts and friendships with the press gallery and the public. He was a gregarious and perpetually practising politician.

Cam Millikin, the political organizer and important Alberta Liberal, was a Young Liberal then and he remembers sitting in the public gallery watching the Commons proceedings, and particularly Turner, whom he'd once run a 220-yard race against when he was at Dublin's Trinity College and Turner was at Oxford.

"There was no reason why Turner should remember or even recognize me," Millikin recalls. (Although Millikin is, in fact, very noticeable. He is almost seven feet tall.) "He'd beaten me in that 220-yard race. I could remember his flailing arms and the way he ran with his shoulders and his whole body, and how he congratulated the losers. Turner had a charisma then in the true Greek sense of the word, meaning a gifted person, and that was the only time I'd ever seen him. But when I was in the gallery that day he saw me and recognized me even though I was a nobody in the Liberal Party or anywhere else, for that matter. He sent me a note asking me for sherry in his office and I've never forgotten that. Although I've had to back a few other Liberal leadership aspirants since then because they called in some notes I owed them, I've been Turner's man ever since that day. For a long time, every Friday, at the expense of the Alberta Young Liberals, I sent a telegram to Prime Minister Pearson demanding that Turner be appointed to the cabinet. And when he was finally appointed I got a wire from Jim Coutts saying he hoped I was happy now."

However, before that day came Turner had to serve a long apprenticeship in the Department of Northern Affairs and Natural Resources with Arthur Laing and his two bright young executive assistants, Jack Austin and Gordon Gibson.

These were the days of the small, squalid scandals: the allegedly unpaid-for-furniture affairs involving Secretary of State Maurice Lamontagne and Immigration Minister René Tremblay; the admission by Minister without Portfolio Yvon Dupuis of a $10,000 "present" from a chiropractor who wanted a licence to operate a racetrack; the Stonehill Affair concerning allegations of requests for payments to party coffers in return for citizenship for flamboyant and controversial American businessman Harry Stonehill; and especially the Rivard Affair, which involved allegations of offers of bribes by two young executive assistants in an attempt to prevent the extradition of drug smuggler Lucien Rivard to the United States. The government almost fell, the careers of more than a dozen people were damaged or ruined, and the House was swamped in bitterness and anger as the two old adversaries, Mike Pearson and John Diefenbaker, glared at each other across the centre aisle, trading accusations and insults, sometimes even quotations from Confucius.

"Perhaps he will recall the quotation from Confucius," Pearson lisped petulantly at Diefenbaker at one stage: " 'He who digs dirt loses ground.' " And the wily old Opposition Leader threw back, "I am also reminded that the same Confucius said: 'He who hides wrongdoing is a wrongdoer himself.' "

"Parliament used to be a club for gentlemen. It has become a jungle," Colin Cameron, the quiet, intellectual New Democrat from Nanaimo, remarked wistfully in the Commons in February, 1965. "Parliament has descended into straight thuggery." But Turner avoided all of this and continued to cultivate friends on both sides of the House. "If you step into some shit, get out of it as soon as possible and throw away your shoes," he used to say.

This was also the time of the long and angry flag debate, toward the end of which Turner strongly advocated closure, and of argument over the sharing of Canadian water with the United States, in which Turner was directly involved as parliamentary secretary to the Minister of Northern Affairs and National Resources.

Turner stressed in many speeches the importance of Canada's abundance of water to the country's future, but also hinted of a possibility that future generations of Canadians and Americans could, in fact, share the waters of the continent "in a spirit of realistic friendship." He invariably added, however, a strict proviso that Canada must determine its own needs as far into the future as possible before committing any of its water to any continental uses. The major water resource proposal at the time was being made by the Ralph M. Parsons Company of Los Angeles, a firm of engineers, which advocated a North American Water and Power Alliance

(NAWAPA) and had strong support from influential U.S. senators. The massive and imaginative $100-billion plan envisaged the collection of surplus water from the Rocky Mountain region and its redistribution to the water-poor areas of Canada, the middle-western and western United States, and northern Mexico. The benefits to Canada, according to the planners, would have been remarkable in terms of irrigation on the Prairies, drainage and reclamation of agricultural land, and creation of seaways from Canadian inland cities to the West Coast and the Great Lakes with an ultimate effect of increasing Canadian production by $30 billion annually and supporting an additional population of 35 million.

Turner found the plan both interesting and imaginative, but he stressed in speech after speech that Canada could not bargain with one of its most precious resources until it knew how much water it had, how much it would need, and what it was worth. In his major speech on the issue, to the U.S. Chamber of Commerce in Washington in December, 1965, he was blunt. He insisted he was giving just "one Canadian's view" on the issue, then informed a somewhat startled audience that Canada was in the driver's seat on any question of water-sharing and intended to drive a hard bargain; that Canada was not even prepared to start water-sharing negotiations without a full inventory of its future needs; that nothing would be done without full federal-provincial co-ordination; and that Canada might insist that population and industry move to the water in Canada instead of allowing the water to go to existing centres in the U.S.

And he added: "If some day we can agree to sharing our water, we might want to insist that if water is to be considered a continental resource, markets should also be considered on the same basis. We might wish to export water not for money, but in return for access to your markets."

The speech was reported widely throughout Canada and unanimously acclaimed in editorials. The *Globe and Mail* thundered:

> Water is probably the greatest resource card – perhaps the greatest card of any sort – that Canada holds in the international poker game. But Canada will not benefit from that card if it is filched, thrown in too early, held too long, or traded for worthless tender. Of late it has seemed that Canada did not know much of these skills of the game.
>
> It is therefore encouraging to note that Mr. John Turner does, and that he has been bold enough to tell the United States that it is on Canadian terms that the game is going to be played. . . .

Knowledge first, says Mr. Turner, and then the bargaining; and there too, his policy is wise. In the past we have traded too many of our resources for mere cash, instead of for the development of on-site industries and markets for them that could have increased Canada's potential as a prosperous place in which we live.

A good policy; but how united behind it are Canadians? . . .

Turner also spoke frequently on relations with Quebec, urging establishment of an equal partnership between English- and French-speaking Canada, and stating that a solution to the problem of the two cultures was fundamental to the survival of confederation. He said equal partnership did not mean equal representation in Parliament but equal opportunity for the development of language and culture, with French-speaking Canadians having access to the federal government in their own language and the right to have their children educated in their own language in public schools where there were substantial groups of French-speaking people.

Some of his English-speaking Quebec followers can still quote from one of his more eloquent speeches in Montreal in 1964, a rousing appeal on behalf of the English minority in the province: "This is our land. We too are Quebecers. We are not aliens on this soil. Our future is here. We too love Quebec. We want a better life, more security and greater opportunity, here and together. . . ."

He travelled to the Soviet Union with Laing and four officials of the Department of Northern Affairs and National Resources, visiting lonely areas of Siberia previously inaccessible to Westerners, to see how Russia was developing its Arctic lands, and he came home impressed with Siberian cities like Norilsk, with a population of over 100,000 and stone buildings up to nine storeys high built on permafrost, and Bratsk, which had hardly existed ten years previously but boasted a huge aluminum plant and a cellulose plant and was planning an iron foundry.

Peter Worthington, who was stationed in Moscow for the old *Toronto Telegram* at the time, says the trip would have been a failure without Turner. "Although the Russians had invited them, they weren't anxious to show them anything once they got to Moscow," Worthington says. "But Turner insisted. When they wanted to go to places like Norilsk and Bratsk, the Russians said it was impossible because the only planes left at three o'clock in the morning, and Turner would say, 'Tell us the way to the airport and we'll be there.' He had them bluffed in the end."

Turner was convinced that the Soviet Union was well ahead of Canada in northern development, although the Russians could learn much from Canada as well, especially about northern railroads and roads, and he advocated a number of steps to help Canada catch up. These included an inventory of northern resources by accelerating aero-magnetic and field surveys; some equalization of market factors for private industry by government construction of access roads, air fields, and railways; labour incentives through payment of bonuses for northern work under federal public works contracts; equalization of living costs for northerners through reductions in costs of heat, light, power, and transportation; and encouragement of investment in the North through tax incentives and tax abatement, including a "northern depreciation allowance."

Politically, he suggested that Canada could become an "honest broker" in diplomatic relations between the Soviet Union and the United States, as it once had been between the United States and Britain.

And his own political star began to rise at home. John Bird, the respected and venerable parliamentary correspondent for the *Financial Post*, wrote in mid-1965:

> On the government side much of the ability is packed into the row of parliamentary secretaries. That's where it ought to be in readiness for promotion to cabinet. These people are not properly back benchers. They are part of the government establishment, although waiting in the anteroom.
>
> Outstanding are John Turner, thirty-five (Northern Affairs); John B. Stewart, forty (Secretary of State's Office); Jean-Luc Pepin, forty (Trade and Commerce); Donald S. Macdonald, thirty-three (Justice); and Larry Pennell (Finance).
>
> Wiry, tough, able and admirably bilingual, John Turner is often tipped as a possible Prime Minister if the day comes when an English-speaking Roman Catholic from Quebec can make it.

And columnist Douglas Fisher commented in the *Ottawa Journal*:

> I would put [in a new cabinet] the following: Joe Greene (Renfrew South), a natural speaker, organizer, and party combatant; Robert Winters (York West), a darling to the business community; Donald Macdonald (Rosedale), an aggressive, bright hatchet man; John Turner (St. Lawrence-St. George), a man with almost every talent except humility; Jean Chretien (St. Maurice-Lafleche), an idealist with push and much charm in his English-speaking role; Jean Marchand (Quebec West), already a cinch for something; Bryce Mackasey (Verdun), a

100

persuasive, forceful, lots-of-blarney kind of man; Pierre Elliott Trudeau, a literate, well-spoken nationalist; Jean Dubé (Restigouche-Madawaska), a stylish, serious speaker; Jack Davis (Coast-Capilano), a cold, incisive, able technocrat; and Ron Basford (Vancouver-Burrard), young, argumentative and a dogged mixer.

But Turner was not to win a responsible cabinet post for quite a while.

11

Minister
without Portfolio

The general election of 1965 was disastrous for the Liberal Party. It was called by Pearson, on the advice of Walter Gordon, in the belief that finally a Pearson government could achieve a majority in the Commons and govern with some strength and confidence. But Pearson and Gordon underestimated the sometimes strange, messianic, and, to many, magnetic skills on the hustings of John G. Diefenbaker. Diefenbaker ranted and raved across the country, drawing huge crowds as he claimed some mysterious "they" were out to get him and how he had "stood" against "them" and all evil things while the Liberals indulged in the many scandals he described in detail, but not always accurately.

Time after time he would support his arguments against the government by telling the crowds they could "just look it up" in the Hansard reports, naming the day and the page, and when members of the press corps dutifully did examine the nominated sections of Hansard they found they had nothing to do with what Diefenbaker was talking about. It caused serious ethical arguments among the journalists about whether it was their duty to report what the man said, what he apparently meant to have said, or what were actually the facts. But the Diefenbaker campaign worked. The country was angry about the scandals and upset about the growing separatist movement in Quebec, and the Old Chief milked both issues so skilfully and constantly that reporters travelling with him could mouth sentences of his speeches seconds before he spoke them.

A report by *Montreal Star* reporter Peter Desbarats, who had described so glowingly and graphically the enthusiastic reception for Pearson in Montreal in 1962, showed how far the Liberals had fallen between these two elections and how much the country had changed. This time Desbarats wrote:

Noisy separatist demonstrators and an incendiary time bomb

102

in a shopping bag ruined the Liberal's high powered campaign in the Show Mart last night.

It was the shortest, noisiest and most chaotic meeting of the campaign – and the worst reception ever given to Prime Minister Pearson in this city.

The bomb failed to ignite. None of the 3,000 people in the hall was aware, as the meeting ended, that the city bomb disposal squad had been called to the Show Mart. The bomb was taken to the laboratory at police headquarters and later disarmed.

Four separatist demonstrators were arrested outside the Show Mart by Montreal police before the meeting started. About fifty young separatists managed to join the 3,000 people inside the hall, safe from city police but subject to the not-so-tender care of burly Liberal "whips." The separatists and the "whips" started a chaotic running battle at the back of the hall throughout most of the meeting, drowning out the main speakers and distracting the audience.

The main clash occurred in the middle of the Prime Minister's fourteen minute speech. Suddenly the separatists' cries of "En Français!" – Mr. Pearson was speaking in French at the time – were interrupted by the clatter of bodies falling over metal chairs.

The "whips" hustled about twenty separatists out of the hall. A few punches were thrown. One connected with the bearded chin of a *La Presse* reporter. At least one nose was split. A young girl was among those bundled roughly through the main doors of the Show Mart. . . .

Mr. Pearson began to speak at 9 p.m. and finished at 9:14 p.m. It was about half the length of his usual campaign speech and only a fraction of the audience was able to hear it. . . .

John Turner was nominated without opposition in St. Lawrence-St. George for this election although the riding was in danger of disappearing in a redistribution, and he immediately went on the road in support of candidates in other ridings, especially in Ontario. One of his Toronto speeches drew a strong reaction from a Montreal citizen named M. Brian Mulroney, who wrote in a letter to the editor of the *Montreal Star*:

Sir, – Speaking at a Liberal Nominating convention in Toronto last Thursday, Mr. John Turner, M.P. is reported to have said:

"If Mr. Diefenbaker were to become Prime Minister again, it would mean one-man government, palace revolutions, economic jingoism, anti-Americanism and a new wave of French separatism."

It's unfortunate that Mr. Turner ran out of breath just when things were getting exciting. As his hindsight is, no doubt, just as well developed as his great capacity for prophecy, I am sure he would have wanted to tell his fellow Grits just how Mr. Diefenbaker stabbed Julius Caesar, started the War of 1812 and caused the Irish Potato Famine. . . .

The Liberals won only 172 seats in the November 8 election, far short of a majority, and Walter Gordon resigned from the finance ministry, stating he had misled the Prime Minister by advising the election.

However, Turner easily won his riding of St. Lawrence-St. George, increasing his plurality over the Conservative candidate and causing the pundits to proclaim him a certainty for a responsible cabinet position in the next cabinet shuffle, which occurred about six weeks after the election. Turner was, in fact, promised by Pearson the major new portfolio of Minister of Resources and Energy. However, six hours before the announcement of the changes an embarrassed Pearson told Turner he had had to bow to pressure from the Quebec caucus and give the post to a French Canadian. So it was given to Jean-Luc Pepin, while Turner was made Minister without Portfolio. It was a major shuffle, bringing into the cabinet five fresh younger faces: Joe Greene, Larry Pennell, Jean-Luc Pepin, Jean Marchand, and John Turner. But Turner was left on the cabinet's bottom rung. *Ottawa Citizen* editor Christopher Young wrote:

Mr. Pearson was bold and original in dealing with departmental organization. But he was cautious in dealing with his ministers. Some of the cabinet appointments are encouraging, some were taken for granted and some are distressing.

For example, John Turner, of Montreal, is easily the most promising Liberal MP under the age of forty. He has ability, high educational qualifications, energy to burn, and three-and-a-half years' experience in the House of Commons, more than several of the ministers. He is the kind of man who can articulate to the country what the Pearson government is trying to accomplish, something that most members of the ministry have lamentably failed to do. Why fob such a man off without a portfolio?

And Peter Newman commented: "The new Resources and Energy portfolio, which was tailor-made for John Turner, has gone instead to Jean-Luc Pepin, a witty, former professor of political science whose talents are sorely needed in this administration, but a man not even vaguely familiar with the terms and problems of Canada's resource needs. Turner, who was easily the ablest Liberal on the backbenches in the Twenty-Sixth Parliament, has been relegated to the limbo of a minister without portfolio."

Turner was disappointed, but he did not publicly complain. He told Peter Newman in an interview, "An apprenticeship is absolutely essential in politics. The worst that can happen to you is to be thrown into the front lines too early. Politics is a game. You've got to learn the rules and gain the respect of the opposing players."

He was still a member of the Young Turks and now its members were not confined only to the Liberal Party but to the opposition and the NDP as well. The younger members of all three parties began to chat in friendly terms in the corridors of power and challenge each other to squash games at the Skyline Hotel. All were bound together by their comparative youth and frustrations and were able to forget their political differences, at least temporarily, in their impatience to improve Parliament in general.

Blair Fraser wrote in *Maclean's*: "There is today a general crisis of leadership in Canadian politics. It is not confined to one party, or even to the two major parties. Most emphatically it is not confined to the personal hostility between two elderly men. It is a revolt in all parties of the young against the old, the newcomers against the Establishment – and the Establishment is as firmly established in Opposition as it is behind the treasury benches."

Reid Scott, the thirty-nine-year-old lawyer who had won three elections for the New Democrats in Toronto-Danforth, probably best expressed the feelings of the Young Turks when he complained: "I don't think there is any hope for Parliament as long as the present older generation is running the political parties. I don't care what party you're in, when you run up against your senior colleagues you run into a wall against change. Their attitude is, 'We'll tinker with the system, but we won't really change it.' They may not like each other but they don't dislike the system. They know it, they're comfortable with it, and they're not going to let any young upstarts turn it into something different."

And John Turner, now the youngest member of the Pearson cabinet at thirty-six, was saying: "Parliament doesn't seem to be able to digest the new, contemporary ideas that should be converted into legislation. Right now we've got a backlog of housekeeping legislation that'll take us two years to get through even without introducing a single new idea." He complained that Canada's Twenty-Seventh Parliament was "pirouetting in a vacuum" and described the state of affairs in Ottawa as "a death struggle of a vanishing generation."

"We have inherited the quarrels of another era and we can not tolerate the situation any longer," he told a meeting of his Montreal riding association. And at a meeting of the Saskatchewan Young Liberals he said: "If the Liberal Party today is arrogant it is not the 1957 arrogance of telling the people what is so, but the arrogance of assuming the people understand and that the party's program is one with the public will. The federal Liberal Party has a serious policy gap. There was virtually no policy during the last election which was fought on the majority theme – but majority for what?" he asked. "You are nuts if you don't start using your political power as citizens of this country and members of a party. You must exercise this power to achieve the aspirations of our generation. Don't be conned into routine work to get the older generation elected," he said. "You are closer to the pulse of change than the older people. You represent a body of informed and dedicated opinion. You must be the watchdog of policy morality; the conscience of the party; the radical vanguard, the militant wing; the impatient people hungry for reform. Mobilize your generation," he urged. "Invade the ranks of the party and take over offices."

Turner's one conservative move in this era – and it shocked his young reformer friends – was to vote against the total abolition of capital punishment for a five-year trial period in a free vote in the Commons in April, 1966, while most of the Old Guard, including Prime Minister Pearson, Trade Minister Robert Winters, Works Minister George McIlraith, Transport Minister Jack Pickersgill, External Affairs Minister Paul Martin, and Finance Minister Mitchell Sharp, voted in favour of abolition. Turner was one of only forty-eight Liberals, including five cabinet ministers, who voted with a majority of Conservatives to defeat the motion by a total of 138 votes to 113.

The vote hung over his head for a long time, leaving him with a conservative image he detested. About a year later he explained to Fraser Kelly, of the *Toronto Telegram:*

I know the consequences of that vote. Some people said it proved I was a right-winger. Others said I did it because I thought that's what the people in my provincial organization wanted. They can't have it both ways. I voted for abolition except in the case of killing of policemen, prison guards or officers on duty. I still believe the government should have supported that position. I thought there was still an element of deterrent. I thought that if we were moving to relieve the

106

doer of the deed from ultimate responsibility, we should also have moved toward penal reform and compensation for the victim. And I felt the opinion of the country would have supported the amendment by about 98 per cent, whereas it wouldn't have accepted total abolition. I'm not an all or nothing guy. I believe in operating within the limits of persuadability.

In fact, the government subsequently abolished capital punishment, but with the limitations involving the killing of policemen and prison guards advocated by Turner.

Now Turner says: "I could support the total abolition of capital punishment as long as life imprisonment meant life imprisonment. What worried me then was that a law must be credible with the people. Most of the people supported capital punishment and still do, and unless a law is credible it is not going to sit well with the people. I said then that intellectually I agreed with abolition, but then life imprisonment had to mean life imprisonment. Ordinary people think capital punishment is a deterrent. They believe in an eye for an eye and a tooth for a tooth, and you cannot have a situation where a murderer comes out in ten years. People are not going to buy that, you know. But it did give me a right-wing image. Oh, Marchand was furious at me. But, of course, I vote the issues the way I see them. I mean, I can't be labelled. In 1968 I set up the Department of Consumer Affairs and business thought I was a Communist. You know, it depends on the issue."

In general, he was ahead of his time, forward thinking, a young man with his life and political career ahead of him and disgusted with the attitude of older politicians who thought life would be the same in his era as it had been in theirs. A speech he gave to the Toronto Kiwanis Club in June, 1966, is worth quoting at length. He said:

I want to talk to you about the challenge of change and something of what it means to political life in this country. During the past ten years politics has been an uncertain game in Canada. We have had four minority Parliaments out of the last five. We are living through unsettled times at Ottawa. My thesis today is that there is little prospect for return to the good, old, stable days.

We may someday manage a majority government but never stability as we once knew it. The reason I say this is that this epoch of change is here to stay. Change moves so fast, one change follows another so relentlessly and intensively that it has become part of the conventional wisdom to say that the only constant factor in our lives today is change. There is little hope for stability in our generation. Traditional roots are being torn up. Old approaches are outmoded. The lessons of the past are no longer applicable. History is no longer a teacher. We need an entirely new framework to accommodate the present and the future.

There are two aspects of change that should particularly concern us. First, technological change, or the march of the machine and the computer, and, secondly, the advances in communications. These revolutions in technology and communications impinge upon the lives of every one of us, and therefore involve the political process.

Take technology. Here we have underestimated the sweep of what is a veritable revolution.

In North America, technology's two twins, automation and cybernation, have become an overwhelming social force. By automation I mean the installation of self-correcting machines that feed back information and adjust themselves. By cybernation I mean making these automated machines capable of responding to a near infinity of contingencies by hooking them up to computers. This twinning of electronic memories and self-disciplining machines has left social chaos in its wake. It has brought chaos in employment, inequality in prosperity, regional decay and a new suspicion between management and labour. . . .

Technology has been called a second industrial revolution. So far it has merely affected the semi-skilled and the unskilled worker. More and more jobs have been mechanized, automated, or cybernated. The machine and the computer have invaded the factory. But the process will not stop there. The office is next. There is now a distinct possibility that machines will replace clerks and even middle-level executives.

What will this do to us? One thing is probable: it will infect more and more people with the feeling of insecurity that comes with automation. It won't be only the blue-collar worker who worries about the machine. The white-collar middle class will share that deep concern. Traditionally there was disparity of interest between the so-called blue-collar and white-collar worker. It wasn't only that one was paid by the hour and the other by the week. It was that the factory man's life was insecure, unstable and cyclic, whereas the office worker had security of tenure and pay.

The machine has dissolved that distinction and will unite worker and clerk in a common cause. This may provoke a new impetus for reform, gripping larger areas of society, and create

108

a classless and positive reaction to this central, economic problem of our age.

What are some of the social consequences of this new technology? One of the principal spiritual consequences may be the "devaluing of all values" as the German philosopher, Nietzsche, once predicted for us. If there is nothing constant and stable in life, what does this do to our beliefs and myths? Automation and its warning of change now affect everybody. The onslaught of the machine, devaluing values, has provoked a crisis of belief and disbelief. If God is dead, as some have said, then man who substituted himself for Him now finds himself spiritually empty and unsure of himself.

An even more fundamental possibility is that work, as we know it, may be abolished. St. Paul says that "if man will not work, neither shall he eat"; but this law, so basic to our philosophy, may now be repealed by the machine. This in turn involves psychological consequences for us that are appalling. The certitude that man must labour by the sweat of his brow was a weary but at least a consoling thought. Machines are now lifting this burden from human shoulders and, in so doing, may be corrupting the central Western ethic of work. Seen in this context the machine is not simply a technological fact, but the stuff of spiritual crisis as well. . . .

This was in the mid-sixties, long before most people were aware of the beginning of the new information era and certainly well before most Canadian politicians were considering its impact, but Turner was even more startlingly futuristic in the role he was given as Minister without Portfolio with special responsibilities to Transport Minister Jack Pickersgill. In one speech to the Canadian Air Line Pilots Association, he predicted:

Shortly there will be supersonic jets which will be so fast that no journey anywhere in this earth will take longer than six hours. It may well be that meals and stewardesses will be outmoded. All planes will have standing room only because of the limited time it will take to travel from one place to another. This is great news for those who have experienced the joys of trans-Atlantic economy flights in the company of a dozen bilious babies. Regina will be ten minutes from London over the Pole.

Air transport is just at the first stages of its revolution. To set the limits today is folly. Although less than one per cent of today's freight travels by air, the day will come when most will travel by air, either hundreds of thousands of feet up in the air or inches off the ground. The air-cushion vehicles riding on air may bring about the passing of the wheel. If such vehicles become workable highways would become obsolete, frontiers will become a thing of the past, electronic guidelines will replace freeways, and interior virgin country will be opened up for recreation, habitation, and development. . . .

The globe is indeed growing smaller when our world can be circumnavigated in ninety minutes. The earth can never be to our children what it was to our fathers. True loneliness will lie between the stars, not between distant countries or oceans. Ours will be a world without distance. . . .

Through all the ages man has fought against two great enemies – time and space. Time may never be wholly conquered. The sheer space may also defeat man when he has ventured more than a few light years from the sun. Yet on this little earth, at least, we may one day claim a final victory. I believe the time will come when we may move from pole to pole within the throb of a single heartbeat.

This is the future that lies open to us. Today we must begin to orient ourselves to the next step in this transformation of our life.

Turner was not an economic nationalist at this time when its father, Walter Gordon, was still a powerful member of the party's Old Guard. There was a friction, mixed with some respect, between the two men. Even before he became a cabinet minister, in an important speech to the Canadian Club of New York in January, 1964, Turner had raised the eyebrows of the economic nationalists by stating:

The current wave of economic nationalism in Canada will have to be resolved. Canada needs foreign and especially American capital for economic growth, and yet it worries about selling its birthright to others. American control of some of our primary and secondary industries has reached alarming proportions in the eyes of many Canadians. This concern has provoked tax and fiscal measures which many have considered to be ill-advised and even hostile to our friends abroad.

I would personally hope that the balance of investment in Canada would not be cured by restrictive, protectionist tax policies. The question of foreign ownership can surely not be resolved by penalizing investment money which came into Canada under certain ground rules. It is neither good politics nor good business to change the rules in the middle of the game.

Nor would we be wise to discourage new investment capital. I would hope rather that the balance might be adjusted by stimulation of investment by Canadians themselves in their own resources and industries. At the moment there is probably not enough private Canadian capital to achieve the kind of balance that many seek between foreign and domestic participation in our industry and resources. We may have to resort to a typically Canadian compromise by channelling certain public investments into the private sector.

The idea of government participating financially in sectors of industry traditionally operated by private industry is not new in Canada. It would surely be preferable to encourage Canadian equity participation in our industry, even by way of public investment, rather than to penalize foreign investment.

Subsequently, when Gordon's book, *A Choice for Canada*, was published in 1966, Turner lost more friends among ardent economic nationalists by telling a press conference in Regina the book "doesn't represent the main stream of Liberal thinking."

This clash with Gordon did not help his chances for promotion in the cabinet. "Walter felt that because I came from the Montreal wing of the party I was more of a free-trader than he liked, and I wasn't as much of an economic nationist as he liked. I think I wasn't on Walter's promotional list and he was the senior Ontario minister," Turner says. "But, you know, Walter and I are very good friends. I find him a very civilized man."

In fact, after Pearson and Gordon argued bitterly in the midsixties and the long friendship of the two old political warriors deteriorated into an almost irreconcilable situation, Turner brought them together again on Pearson's deathbed. "I used to keep in touch with Walter, particularly when I was Finance Minister," Turner says. "I used to come up to Toronto and see him about every six months or so, and he would take me to the York Club and we'd dine in a private room and talk about things. We'd agree to disagree on some things and agree on others.

"Well, once I met Walter like this just after I'd seen Mr. Pearson at his retirement home in Ottawa and had learned that he was dying. The next night after I saw Pearson I was having a dinner with Walter in Toronto, which had been scheduled for some time. And at the end of it I said to Walter, 'I know you and Mr. Pearson have had a falling out, and I know the reasons why, and I know his side of the story and I've never heard yours, Walter. But if you want to repair that you haven't got many days left to repair it.' Walter took the plane to Ottawa the very next day and had lunch with Pearson and they got together again."

But in the sixties Turner was not in Gordon's good books, al-

111

though he consistently claimed he was a strong Canadian nationalist and that his only argument with the Gordonites involved the methods they proposed to reaffirm economic independence. He wanted to use an inventive approach rather than the punitive measures advocated by Gordon.

He expressed concern in several speeches about talk of a free-trade union with the United States and the fact that resources were being discussed in continental terms. "We reject the word continental from our vocabulary and feel that our resources and our water are national assets," he said. "Americans control a good deal of our primary and secondary industries by way of equity and debt and we are having a great debate about the fact of foreign ownership of our businesses and resources. Although we have argued sharply about the methods of dealing with it, Canadians are at one with the objective; that we must reaffirm economic independence if we are to maintain political independence. We must be more than just a branch plant economically if we are really to fulfil ourselves among the company of nations." Thus he was prepared to meet the economic nationalists part of the way, but his popularity with them and the Old Guard didn't improve much at the important Liberal policy convention in Ottawa in October, 1966.

This was the conference in which medicare was postponed and Mitchell Sharp's moderate economic philosophies prevailed over Walter Gordon's radical economic nationalism after bitter debate, leading to a Turner-like compromise policy position urging encouragement of Canadian investment rather than discouragement of international capital. As one wag put it at the time: "The Liberal party has resolved that it is all for Canadian ownership of industry as long as it doesn't interfere with foreign investments."

Turner voted against postponement of medicare, then made his mark at this conference by virtually ignoring the main argument on economic nationalism and pushing through a forward-looking, pragmatic motion on reform of labour relations, including the ending of ex-parte injunctions in labour disputes, which allowed struck employers to get an order limiting the number of pickets without the affected union being heard in court. The other major planks in the Turner platform were: strengthening of the labour relations services of the federal Labour department by expanding regional offices and providing them with facilities to conduct continuous free collective bargaining; extension on an industry-by-industry basis of labour, management, and government councils to provide a forum for discussion, education, and research and to co-ordinate national economic policies; a study of special legislation for the settlement of disputes affecting the general public interest; provision of adequate facilities for adult training and retraining, including payment

112

of allowances; establishment of obligations for employers to provide advance notice in case of shutdown or relocation; government provision of relocation expenses for workers displaced through automation or technological changes; proper consideration by a royal commission of the status of women.

"The whole nature of work and its utilitarian effect on the economy must be re-examined," Turner said. "Labour is no longer a commodity to be exploited. Management no longer has the right to freely manipulate men as it manipulates money and machines. It is important in times of technological change to protect not so much the job as the workers. The basic assumption in our society of two equal and competing forces of labour and management must be re-evaluated." He had previously advocated a guaranteed annual income in Canada and now he said society must provide work for all who are prepared to work or "guarantee a minimum level of material life for those unable to find work."

"Is there any reason why there should be a distinction between the blue-collar workers and the white-collar workers based on the method of payment?" he asked. "Why should a blue-collar worker continue to be paid for his efforts on an hourly basis instead of a yearly guaranteed basis coupled with increases based on individual productivity and cost of living?"

At first the convention toyed briefly with the Turner motion, then shelved it with distaste. But to the annoyance of the Old Guard, Turner and his supporters lobbied behind the scenes and finally won a vote by a narrow margin for Turner's right to speak on the motion, forcing a session of the convention to extend until 1:30 a.m., when the controversial policy was approved with about a third of the delegates voting against it. The policy was never implemented by the government, but Peter Regenstreif wrote in the *Montreal Star*:

> The Minister without Portfolio made gigantic gains at this meeting because he was virtually alone in fighting for issues dear to the hearts of urban Canada, especially in connection with labour. More important, he was seen by the delegates and they liked what they saw.
>
> Mr. Turner began this party conference as a "dark horse" with a small band of devotees. Liberals across the country knew him as a coming man – but perhaps for next time. That has all been changed. He is now a definite contender with time on his side. A portfolio is coming his way shortly. If he continues to perform behind the scenes as he has so far, his progress to the front rank is assured.

Turner was mildly critical of the conference in a subsequent speech to the Manitoba Young Liberal Association. "The substance of the policies debated were largely echoes of the past, echoes of policies which have been debated before," he said. "In terms of policy, the meeting was not a success. Events are outrunning the policies."

And in this same speech he called for a set of "Canadian Rights." "They must be enshrined in the constitution so that no one can challenge a person's right to live freely in Canada," he said. "They must be carved in stone, so they never can be swept away by the tides of time or the forces of technology."

Turner also represented the government at a Commonwealth Parliamentary Association Conference in Ottawa in the fall of 1966, revealing there for the first time an attitude to foreign affairs and foreign aid.

"We are a fortunate people, it is true," he said in a major speech to the conference. "But we do have our own problems of poverty and uneven distribution of our national wealth. We have our problems of vast distances, regional biases and cultural diversity. But Canada is at times neurotic in its self-analysis. We constantly worry about relations between French-speaking and English-speaking Canadians. We worry about the almost overwhelming neighbourhood of the United States. We worry about our federal-provincial relationships. We are all tempted to overestimate our own importance in the world and to exaggerate the gravity of our own problems, and Canadians have surrendered to that temptation all too often," he said.

"It is trite to say, in the space age, that the world grows smaller and closer. The bad breath of poverty is felt throughout the world. Over half the world's population is illiterate; over half the people of the world are chronically ill; a large part of the world is hungry most of the time and most of the people of the world cannot afford decent clothing, housing or recreation. The gulf between the 'have' and 'have-not' countries grows larger rather than smaller. As the gulf widens the dangers grow. Strides in economic development are offset by the population explosion. Surely this is a race to disaster. Therefore," he said, "it is not only our duty but it is imperative that those countries in the Commonwealth blessed with relative prosperity and affluence share this abundance."

Peter Newman summed up Turner's period as Minister without Portfolio in a column in *The Toronto Star*:

> Turner is a man of our time, born at the beginning of the Depression, highly educated, articulate, unsentimental, handsome enough to illuminate a million television screens and, one

begins to suspect, intellectually substantial enough to back his image up.

The mind that emerges from an analysis of his speeches is that of a young man bored by abstractions, interested more in workable ideas rather than grandiose ideologies. Turner is no romantic perpetuating the conditioned reflexes of small 'l' liberalism. Committed more to existence than to essence, he is slowly forging a brand new, swinging vision of this country and its potential. . . .

There are words and phrases . . . seldom heard before in Canadian political speeches, and on occasion, his oratory achieves a shimmering cadence reminiscent of John Kennedy . . . .

There's still a gap between Turner's private and public impact. Visitors to his Parliament Hill office go determined not to be charmed because his charm has been too much heralded, yet few can talk to him without being stimulated, and most leave, despite themselves, charmed. Turner's problem in confronting the public is that under our parliamentary system, no junior member of cabinet can stake out meaningful positions without entering the bailiwick of a fellow minister, and thus risking resentment and party discipline. . . .

At the same time Turner is pragmatic enough to be totally loyal to his party. He looks on the Liberals' recent internal squabbles as being nothing more than "pillow fights." . . . He does take sides in the continentalists versus nationalists issue, however.

"Continentalism is not part of my political vocabulary, particularly when it comes to resource policies," he said. While he disagrees with the restrictive measures that have been advocated by Walter Gordon, he supports Gordon's objectives. "I think that Walter Gordon's national conscience is an essential ingredient for my country – and for my party," he says.

Turner is then a patriot, but a realistic patriot. His main policy thrust is to find ways of improving Canadian society because he says, "without excellence in all things Canadian, this country will never have an identity and will be unable to compete in the world." To achieve that excellence he is for the ripping away of all social and financial barriers to higher education and the expansion of the federal government involvement in research. He also wants a further relaxation of our immigration policies to allow into the country not only the skilled but those who can demonstrate the ability to learn.

"Canada needs not only qualifications that fit on a printed

certificate: it needs muscle, energy, hard work. We need fifty million people because if the eleven to one ratio in population continues, we'll never be able to exercise any leverage against the Americans."

Turner's future is bright but the path he'll take to power is still winding and of undetermined length. He is not openly running for the leadership of his party though there's little doubt he'll make the attempt when the opportunity presents itself, and with half the electorate under thirty-five, his chances of becoming the candidate who can give the new generation political expression are excellent. In the meantime, he's churning the political water like some sleek speedboat, discreetly buzzing the smug harbor of Ottawa's Establishment Liberalism.

12

Centennial: The End of the Pearson Years

In five long years of sustained and unparallelled prosperity, Canada's political affairs had been in almost continuous uproar. By denying confidence to any of the national parties through three elections, the people had ensured a weak and distracted government at the centre at a time when the provinces grew stronger and the startling renaissance of Quebec became angrier.

But in spite of all this the Pearson government had achieved most of its major objectives in social welfare legislation, which provided an important buffer in the hard times to come in the eighties, and after a remarkable series of adventures in federal-provincial relations, it had set a firm, soundly constitutional course that the people seemed to understand and appreciate. So there was much optimism in the country and in the Liberal Party as Prime Minister Pearson lit the centennial flame on Parliament Hill on New Year's Eve of 1967 and proclaimed Canada's 100th birthday to be underway. After all, the previous year had been pretty good for Pearson's Liberals. Not a single cabinet minister had been forced to resign because of a scandal, which was an achievement, and the image of fumbling ineptness that had plagued the party almost since Walter Gordon brought down his first budget in 1963 had faded.

The Liberals had been able to sit back and chuckle merrily while the Conservatives pulled themselves apart in their attempts to dump their leader, John Diefenbaker. There was as well a stability in their own ranks, due mainly, the pundits said, to changing patterns of power through the emergence of political unknowns to new positions of influence, and an unspectacular efficiency by members of the Old Guard now moved into new positions of authority. Finance Minister Mitchell Sharp stood out in this regard, bringing a new, calm credibility to the post. As Maurice Western wrote in the *Winnipeg Free Press*:

The Pearson government, in unrelenting parliamentary struggles, has suffered a good many casualties. But any government suffers some attrition in four years and the present ministry appears considerably more competent, better balanced and tougher than the overrated original "team."

There is a core of steady veterans such as Messrs. Pickersgill, Martin, Winters and Laing. Behind them are some young ministers (Mr. Turner is an outstanding example) who have already gained much valuable experience in government.

Finally, Mr. Pearson has at last found in Mr. Jean Marchand a Quebec lieutenant of stature and developing parliamentary skill.

In January, Pearson brought Walter Gordon back into the cabinet as Minister without Portfolio and then appointed him head of a special cabinet committee to study foreign ownership of Canadian industry and ways to encourage greater Canadian ownership. The other members of the committee, obviously chosen to balance Gordon's radicalism, were Finance Minister Mitchell Sharp, Gordon's chief opponent on economic nationalism, Manpower Minister Jean Marchand, representing Quebec, Minister without Portfolio John Turner, who held middle ground on the issue, and Veterans' Affairs Minister Roger Teillet, of Manitoba, who was apparently thrown in in case western Canada should feel ignored. Trade Minister Robert Winters was also reported to have been invited to serve on the committee. He refused because, he felt, the committee's report would likely reflect Gordon's views and he had no wish to be associated with any move to further disturb U.S.-Canada economic relations by endorsing proposals for additional restrictions on U.S. capital investment in Canada. The committee was to preside over an inquiry to be conducted by a task force of economists outside the government service. This group was eventually headed by left-wing University of Toronto economist Mel Watkins.

In the meantime Turner hit the headlines and editorial pages across the country with a provocative address at the Osgoode Hall Law School in Toronto, in which he lashed out at his own legal profession and urged drastic and imaginative law reforms. He told the law students:

I do not believe in simplistic solutions to complex problems. One mechanism cannot do the job. Law reform is beyond the scope even of centres of research. What is required above all is a change in the lawyer's attitude. We must start first with the law profession.

Where are our social reformers in law? Where is there a

program of public education to change the public attitude towards the law and lawyers?

Too few lawyers are in the vanguard of social progress. Too few lawyers are explorers for social justice. Today the lawyer is too wedded to major business interests.

Today young lawyers seek only to join big law factories. We have lost the tradition of the lawyer as a professional loner acting for any individual client, big or small.

Lawyers seem to have lost their interest in individual freedom and reform. They have become time-sheet lawyers – working on a meter. It is little wonder that the Canadian Civil Liberties Association has been unable financially to maintain the services of full-time counsel. Did the legal profession massively move in to support this organization?

Now, what about you, the law students? In my travels across Canada I have looked for progressives and reformers amongst law students. But you want to play it safe. You seem afraid of the hierarchy of the profession. You seem complacent about the status quo. Where are the Caesar Wrights and the Frank Scotts of your generation to prod and kick the legal profession into action on law reform? Are you going to avoid reform or embrace it?

Be critical of the law! Write and debate about changes in the law! Let's read a radical piece or two in our legal journals. Case-law is not the gospel. Is the law right? Are the judges socially aware of the changing conditions? Can judge-made law move faster than the legislatures? Should it?

These are questions you must ask yourselves if we are to reform our laws. We need law students who are activists, not pacifists, about law reform.

Some people say that if you go to the law schools in Canada there you will find future judges and senators. I want people to say that you should go to the law schools if you want to find social reformers who want to change our society for the better. This is your challenge. It is a personal one. Decide now to spend at least two years of your career in the public service to make laws as they should be. How we would benefit from such dedication! How you meet this challenge will determine, in large measure, how far and how fast the law will be reformed and how quickly we achieve a better life in the Second Canada.

Mr. Justice Cardozo once wrote: "The process of justice is never finished, but reproduces itself generation after generation in ever changing forms."

What will your generation do to produce a newer and better form of justice in Canada's future? That will depend on you.

Rather than become an agency for change, the law too often has become a barrier to change. The technology of law reform in Canada is rusty and obsolescent. Efforts to keep the hopes and dreams of society are lagging behind because of small vision, limited resources, lack of desire for reform, overworked public officials and complacency.

Then Turner outlined his own proposals for change, starting with reform of Parliament, where the laws are made, by modernizing the cabinet with inner and outer segments to separate policy-making from administration; then a Bill of Rights, enshrined in the Constitution, to deal with old political freedoms, new economic rights, and invasion of privacy; and a national program of "legicare," similar to medicare, to end a double standard for the rich and poor in matters like bail, compensation for automobile accidents, and sentencing of offenders.

He described Canada's laws regulating business and protecting consumers as "woefully inadequate," allowing management in corporations to become a law unto itself, and he urged new laws to deal with rights of minority shareholders, takeovers, mergers, stock trading by those with inside knowledge, the relationship of auditors to companies, proxy solicitation, and disclosure of stock dealings by company officers. He also advocated updating of the Criminal Code so that it would not legislate anyone's private morality.

In other speeches, like one to the North Vancouver Seymour Liberal Association, he continued to be aggressive, even abrasive. "We're going to have to turn around for once in our lives and face the future swearing," he told this Vancouver meeting. "When Centennial slips away, what will be left? A few frayed flags? A collective hangover? Will we have a fresh feeling of national pride when this giant birthday party is over? Or will we fall back once again into the gloom of regional alliance?" He said he was optimistic that Canada could take its place as a leader among nations despite its size. "We can't compete in numbers. We can't compete in military power. But we can compete in terms of quality and excellence."

He spoke persistently around the country as Minister without Portfolio and the press was good to him. An article by Gordon Pape in the *Montreal Gazette* in March, 1967, is representative of the media reaction at the time.

OTTAWA—Montreal's John Turner may be too good-looking ever to become Prime Minister of Canada.

Unlike their neighbours to the south, Canadians tend to be

naturally suspicious about ruggedly handsome men who look like they just stepped out of a television commercial for Vitalis.

The suspicion becomes even stronger when good looks happen to be combined with a Rhodes Scholar background, a cabinet post at thirty-six, and the ability to write and deliver speeches that are so dynamic and idea-packed they sound more like a product of Madison Avenue image makers than the genuine thoughts of a real-live Canadian politician.

"His problem is he's too good-looking," one of his closest associates candidly admits. "People see him and they think there must be something phoney. If he were just a little uglier, he'd be a lot better off."

But Turner is stuck with his appearance. If youthful good looks combined with a touch of grey in the hair are really a drawback in Canadian politics, he'll have to make it to the top in spite of them.

And the top is clearly where he's aiming. Turner is one of the fastest rising stars in Parliament; even some Conservatives, frustrated by what they regard as a mediocre crop of candidates for the leadership of their party, have been heard to mumble when there's no one else within earshot just how great it would be to have Turner as a Tory.

Many young Liberals are every bit as enthusiastic – and not as reluctant to admit it. They regard Turner as having many of the characteristics they want in a leader – ability to attract young, sophisticated voters; creative thinking and imagination; long range vision; effective speaking manner; awareness of the techniques of modern communication; good education; and an easy mastery of the winning smile and the fast, firm handshake.

As an added bonus, Turner is probably the most fluently bilingual of all English-speaking politicians in Ottawa. He is capable of delivering an hour-long speech in French without notes and exchanges banter with the waitresses in the Parliamentary Restaurant daily in a relaxed, colloquial French. . . .

One of Turner's great advantages is that he inspires tremendous loyalty in the people who work for him – loyalty which is sometimes so fierce that it loses all sense of proportion. One member of his staff went so far as to call him "greater than Kennedy." Certainly a casual visitor to Turner's Centre Block office can't help but come away with the impression that the people who work for him are convinced that their boss will one day be Prime Minister of Canada. . . .

In recent months Turner has been using his speeches across the country to carefully piece together the picture of the Canada of the future as he wants it to be. He calls it "A Second Canada."

The Turner speeches, which are clearly the basis for his future political philosophy, lay constant stress of the need for Canadians to look to the future and live their destiny to the fullest. The ideas he throws out are imaginative, sure to appeal to the young – but he's careful to always blend in a degree of moderation to show cautious businessmen he isn't going to throw out everything the country has already built. . . .

He has given a great deal of thought to the future use of Canada's water resources, and is probably the single most knowledgeable politician on the subject in the country.

He has worked out what he calls "an economic bill of rights for Canada" aimed at updating the traditional rights of citizens to include the rights of economic security, freedom from the fear of automation, the right to privacy, freedom from noise, the right to clean air and water etc.

He has proposed plans for revamping the creaking Parliamentary system; called for a drastic overhaul of Canada's legal system and outlined specific fields where reforms are needed; probed at depth into the problems of leisure that will grow in the next decade; attempted to put forward some policies for ending labour strife; examined the growing needs of education and proposed some solutions; and looked long and hard at Canada's tendency to regionalism, something that disturbs him deeply. . . .

Turner's great need now is a good, solid ministry that he can get his teeth into and prove to himself and everyone else whether he has the administrative ability needed in any leadership aspirant.

There have been persistent rumors in recent weeks that a cabinet shuffle is in the offing – perhaps even during the Easter recess. If Turner comes out of the shake-up with something resembling a major portfolio, or even with an intermediate one, he should finally have his chance to show the country whether he is really leadership material, or just a flashy, fast-talking lightweight.

The cabinet shake-up came on April 4, 1967, and Turner was given the intermediate portfolio of Registrar General. He was told, however, that the department would shortly be expanded to include consumer affairs and thus become much more powerful and important.

It was a popular shuffle, which also brought two other young "swinging Quebecers" into the cabinet. Pierre Trudeau, forty-six, the MP for Mount Royal and parliamentary secretary to the Prime Minister, was appointed Minister of Justice, and Jean Chretien, thirty-three, the MP for St. Maurice-Lefleche and parliamentary secretary to Finance Minister Mitchell Sharp, became Minister without Portfolio. The only other move was the promotion of Walter Gordon to President of the Privy Council, giving added status to his role as head of the cabinet study of foreign investment in Canada.

The appointment of Trudeau to the prestigious Justice portfolio was the only real surprise. The press described him as "a colorful, free-thinking intellectual," and wrote stories about his taste for sandals, bright shirts, and casual ascots. At the swearing-in ceremony Pearson quipped that everybody knew Trudeau was going to be appointed to the cabinet because he had shown up in the House wearing a tie. "And shoes too," John Turner added. It was the last time he ever joked publicly with or about Pierre Trudeau.

In almost his first act in his new portfolio, Turner created an image of himself that was so far to the left it startled even his closest supporters. In a television interview with Pierre Berton he was asked if he believed in free housing. Yes. Free university education? Yes. Free medical services? Yes. With a means test? Not really. Are you in favour of the guaranteed annual income? Yes. How much a year. About $3,000. A capital gains tax? Yes. Increased inheritance taxes? With some reservations. Do you think taxes will ever go down? No. Dennis Braithwaite asked in his *Globe and Mail* column if this man who could someday be Canada's prime minister also believed in free lollipops.

"Is it really 1984 already," Braithwaite asked, "an era of doublethink in which a politician, a man seeking the highest prize within – as we used to naively say, the gift of the people – with utter confidence tells the TV audience, in his first solo flight, that he intends to go on taxing, taxing, taxing, until he has taken all our money, at which point he and his buddies in the cabinet will generously return certain amounts in various programs designed to keep us from starving or going without a roof over our heads? And all these awful disclosures are made voluntarily, without coercion. Pavlov never had a more tractable respondent than Pierre had on this night."

Other right-wing columnists and editorialists blasted away at Turner's "almost Communistic" attitude and Colin Brown, founder of the Citizen's Coalition, spent several thousand dollars on newspaper advertisements reproducing the Braithwaite column across the country.

Only the veteran liberal writer Bruce Hutchison came mildly to

Turner's defence, stating that reports of the TV interview had been oversimplified and that Turner deserved credit for "this act of courage." "But now," Hutchison added, "Mr. Turner, a liberal in the full Wilsonian sense, has loaded his boat heavily with the freight of positive commitments. Perhaps, indeed, he has burned his boat altogether, and irrevocably placed himself far on the left of the political spectrum. It is here, he evidently thinks, that his own generation is moving towards ultimate power."

Turner didn't worry much about all of this, however, and his left-wing image remained undiluted as he attacked his new job with almost a frenzy. He set up a task force to study the Canada Corporations Act, which had not had a serious overhaul in thirty years; encouraged uniformity of securities legislation across Canada; threatened to bring the National Hockey League and the Canadian Football League under the jurisdiction of the Combines Investigation Act after Vancouver failed to get an NHL franchise when the NHL expanded to six U.S. cities; pressured the major oil companies to stop refusing to supply gasoline to dealers who would not buy associated products from named suppliers; attacked the advertising industry for misleading consumers; organized an interdepartmental committee to watch over consumer affairs; removed barriers against import of low-priced foreign drugs in an effort to reduce drug prices; and eventually steered through the House the bill setting up Canada's first Department of Consumer and Corporate Affairs and became its minister.

In the House he voted in favour of limited abolition of capital punishment, switching from his anti-abolition position eighteen months previously because of exemptions in the new bill for the slaying of policemen and prison guards. The motion carried by a vote of 114 to 87.

He also made several forays into Quebec, calling on Quebecers to negotiate a non-separatist option that would permit expansion of French culture throughout the country with guarantees of linguistic and cultural rights of both French and English Canadians. "These guarantees would necessarily reflect a return to French cultural expansion in Canada and would also guarantee to the English-speaking minority in Quebec the continuance of their rights," he said. But he also warned: "French-speaking Canadians should realize that the rest of Canada is not ready to make any compromise for the sake of keeping Quebec. Sometimes one must water one's wine. To forget this aspect would be to set any negotiation off on a wrong foot."

When the Watkins Report on foreign ownership was released, supporting some of Walter Gordon's tough positions, he remained diplomatically mum for a while, having backed Mitchell Sharp's more moderate stance in the cabinet committee discussions, and then gave the report lukewarm support by saying he was in complete agreement with its objectives, but that Canada still needed all the capital it could get, both foreign and domestic. "I was on Sharp's side in that argument," Turner says. "I just didn't believe in Walter's theories of buying back the economy. I thought there were better uses for the country's resources."

Then when Gordon stepped out of line with a speech sharply condemning U.S. policy in Vietnam, causing much cabinet and public controversy, Turner indicated in an almost simultaneous but more guarded speech that he was on Gordon's side at least on that controversial issue.

Centennial year turned out to be another hectic period, another year of crisis in Canadian politics. Inflation began to increase at a worrisome rate and interest rates rose. Taxes had to be increased to pay for the rising demands of the welfare system. Radical changes in public attitudes were reflected by the unanimous support accorded Justice Minister Trudeau's divorce reform measures. The armed forces were unified after much bitter controversy, and collective bargaining was introduced into the public service. The report of the Bilingualism and Biculturalism Commission proclaimed the country to be in serious danger of disintegration and General Charles De Gaulle's cry of "Vive le Québec libre" in Montreal didn't help. The Liberal Party's caucus again divided sharply with the return of Walter Gordon to the cabinet, but the Liberals still remained almost friendly in comparison with the civil war in Conservative ranks that arrayed Diefenbaker "loyalists" against rebels backing Party President Dalton Camp's successful campaign for a leadership convention. Diefenbaker was dumped at the convention and replaced by Robert Stanfield.

And in the end, on December 14, Lester Bowles Pearson called it quits and started the scramble for power that saw Pierre Elliott Trudeau rise on an unusual, adventurous wave of combined English and French support to the country's top political position.

John Turner saw Pearson for the last time almost exactly five years later, in early December, 1972. "Mrs. Pearson called me up and said, 'Mr. Pearson would like to see you,' " he recalls. "So I went over to see Mr. Pearson. It was the first snowfall, just a light snowfall, and I walked over from my house, which was about half a mile away. It was about 5:30 and I chatted with Mr. and Mrs. Pearson for a while and then she left and we poured ourselves a couple of Scotches. He knew he was dying. For the first half hour he talked about his life and our government. He was very,

very distressed about Trudeau's foreign policy and attitude to the alliances. You know, Trudeau was questioning NATO and our defence commitments in those days. And then he talked, I guess for the last twenty minutes, about what I should do and where I would go. He said someday I would be Prime Minister and that I should be patient and just wait it out. And I told him I anticipated I would be having troubles with our great leader before it was over. He said he could understand that.

"It was a very warm conversation, very warm. He had deliberately called me in and I knew when I left that it was the last time I would ever see him. He took me to the door and as I walked down his driveway he kept the door open and I could see his face in the light. As I left the driveway I turned back and waved to him and he waved to me, and I could still see his face in the light of the door. And I told Geills when I got home that was the last time I would see Mr. Pearson."

13

Two Very Different Men

The two men were about as different as men could be. One was highly educated, an intellectual loner with few close friends and an admitted inability to get along with people; the other was a gregarious sentimentalist, as well-educated and intellectual, though less assertively so, but who never forgot a friend and could boast that he'd meet one on almost any main street of the country, a man so anxious to get along with others of all classes he could adapt automatically to the bawdy dialect of jocks or to the polite phrases of princes and princesses and not feel out of place anywhere. Both were Catholics, but one was influenced by the classicist Jesuits, the other by the man-of-the-world, more pragmatic Oblates. One was born to wealth, while the other earned some of its benefits only after the experience of insecurity. One had been around the world more than the other, but the second had been around Canada much more than the first. In sports, one competed almost invariably against himself; the other relished in the rivalry of other men. One loved to drive a flashy antique Mercedes sports car while the other owned an old station wagon, and in later years, took the subway to work and drove his five-year-old Volkswagen Rabbit when he had to. Both took care of their health and their bodies, one austerely, taking only an occasional glass of wine, the other loving his long cigars and lunchtime martinis and sweating them off on the tennis and squash courts. On the few occasions they dined together one never picked up the tab, the other always had to. The personality of one was laid-back, "cool," mysterious; the other's unsubtle, transparent, and "hot." There was even a genetic difference: one was right-handed, the other left-handed. Both were bilingual, but French was the first language of one and English was the first language of the other. There were some similarities about them but deep down they were very different men and they found it hard to adjust to each other.

When Pierre Trudeau's arm was raised in victory at the April,

127

1968, Liberal leadership convention and he became Canada's fifteenth prime minister, John Turner described him, in seconding the motion to make the vote unanimous, as "the greatest Canadian of this generation," and he meant it. Turner respected Trudeau. But he did not like him much. And Trudeau did not know what to make of Turner. Here, after all, was a rival who had refused to make him King when he had the power at the convention to do it, and yet to whom he was in debt because he had also refused to transfer his delegates to the main challengers, Robert Winters and Paul Hellyer, when they had tried to gang up to defeat him. By preventing a complete polarization between its left and right wings, Turner had made his leadership of the party tenable. Also, here was a man who had kept his own small power base of 195 delegates even at the end and robbed him of a little of the victory, a man still his own man, admirable but troublesome, a threat.

After the convention, Trudeau kept Turner on as Minister of Consumer and Corporate Affairs until the party swept to victory in a snap June election, in which Turner contested the riding of Ottawa-Carleton. His Montreal seat had vanished in a redistribution but his margin of victory in this new riding was so wide that both his Conservative and NDP rivals lost their deposits.

Then when Trudeau formed his first real cabinet in July, 1968, he appointed Turner, who had just turned thirty-nine, as Minister of Justice. It was a new type of cabinet, with an inner sanctum of senior ministers and an outer sanctum of lesser authority, and it included most of Trudeau's leadership rivals in the powerful positions. It was also the youngest cabinet (average age: forty-seven years) since Confederation, and it set the style of Trudeau government for years to come, although many of its senior members would resign in weariness or frustration. But Trudeau's appointment of Turner to the prestigious Justice portfolio, which he had held himself, was a little like the appointment of a Secretary of State for External Affairs under Mike Pearson. His decisions were likely to be second-guessed, and they were. To begin with, constitutional affairs were usually an important responsibility of the Justice Department, but Trudeau reserved them for himself, a move that reflected the differences between Trudeau and Turner in the leadership campaign when Turner had attacked the Trudeau appeal for cool logic on national unity and advocated instead a flexible and emotional approach to the problem by insisting, "You solve it by the heart and you solve it by the gut, because that's what Canada's all about."

Then Turner was publicly slapped down by the Prime Minister when he said in his very first statement as Justice Minister that he favoured separate votes in the Commons on the controversial issues of homosexuality and abortion instead of their inclusion in the omnibus bill on the Criminal Code, which had been introduced by Trudeau when he was Justice Minister. "I want to make sure that an MP who is against abortion but for a tougher firearms law doesn't lose his vote," Turner said, reflecting a position already taken by Opposition Leader Robert Stanfield. Trudeau retorted haughtily: "I still regard the bill as a single item. But if Mr. Turner has grave reasons for changing it, I suppose we'd consider them." The cabinet was split on the separate vote issue, but Trudeau won. The bill was introduced as a single item.

Despite these setbacks Turner tore into the fusty old Justice Department like a small tornado, upsetting a few of the inmates but endearing himself to most of them. "Put a charged-up guy like John Turner into the Justice Department and something is bound to happen," wrote Bruce Phillips of Southam News Services. "Something is. Turner is riding into the department like that television knight dispensing gallons of foaming cleanser, blowing the dust off old law books and shaking up some greybeards who haven't changed their way of doing things since the day Blackstone bought his first frock coat. It's hard to imagine anyone injecting any sex appeal into something that by definition is as dry and dreary as the Justice Department, all clogged up as it is with ancient torts and yellowing writs of Mandamus. Nevertheless, Turner is going to try, and although he is marginally thicker around the waist than he was when he burst on this scene six years ago, he has lost none of his patented go-get 'em style."

Turner started by recruiting new talent and ordering computers to provide case law and legal precedents and keep track of the progress of cases before the courts. Then he departed dramatically from tradition by abandoning party patronage in the naming of judges, a process Trudeau had also encouraged, so that half of the judges appointed by Turner in his first six months in the portfolio were non-Liberals. Whenever there was a judicial opening Turner sent a short list of suggested names to the Canadian Bar Association. The Association then divided the names into three categories; well qualified, qualified, or not qualified. He then made the appointment from the first two categories after much further consultation, but the candidate's politics was not one of the deciding factors.

One of Turner's first judicial appointments, for instance, was that of John Osler to the Ontario Supreme Court. Osler was a member of an old and well-to-do Ontario family and he had an outstanding reputation as a labour lawyer. But he had a serious blot on his record at least in terms of a judicial appointment. He had been associated with the old CCF Party and, even worse, the other senior partners in his law firm, David Lewis and Ted Jolliffe, were socialists. When asked why he had appointed Osler, Turner replied: "Because he was what I wanted; a man with views on labour matters, lots of experience before boards, and an obvious sensitivity to injustice. I'm not sure what Osler's politics are now but I doubt he's a Liberal. Certainly David Lewis has been soliciting his appointment. The first factor in a judicial appointment so far as I'm concerned," Turner added, "is competence. Political affiliation is much less relevant. The choosing of judges is the toughest thing I have to do. After all they have more power than anyone else in our system." Still, quite a few of Turner's friends were made judges during his tenure. He had friends of all political persuasions.

His main early task was to push through the Commons Bill C-150, the massive omnibus bill on the Criminal Code, despite strong opposition even from some members of his own party, his own firm belief that it should have been split, and much bitter controversy. The 120 clauses of the bill amended Canadian law on a range of matters from sexual mores to gun control, harrassing telephone calls, drunken driving, and legalized lotteries. In effect, it wrote a new legal charter for Pierre Trudeau's "Just Society." Its most controversial sections sprung from Trudeau's statement eighteen months earlier that "the state has no place in the bedrooms of the nation." Eliminated were penalties against any sexual acts in private, including homosexual acts, and hospitals were permitted to perform therapeutic abortions in cases where a committee certified that the continuation of pregnancy "would or would be likely to endanger the life or health" of the mother. These were to replace current clauses that made buggery an indictable offense with a maximum penalty of fourteen years' imprisonment and outlawed abortion for any reason, on pain of up to life imprisonment for a convicted abortionist and two years for the patient.

Turner, who had come so close to becoming a Catholic priest, had to examine his conscience closely before proceeding on both issues, but particularly on abortion. He sought theological advice from two separate church sources, one in Quebec City and one in Toronto, one in French and one in English, on the duties of a Catholic legislator in a pluralistic society. "The duty," he says now, "is to achieve the common good. You have to give away a little of your Catholicity. You don't have to surrender your commitments, but you have to understand that there are others who don't share them, and you have to work out a result in the civil sphere that accommodates the duty. We are going to have similar issues in future that are going to be just as tough," he says. "Euthanasia.

Genetic engineering. Those are just two I can anticipate. I believe fundamentally in the sanctity of life, and that really you don't have too much human authority to tinker with it. I mean, what are the justifications for that. To purify the race? We went through that in the thirties in Germany. You know, put those issues in human hands and you're on dangerous ground."

Turner received thousands of letters, mostly from Catholics, protesting the proposed relaxation of the abortion legislation. His own riding president in Ottawa-Carleton, Dr. Dalton J. McGuinty, a staunch Roman Catholic and father of eight children, resigned after pronouncing that the abortion law would be "a dark day for our country," and at one stage a delegation of concerned Catholic bishops called on him. "I asked the boys," Turner says, "whether they had a legal opinion as to what the bill really meant, and they didn't have one. So I said to them, 'Here's what it really means,' and I told them what it meant. And I said, 'Gentlemen, I happen to have two theological opinions as to what my duty is.' I had them and they knew it."

Turner personally abhors homosexuality also, and on that issue he told the Commons: "The nub of the matter is who is to decide what moral behaviour or conduct is to be reflected in the Code? That is the point. In a pluralistic society there may be different standards, differing attitudes, and the law cannot reflect them all. Public order, in this situation of a pluralistic society, cannot substitute for private conduct. We believe that morality is a matter for private conscience. Criminal law should reflect the public order only. Despite the fact that most of us in our personal convictions have a complete repugnance to the conduct from which we are lifting the taint of criminal law, this does not to my mind interfere with the validity of the principle we are trying to submit to the House. The bill does not endorse such acts. It does not popularize such acts. It does not even legalize this kind of conduct," he insisted. But his arguments were questioned at length and strongly opposed by many Conservatives and all Creditistes. The opposition could be summed up in one exchange:

John Diefenbaker (PC, Prince Albert): "What has the government done for the people of Canada since December 13 last?"

George Muir (PC, Cape Breton-The Sydneys): "Made them all homos."

The Catholic Quebecer Creditistes filibustered the bill for twenty-one days, claiming, among many other things, that it was "a Communist plot to prevent us from reproducing ourselves so as to be able to seize the country without any trouble." But eventually, on May 14, 1969, almost eighteen months after Trudeau first introduced it, after the Creditistes had no talk left in them, and after forty-four attempts at amendment, Turner secured passage of a slightly redrafted version of the omnibus bill, with the abortion and homosexual sections unscathed. The vote was 149 to 55. Former Prime Minister John Diefenbaker voted against it along with forty-two other Conservatives, one Liberal, and eleven Creditistes, while Conservative Party Leader Robert Stanfield voted in favour. It was by far the most massive law reform in over fifteen years.

Turner's basic task in 1969, however, was to see that the Official Languages Bill, Trudeau's main plank in his June, 1968, election campaign, became law. In the process of doing this he clashed again with Trudeau and with Secretary of State Gerard Pelletier, creating a serious division in cabinet, including threats by Turner to refuse to take responsibility for the legislation in the Commons if it was not in a form he considered satisfactory.

The original terms of the bill guaranteed the use of both English and French in the civil service, courts, and public buildings wherever there was a minority population of 10 per cent or more. Pelletier had publicly insisted that this would be extended, under planned amendments, to any major city like Toronto or Vancouver, although French Canadians made up only 2.5 per cent of the population in Toronto and an even smaller segment in Vancouver. Also provided for was the appointment of an Official Languages Commissioner with ombudsman-like powers to investigate any complaint under the Act. These terms caused a furore among western premiers, particularly because of the expense involved in a requirement that "every court in Canada" must ensure that "any person appearing or giving evidence before it may be heard in the official language of his choice." There was also serious concern among westerners that they would be forced to become bilingual and that civil service jobs would be restricted to a small elite of bilingual people.

Turner travelled frequently to the West, talked to the premiers and their attorneys general, and pushed amendments through the cabinet that mollified the provinces, most significantly an amendment that left it up to them to decide whether or not they would make criminal court hearings bilingual. The opposition in the Commons praised the amendments, but they rankled the hardliners in cabinet, especially Pelletier, who felt Turner was caving in to bigotry.

Turner's main fear was that the provinces would contest the legality of the Act in the Supreme Court. He was certain the court would decide in its favour and even offered to appear personally before the court to defend it. But he was also convinced that bilingualism should not be rammed down the throats of the people by court order; that its full benefits could not possibly be secured if not accompanied by a reasonable amount of national goodwill; and that the original bill wouldn't work anyway because people would not respond well to legislation for which they had developed a hatred.

John Diefenbaker and sixteen other Conservatives opposed even Turner's watered-down version of the bill on second reading, but in the end, on July 7, 1969, the Commons approved it without a formal vote.

In a commentary on the performance of the Trudeau cabinet in its first year, John Walker of Southam News Services wrote:

> Only Justice Minister John Turner, of the Trudeau opponents [at the 1968 leadership convention], has managed to keep his cool in the cabinet-Commons testing ground. His efforts to water down the Official Languages Bill for the Westerners had to be modified to meet the strenuous objections of Secretary of State Pelletier, but he guided this much revised bill through with reasonable skill, as he had earlier the Criminal Code amendments.

And the *Montreal Gazette* editorialized:

> Mr. Trudeau and his government avoided a major, public confrontation on the law. The negotiating which was done with the provinces (on the language bill) was done – as it should be – quietly and with reason. Both the provinces and the federal government deserve credit for their moderate approach, and perhaps Justice Minister John Turner deserves as much credit as anyone.

Turner tells his own story of his part in the Official Languages Act this way: "I was always in favour of the Official Languages Act, but I always said in cabinet that we had to sell it to the majority of the country and we had to sell it to the public service. You know, one of the difficulties in implementing it was that Trudeau and Pelletier were always coming in saying that it was a matter of right and that the majority had mishandled the minority, and they weren't going to give the public service credit for the efforts they were making to learn French, and this was at a time when people were making immense efforts to try to do something about it. But, you know, the government was hammering them all the time and not once did the Prime Minister or Pelletier ever thank the public service or ever thank the English-speaking majority for their understanding and tolerance and that made it very difficult for me and the English-speaking members in the Ottawa area and across the country.

"But I approved the Official Languages Act," Turner continues. "I helped draft it, and it was introduced in the House by Gerard Pelletier. But some of the members didn't think Pelletier was doing very well in the House with it, that he was getting clobbered. So Jimmy Walker – you remember Jimmy. He was the member for York Centre and chairman of our caucus. He came to me with a number of members of the caucus and said, 'John, you've got to take this bill over.' And I said, 'Fine, I'll be glad to take it over, but you'd better take that to the Prime Minister.' So the Prime Minister did ask me to take it over after caucus had made its representations. He left me jointly responsible for it with Pelletier, but I took the damn thing over. I talked to the opposition boys and we got it moving. Then, of course, the four western attorneys general challenged some of the provisions, so I called the boys and I went out to see each one. And I sold the amendments to the government and I sold the amendments to the opposition and I sold them in Parliament.

"I can remember taking a big beating in the lead editorial in the *Globe and Mail* that I'd sold out on bilingualism," Turner says. "Keith Spicer, who later became Language Commissioner, was then writing editorials on the *Globe and Mail*. And I just told [the editor, Richard] Doyle, and those guys, 'Look, if you want a bill that satisfies this country and doesn't have us in a court action like the Manitoba situation in 1870, then this is the way it has to be done.' The purists said it should be done differently but I said this was the way it had to be done. And the provincial attorneys general backed down from the Supreme Court. And I talked to the opposition boys again – Gordon Fairweather, Jed Baldwin, Don Mazankowski, Jack Horner – I even got Jack to cool off – George Hees, Pat Nowlan. You know, I knew those guys well. They were very good friends and I said, 'Come on, you guys,' and once I had a few drinks with the guys and we gave them a few amendments, too, the thing got through.

"If the Prime Minister had recognized that he needed the English-speaking majority to help him sell the bill, instead of having Marchand and Pelletier and Lalonde and himself try to push it through, we would have solved the problem a lot easier. This is a complicated country, you know, and this black-and-white approach, this ultra-logical approach, this Cartesian approach of the Prime Minister's, of course, caused us problems in western Canada. And then I had to sell it to the public service and Claude Edwards, the president of the Public Service Alliance, and Lloyd Francis, the Ottawa member, and I made it work. I've got to give a lot of credit to the statesmanship shown by the Public Service Alliance on that. And here again, the government never gave the public service the credit that it should have got for really trying to live with national policy, which was very, very difficult for them to sell to their own members."

But everything did not go this smoothly for the young man who was already being touted in the press as Trudeau's probable successor. Separatism continued to smoulder in the shadow of violence in Quebec and in late March a crowd of about 5,000 militant students and separatists planned to march on Montreal's McGill University, the city's bastion of English-language education for 148 years, to demand that it be turned into a French-language school by 1972.

The Students' Society of McGill, representing all but a few of its students, strongly opposed the march, stating it was keyed to the issue of "national linguistic domination." The St. Jean Baptiste Society disassociated itself. So did René Lévesque's separatist Parti Québécois, describing it as "ill inspired." Even the students' society at Montreal's Sir George Williams University, where a riot had done damage worth $2 million the previous February, denounced the demonstration as "a dogmatic, provocative act that can serve no useful purpose and which can easily lead to violence." The Quebec government panicked. The Deputy Attorney-General of Quebec telephoned the Deputy Minister of Justice in Ottawa, advising him of the situation and warning that a formal request for the assistance of the armed forces and the RCMP in controlling the situation might follow. Technically, however, he made no formal request.

Then, in reply to a question in the Commons, Turner revealed that the federal government had been given notice of a possible request for the use of troops "if violence got out of control," and he immediately issued an appeal by television to both the McGill student body and "the forces of law and order" to show restraint. This disclosure of the Quebec phone call sent Quebec Premier Jean-Jacques Bertrand into a paroxysm of anger. At first he categorically denied any request had been made, then he accused Turner of violating a secret. "It's disgusting. No minister of the crown should have said what Mr. Turner said," Bertrand complained. "It's the sort of stuff that provokes people. It's appalling." In the end, the march was peaceful. No troops were necessary. And many MPs and cabinet ministers thought Turner had committed a serious gaffe by disclosing the warning of the possible request instead of merely alerting the ministers responsible for the army and the RCMP, which he had also done, and who had arranged for men to stand by in case they were needed.

Gordon Pape, the associate editor of the *Montreal Gazette*, and usually a strong Turner fan, wrote:

John Turner didn't do himself any favors with that blurt last week about sending troops into Montreal.

There's been a week now to allow the dust to settle and to assess Ottawa's reaction to Turner's startling House of Commons statement.

It's bad, all bad.

And while it will undoubtedly be forgotten in time, it hasn't helped Turner's short-term credibility one bit. . . .

There have been occasional lapses from grace, of course. His original stand in favor of retaining the death penalty (which he later reversed) didn't quite fit with the image of the dedicated young reformer.

But on the whole Turner personifies just the right blend of caution and daring; a careful young politician weighing the impact of everything he says on his political future.

That's why it was especially surprising that he should have goofed so badly during the Commons question period a week ago Thursday.

But goof he did, and as a result his stock has fallen to an all-time low among his Liberal Party colleagues.

Cabinet ministers and backbenchers alike are openly critical of his actions in telling the House that Quebec's deputy attorney-general had asked for the "potential aid" of the RCMP and the armed forces in the event the McGill Francais demonstration last Friday got out of hand.

No one can figure out why he did it. There are dozens of ways of sidestepping embarrassing questions in the Commons; it's an art the cabinet minister must master quickly if he hopes to survive. . . .

But advisors and friends insist it wasn't really all the Justice Minister's fault.

Premier Bertrand, they suggest, overreacted and didn't really pay any attention at all to the careful way in which the minister worded his reply.

That made the issue much bigger than it really was.

Furthermore, Turner had to make an instant decision in the Commons whether to answer the question or be evasive and risk having the questioner, Creditiste Gilbert Rondeau, set off a bomb in the government's face by revealing everything.

"Turner knew by the look on Rondeau's face that he knew the answer before asking the question," one associate says.

"It was a dicey political situation and he had to make an immediate decision: Either answer Rondeau directly or let him make a fuss about it and perhaps make accusations that the government was misleading the Commons. Turner decided the best course was to give the House the facts."

"That was a mistake," Turner admits now. "It could have been handled better."

But such criticisms of Turner as Justice Minister or performer in the Commons were rare and the matter was soon forgotten, particularly by Turner, who set off within a few weeks on a tour of the Northwest Territories with the travelling court of the area's only judge, Mr. Justice W.G. Morrow. No Canadian Justice Minister had ever been on this lonely court circuit covering a jurisdiction of over 1,300,000 square miles between the Mackenzie River and Baffin Island, north of the sixtieth parallel, but Morrow had submitted a report to Turner urging many reforms of the northern judicial system, including an end to the "barbaric" method of paying justices of the peace out of fines and court costs. This meant they got no fee if they acquitted the defendant. Turner decided to see for himself. He and his wife travelled with the court in an old DC-3 from Frobisher Bay to Pond Inlet and across the frozen wastes to Resolute Bay and Igloolik, carrying the coat of arms and no-smoking sign that temporarily turned little schoolrooms into courts in which Justice Morrow presided in black robes while his Eskimo interpreter wore a green sweater emblazoned with the words, "Here Comes the Judge."

Turner still says that probably the proudest moment of his career as Justice Minister was his admission to the bar of the Northwest Territories at Pond Inlet, above the Arctic Circle, at a ceremony attended only by the officials of the Territorial Court, his wife, a few newsmen, and many curious Eskimos. It was a long way for a young lawyer to have travelled from Gray's Inn, and there were tears in his eyes when he made his acceptance speech:

May it please the court. My Lord, I wish first of all to thank you for your courtesy in admitting me in what you have termed a rather historic occasion, the first member of a bar perhaps, surely in this country, to be admitted within the Arctic Circle, where some parts of the year the sun never shines, and other parts of the year it shines every day, and if I may, in personal terms, thank you for the membership in the bar of the Northwest Territories, and on behalf of my wife and myself I thank you for this wonderfully carved Coat-of-Arms of Canada so that those who have occasion to visit me in my official capacity will understand that the office also bears the responsibility of Attorney General of the Northwest Territories. . . .

May I say to you My Lord it is a rather moving experience to me, and I am sure for those who are accompanying me with you on your circuit. As we flew up from Frobisher Bay today I really thought about you as a judge on top of the world, and this court, meeting for the first time as a court in the village of Pond Inlet, and looking out through the schoolhouse, and probably on as magnificent scenery as any man or woman could see anywhere, bright, white clad, a land of glacial wonder, mountains and fjords, and you are the judge who must take the longest circuit and the longest trip in the world, bringing justice to the people.

I listened, of course, with great interest, and will continue to watch this court in operation with great interest. The law should play no favourites, and everyone should be equal before this court, and I feel confident that is so when it is presided over by you, be the litigant or the accused Eskimo or Indian or White. It is not only the law in this area which is important, but surely even more important the justice which is supposed to be enshrined in the law, and here before this court come men and women who are to be judged by the law of Canada, sometimes a law which they don't know, and in that they may share a lack of experience with other Canadians, but a law which may in certain respects be foreign to their traditions and customs as a proud and independent people.

In order to administer the law in these circumstances, circumstances in which we found ourselves this afternoon, it needs boundless patience and understanding and compassion. . . .

Turner had already appointed an assistant deputy minister of the Justice Department as an unofficial deputy attorney general of the Territories, a move that Morrow said had cut the time Ottawa took to make decisions on his requests from six months to forty-eight hours. And when he got back to Ottawa he stopped the pay-for-conviction system for the justices of the peace.

Turner was enjoying the job. He particularly liked his big West Block office, which had once been Sir John A. Macdonald's with a secret staircase used by Macdonald to escape the politicians, businessmen, and journalists of the day, and he revelled in the political constituency he was building up among the country's tens of thousands of lawyers, many of whom he knew by name and whom he'd phone regularly with a "Hello, Bill, how's the boy?" type of call, just to keep in touch and to hear what was going on around the country. He was efficient. Every morning he wrote on small index cards reminders of the tasks that had to be performed that day, with thoughts on how to go about them.

He described his work philosophy in an interview with Barbara Frum in August, 1973:

I know how to say "No" quickly. You'd be surprised how much time that saves. I never second-guess myself. I make the decision and that's it. There are only two kinds of problems, those that get better and almost solve themselves and those that get worse. You can afford to let the first type ride, but you'd better get at the second type fast. The trick is, of course, knowing which is which. And you have to be able to identify time wasters. I schedule them close to other appointments so the pressure's on them when the other people arrive. I don't keep trivial things in my mind. I've solved that problem by having a very good system of indexing and bringing matters forward. If I want to think about something tomorrow, I write it down on a piece of paper and have somebody hand me the piece of paper tomorrow. And I don't let my secretary type them. I don't want her to waste her time either. She just hands me back my pieces of paper, I write things like grocery lists, things to bring home, things I have to do of a routine domestic nature, uh, get the dog clipped, get tickets for Sonny and Cher. I write those things down on separate pieces of paper and stuff them in my left pocket. So I don't clutter my mind with those. I take those off my mind. I write a lot of other things down on little white cards, speech notes, things I want to talk to the PM about so I don't waste his time and he doesn't waste mine, commitments to constituents at public meetings. They go in my inside coat pocket. So you've got a mobile office. It sounds chaotic, but it works. You've got to keep track of what you've said, and if you've made a commitment, you've got to have what you've promised quite clear, because they are going to have it clear.

Correspondence is something I get out of the way first thing. I want it off my mind early. Later, the telephone calls start and then the meetings start and I want to stay loose for those, you see. I get on the phone with people to find out what they're thinking every morning, how they're reaching out to what the government is doing and what Parliament is doing or what one is doing oneself. I do it every day. Just throw a couple of calls in. No regular pattern because I don't want them to prepare for the conversation. I feel more in touch that way and also it restores one's sanity, you know.

I never write a memo. And I never dictate a memo. There's a lot of time wasted in writing memos. It's a favourite game of governments and big corporations to try to protect yourself. I pick up the telephone. Or I see somebody. I like a clean desk. The more things you have on your desk the more time you're wasting because you spend most of it looking to see what's there. I can't control my days because I can't control events. But I can control my responses to them. I can choose between meetings, between appointments. This job you could go twenty-four hours a day on. But you don't have to be at every meeting, you know. A lot of people go to meetings because they're insecure. They feel if they're not there somebody's going to cut them out. Or cut them up. And if I'm getting stale on a day, either because I haven't had a holiday or I'm tired or I'm just cheesed off, then I just walk out of the office and go to a movie or play tennis.

I'm sure there are lots of more efficient ways of doing things than I do them, but there's got to be a quotient of inefficiency, a quotient of spontaneity, a quotient of chaos every once in a while to keep you used, involved, to keep you from going absolutely hygenic and sterile. You've got to be efficient enough to get rid of the anxiety and frustration so you can concentrate on the really innovative things, the people things, the imaginative things, the new and lively things. If you have a sense of anxiety when you walk home the job's too big for you. You should have another job.

Turner's working days, sometimes eighteen hours long, didn't end until the last of the cards had been pulled from the side pocket of his coat and acted upon. His staff loved him. The press was generally good to him. And his family had grown to three fine and healthy children in the nice, heavily mortgaged home in posh Rockcliffe, where wife Geills presided over the entertainment of important and interesting people with a charm and sophistication noted by Ottawa socialites.

But in the background there was a growing unease and an increasing number of often minor differences between two very different men, one in the office of the gregarious, hard-drinking first Prime Minister and the other in the office of the austere and remote fifteenth.

14

Justice Minister
and Reformer

Whⁿen Turner finished with the Trudeau-inspired Criminal Code changes and Official Languages Act and became his own man, he started a frenzy of law reform based mainly on a belief that the Canadian law system favoured the rich and punished the poor. He first pronounced this philosophy in a keynote speech at the opening of the North American Judges Association in San Francisco in December, 1969, and then at a meeting of the Vancouver Bar Association, where his ideas were booed by some lawyers but in the end earned him a standing ovation. He said:

> Justice in a society such as ours, a society marked by wide differences in wealth and power, requires a legal system that compensates for those differences. What is so necessary is an enlarged conception of the rights of the poor and a changing conception of the role of law in providing, protecting, and implementing these rights. We must disabuse ourselves of the myth that poverty is somehow caused by the poor. We must recognize that the law often contributes to poverty. We must understand that whereas the law for most of us is a source of rights, for the poor the law appears always to be taking something away. That, we have to change.

He said some particular laws – such as vagrancy and public drunkenness – "have made it virtually a crime to be poor in public" so that the very condition of poverty had become a rationale for criminalization.

> Our governments have one set of rules for dispensing benefits to the poor in questions of public assistance and welfare law and another for dispensing largesse to the rich in questions of licences, subsidies to the economy, and government contracts. Substantive and procedural law benefits and protects landlords

over tenants, creditors over debtors, lenders over borrowers, and the poor are seldom among the favoured parties. I believe the poor are less equal before the law; yet their need is greater.

It was the poor, he said, who were victimized when urban renewal arbitrarily disrupted a neighbourhood and when creditors garnisheed wages or repossessed furniture. "The poor are rarely plaintiffs, but they are often defendants, and they are bewildered and bemused by legalities," he said. Then he quoted eighteenth-century Anglo-Irish writer Oliver Goldsmith: "Laws grind the poor and rich men rule the law," and then U.S. Supreme Court Justice William Brennan: "Can we honestly protest as untrue the charge that our legal system has a built-in bias against the poor, not merely procedural but substantive as well."

This belief was basic to Turner and thus to the Justice Department from 1970 to 1972. It led to vast changes in Canadian law and the way it was to be administered. A new Expropriation Act introduced by Turner ended archaic and unfair procedures that had been largely unchanged and unfair since 1896. This legislation provided a comprehensive code for determining compensation payable with a market value minimum plus cost of relocation – "a home for a home" – and new rights to object to any proposed expropriation at a public hearing.

He replaced the Tax Appeal Board that had become bogged down in bureaucracy and precedents only the rich could handle with a new Tax Review Board that was to be informal and not bound by any legal or technical rules of evidence. "This means," Turner explained, "a taxpayer can come in by himself, or with a next door neighbour, and just explain to the board what his problem is and why he doesn't agree with the tax department. He can say it in his own words. And, under the bill, only the chairman or the vice-chairman need to be lawyers. It is going to be, in effect, a lay court." In a further step that brought the government down to the level of the average citizen, the Act provided that in any case involving $1,000 or less, where the taxpayer won his point and the tax department appealed, the taxpayer's legal costs had to be paid by the department.

He expanded the Ottawa-based Exchequer Court into the new Federal Court, thus creating a federal circuit court with both trial and appeal divisions, making access much easier and less expensive, and increasing the power of the ordinary citizen to challenge the actions of the state and its vast assortment of regulatory agencies and quasi-judicial tribunals. The Federal Court Act also allowed a citizen to sue the Crown without the Crown's consent, thereby eliminating one of the most archaic restrictions on freedom in the country, and it limited the power of cabinet ministers to refuse to produce official documents in court or to withhold evidence except in cases involving national security or Privy Council confidences.

Turner consistently advocated a federal legal aid system to cover legal costs for the poor in both civil and criminal cases. The plan was to be similar to medicare with federal money funnelled to the provinces if they met certain standards, but it ran into cabinet and constitutional problems and was never implemented.

His arrest and bail reform measures were made law, but only after much opposition from police and advocates of stern law and order. The main aim of these measures, consistent with so many of Turner's other reforms, was to end a situation where the rich were literally able to buy their freedom when their cases were pending. The poor, on the other hand, had to languish in jail, even though innocent until proven guilty, until their turns came up in the overcrowded courts. Basically, the Bail Reform Act provided that a police officer should not make an arrest if the public interest could be served simply by ordering a person to appear in court on a given day; that when a person was arrested and jailed he must be taken before a justice as soon as possible; and that the justice must release the accused person on receiving his promise to attend court. It was revolutionary but it worked. Editorials across the country hailed the law's "humanitarianism." The police became accustomed to the additional responsibilities imposed on them, and the jails became less crowded.

Turner also cracked down hard on drunken driving by legislating breathalyser tests, but the legislation was challenged in many courts, scores of cases were dismissed on technicalities, and the use of the breathalyser almost didn't survive although Turner firmly believed the public backed it. When the legislation was eventually challenged before a county court judge in southern Ontario, Turner and his Deputy Minister, Donald Maxwell, decided, somewhat desperately, to try to salvage the law by referring it to the Supreme Court for a reference on its validity. Both thought there might have been a gap in the drafting of the bill and they knew that its defence would be difficult, so Turner said he would conduct the Supreme Court case himself. Maxwell, however, talked him out of that by promising that he would take the case personally and he did.

They knew the decision of the nine Supreme Court judges would be close. So did John Diefenbaker. Turner recalls: "Mr. Diefenbaker came over to me in the House and said, 'You know, you're going to lose that reference before the Supreme Court, John. I've figured out how each judge is going to vote.' 'Oh,' I said, 'is that so, Sir? Well, so have I.' And he said, 'Well, I think you are going to lose by five to four.' I said, 'I think I'm going to win by five to four.' Gordon Fairweather was there and we made a bet. Dief wrote down the names of the judges and the way he thought they would decide and I wrote down mine and we each put ten bucks in a sealed envelope and gave it to Gordon. And I won five to four and the judge I had on my side and Diefenbaker had on his side was Emmett Hall. Now Emmett Hall was Dief's old friend from Saskatchewan. Dief had put him on the Supreme Court of Saskatchewan and when Dief was a jury lawyer in the early days out there Emmett would help brief him on some of his cases so he knew Hall well. And Dief said to me, 'How did you know that you had him? If anybody would have struck down that legislation, defending the citizen against the state, all of Emmett's career would underline that he would strike that piece of legislation down.' 'Well,' I said, 'you forgot one thing, Mr. Diefenbaker. You know that Emmett and Belle Hall had no children.' He said, 'That's right.' 'Don't you remember,' I said, 'that his favourite nephew was killed in a drunken driving accident on the road from Yorkton to Saskatoon?' And Dief said, 'Goddamn it, I forgot about that. You're perfectly right.' "

Turner brought in another controversial bill to outlaw the advocacy of genocide but he introduced this one under pressure from cabinet and was not personally comfortable with it. The bill became known as the Anti-Hate Bill and it split Liberal against Liberal, Conservative against Conservative, and New Democrat against New Democrat in a passionate Commons debate. In essence the bill, which was eventually passed, made anyone who "advocates or promotes genocide" liable to imprisonment for five years; anyone who "incites hatred against any identifiable group" in a manner likely to lead to a breach of the peace by "communicating statements in any public place" liable to a prison term of two years; and anyone who "wilfully promotes hatred" against an identifiable group by "communicating statements, other than in private conversations," liable to a prison term of two years. The Act defined an identifiable group as one "distinguished by colour, race, religion and ethnic origin," but it included some important exemptions from conviction, including persons who could establish that their statements were true, or made in good faith, or relevant to a subject of public interest.

Turner was particularly concerned about wiretapping and the use of all forms of electronic eavesdropping. He warned in many speeches that, "Our telephone can be tapped, our office bugged, our files photographed, our physical movements monitored, our communications recorded – all this without knowing anything about it or having any recourse or any protection in law," and he described this erosion of privacy as "the beginning of the end of freedom." So he introduced the Protection of Privacy Act, which banned electronic eavesdropping by anyone except police in special situations or by the police or armed forces to protect national security.

He set up the Law Reform Commission, with Justice Patrick Hartt its first chairman, to clear away the cobwebs in Canada's century-old collection of statutes and make the law a variable thing, responsive to the society it served, changing as society changed. "The law," Turner said, "will never stand still again." The commission went to work tossing out sections like 304 of the Railways Act, which required diesel locomotives to carry steam whistles, and eliminating words like "servant" from the labour laws and "lunatic" from the laws governing mental health. But in the long run the commission didn't achieve much more than this and was a disappointment to Turner.

He pressed constantly for what he called a "liberation manifesto" in the form of a Bill of Rights entrenched in the Constitution and he appointed the first woman, Réjane Colas, to the Superior Court of Montreal and then Mabel M. Van Camp as the first woman on the bench of the Ontario Supreme Court. He appointed the late Bora Laskin as the first Jewish Justice of the Supreme Court.

So his record as Justice Minister was that of a very small 'l' liberal reformer. Except, of course, for the draconian, freedom-destroying War Measures Act of October, 1970, which Turner steered through the Commons and which represented the exact opposite of everything he was trying to do.

Turner was attending a meeting of the Commonwealth Parliamentary Association in Australia on October 5, 1970, when political thugs armed with submachine guns and dynamite kidnapped British diplomat James Cross from his greystone house in Montreal. They made a set of demands on behalf of the Liberation Cell of the separatist Front de Libération du Québec, including the release of twenty-three prisoners. Turner arrived back in Ottawa on October 11 to learn that FLQ terrorists had also kidnapped Quebec Labour Minister Pierre Laporte and that Trudeau was considering invocation of the War Measures Act, which would not only outlaw the FLQ but also "any group of persons or association that advocates the use of force or the commission of crime as a means of or as an aid in accomplishing governmental change in Canada." It would also allow for the arrest without warrant of any Canadian, who could be held in jail for ninety days before appearing in court to state his claim for trial. The enormity of this suggestion startled the young, reform-minded Justice Minister and devastated him.

But then Laporte wrote a pathetic, hand-written plea for his life to Quebec Premier Robert Bourassa:

> My dear Robert. . . . you have the power to dispose of my life. . . . I have two brothers; they are both dead. I remain alone at the head of a large family. . . . I don't see why, by taking more time about it, you would continue to make me die little by little in the place where I am held. Decide – my life or death.

Bourassa and the Quebec government seemed to be weakening, to be willing to negotiate with the FLQ. So after attending several meetings of the Cabinet Security Committee, Turner agreed to defend a government decision on the War Measures Act in the House. He argued, however, that such a drastic break in Canadian tradition had to be strictly temporary.

Turner did defend the Act for more than an hour in a tense and suspicious House of Commons on October 16, the day it was invoked. He insisted emotionally that the government had acted with reluctance because it had no other choice, and that Canada was "facing the gravest hour in our history." He was still stoically and, many said, brilliantly defending the government's action two days later when Laporte's body was found in the trunk of a green Chevrolet, under rags, hands folded across his chest, strangled with his own religious chain. Turner announced the murder in the House, then sat in his seat with his head in his hands.

Turner delivered another major defence of the War Measures Act in the Commons on November 4, 1970, a month before Cross was released unharmed and five terrorists were apprehended and given safe passage to Cuba. His Commons speech was titled "There Is No Freedom without Order under Law," but a subsequent speech to the Canadian Club of Ottawa on November 12 better revealed his personal thoughts and emotions about the FLQ threat and the government's reaction to it. Turner said in part:

> The action the government took was drastic. I have no intention, nor has the government, of evading or attempting to minimize that fact. It was a drastic measure because it was precipitated by persons with an utter contempt for the rights of others. It was a measure brought on by persons with an utter contempt for the democratic process. They seek to mutilate and destroy our social institutions, including that of representative government.
>
> Their chosen instruments for this purpose – and this is well indicated by the communiqués – are not instruments of per-

suasion. They are not the instruments of free dialogue and discussion to attempt to convince their fellow citizens. They are the instruments of hatred, violence, turmoil and chaos. This society in Canada cannot long endure if the time comes when the right of individuals to life and personal security can be rendered meaningless by criminals – not by "political prisoners," but by criminals – through acts of terror directed at the government.

There was rapid escalation. The climate had been set by an attempt to negotiate, by the vocabulary of "political prisoners," and by the use of the word "execution" of those who had been kidnapped instead of "murder," as if to imply some legitimacy. The government had been placed in a position of immobility. All the action in terms of public opinion was left to a bunch of renegades.

I could recite a list of events that contributed to the rapid acceleration of this dangerous situation in Quebec. There were the kidnappings, which in themselves, if they were isolated, would be a purely criminal affair, but within the context of a wider conspiracy and being used for ransom against a legitimately constituted government, were something else. We had the continuous threats to life and property by way of the communications of the FLQ in a seditious, violent and inflammatory language.

We also had a series of bombings and violence, a rising increase in thefts of dynamite. More disturbing, we had an erosion of the public will, a feeling among some sincere people that an exchange of prisoners for the victims of the kidnappings would somehow ease the situation.

People resent violence. But generally, we are not organized to meet it. A campaign of blackmail had to be stopped.

The FLQ literature lays out a pattern of revolution, escalating through different levels of action, violence and confrontation to the ultimate overthrow of the established order in Quebec and Canada. These men have demonstrated an arrogance, a disrespect for law and order and a degree of inhumanity that our ordinary democratic processes cannot continue to tolerate. Intimidation of government and of the public by means of kidnapping and murder have become their modus operandi . . . .

The government recognized, and from the beginning expressed the opinion that the War Measures Act was "too blunt an instrument." We recognized the need for a more specific statutory instrument. The action taken by the government was taken reluctantly. Throughout his life and throughout his career as a Member of Parliament, the Prime Minister has tried to advocate those measures of law reform that are needed in an age of confrontation, this age which is dominated by a conflict between freedom and authority. The law is caught in the crunch. On the one hand the law is the symbol of authority; on the other hand it is the guarantee of freedom.

We did what we did because it had to be done. Some of the measures we have had to adopt in the short run and for a short term are philosophically abhorrent to us. We intend as soon as we can to turn once more to the road of law reform and the continuing enhancement and protection of civil liberties.

Turner did try to bring Canadian civil liberties back to normalcy as soon as possible, and he succeeded, but again he found himself in conflict with Pierre Trudeau. The government introduced a less drastic Public Order Act in December to replace the War Measures Act and Turner insisted that it contain a "sunset clause," making it lapse on April 30, 1971. But as this deadline approached Quebec Premier Bourassa, Trudeau, and other cabinet ministers argued for further equally tough laws to continue the outlawing of the FLQ. Turner strongly disagreed with them at an angry cabinet meeting in late April and there were reports that he had threatened to resign if similar oppressive legislation remained on the books. Turner denied the resignation rumours but admitted there was friction. And he won his point. The Public Order Act died on April 30, without a replacement and with Turner arguing against keeping the special powers in much the same terms government critics had used against them in the first place: that the Criminal Code's provisions on conspiracy and sedition were adequate to counter the FLQ or any other organization dealing in murder, kidnapping, blackmail, and revolutionary violence. Bourassa angrily accused Turner of being "soft, illogical, and inconsistent," but Canadian law returned to its usual merciful state and Turner returned to his liberal law reform.

Toward the end of his three-and-a-half-year period as Justice Minister in January, 1972, he was presented with the twenty-first annual Brotherhood Award at the Beth Sholom synagogue in Toronto. Afterwards *Toronto Star* reporter Rae Corelli, who is a close friend of Turner's, sat in the synagogue's boardroom with him and chatted over a bottle of Scotch about the speech and his personal philosophy. Corelli reported:

He delivered a fifty-one-minute acceptance speech in which he talked with an almost evangelical zeal of the mission that totally absorbs him – the fundamental and ideological reform of the nation's criminal and public administrative law.

"Canada needs a more contemporary criminal law – credible, enforceable, flexible and compassionate," he says, and the words come chopping through the microphones in the style of a sermon, not preachy, but fluidly, with deliberation and sometimes near-eloquence.

The art of making speeches has finally come to Chick Turner, the Irish Catholic Rhodes Scholar, one-time sprint champion, one-time college sportswriter.

But there is more. There is a new bluntness. There is more gray in the hair. The eyes are harder, less compromising. There is less apparent concern with image and more with objectives. John Turner seems to have discovered sometime during the past few months that he really can handle himself as well as he had been trying to lead everyone – probably including himself – to believe. One gets the feeling that the discovery may even have surprised him.

"Hell, why wouldn't he believe it by now?" asks a prominent member of the Ontario Liberal caucus. "He carried the can for the whole War Measures Act almost from the beginning. They stuck him with selling that Official Languages Act in the West and he sold it. He's got a wad of legislation through or pending in the Commons that would choke a goat."

But the impression he creates of having somehow undergone a profound shift in his attitude is persistent, which probably explains why, as John Turner sits there chatting and sipping his Scotch, someone blurts: "You really believe in this pursuit of the philosophical reform of the criminal law, don't you." It is not a question, but a conclusion.

"I believe in it because it's absolutely essential that people in this country and everywhere start believing in the law again," Turner says grimly. "Really – in the law as a fair way of regulating disputes between people and between state and citizen. I didn't have that crystallized into a coherent thought until a couple of years ago. But I'm convinced you don't solve violence just by law. You don't polarize society out of existence. And if the criminal law doesn't meet the instincts of the ordinary citizen, then I don't give a damn what the law is, it's not going to work."

In his Beth Sholom speech, Turner said he wanted to speak about "a new consciousness that I sense among Canadians, about a human rights consciousness, about a human rights revolution . . . .

"The legitimacy of the administrative state is predicated on maintaining equilibrium in the relationships between the individual and the state. The bigness and remoteness of the government must not be allowed further to obscure or dwarf individual rights. If there is a risk between freedom and order, I'll choose freedom. If there is a risk between the individual and the state, I'll take a chance on the individual. . . ."

Donald Maxwell, who was Deputy Minister of Justice under both Pierre Trudeau and John Turner and is now general counsel for Canadian Pacific Railways, says he liked both men, but found Trudeau, removed and professorial, an enigma, while Turner, although equally bright and intellectual, was an "ordinary guy." "I had a better rapport with Turner," Maxwell says. "He was able to grasp ideas and deal with them. He wanted to improve things, to move them forward. He was very liberal in this way, but there was also a touch of careful conservatism about him. Between us we ran the Justice Department like a big law firm rather than a branch of government, and morale in Turner's time was never higher. When there was talk of his going to Finance I had a long talk with him and told him that if he had any further aspirations he should forget about Finance. I told him it was a graveyard."

Trudeau promoted Turner to Minister of Finance in early 1972 in a move that some observers described at the time as logical because he was the best man for the more difficult and responsible position. But others described the move as Machiavellian.

15

Finance:
The Political Graveyard

Turner did not want to be Finance Minister. It was a grave-yard, as everybody said. He was by now one of the most astute and popular politicians on Parliament Hill. He was constantly being touted as the next Prime Minister and deep down he believed he could do a better job of it than Trudeau. He considered Trudeau to be an aberration in the Liberal succession anyway, not really a Liberal at all. And hadn't Mike Pearson expressed his concerns about Trudeau on his deathbed and belatedly passed the baton to the younger man, as he should have done in the first place instead of treating him like a kid he had known all his life, a kid who needed experience?

After all, that was the way it was done before. The Liberal establishment always had a successor to the present leader, certainly at least since Mackenzie King, who had hand-picked Louis St. Laurent as his successor. And then St. Laurent had designated Lester Pearson and Pearson had given his blessing to Pierre Trudeau, partly because he wanted to continue the alternation of English- and French-speaking leaders. Since 1948 the laying on of hands had been the way of doing things. And Pearson had suggested on his deathbed he might have made a mistake in this most important matter because his chosen man was blasting away at NATO and the other Canadian alliances the great diplomat had spent a lifetime building. He had told Turner he was saddened by this and that he should just wait it out because the system would right itself in the end and he, Turner, would be Prime Minister.

Turner was young and could afford to wait. But he knew that the Finance Ministry could be a trap, a move by Trudeau to rid himself of a rival so strong that sometimes in the Commons opposition members were telling Trudeau to consult with "the boss," and pointing at Turner, because Turner, they said, knew what was going on.

Turner knew that since Confederation only two ministers of finance had made it to the awesome pinnacle of Prime Minister, Sir Charles Tupper, who was the sixth Prime Minister, and R.B. Bennett, who was the eleventh. At least seven finance ministers who had designs on the top post had left their political careers or their health in ruins. William S. Fielding, who was Finance Minister under Laurier, was personally defeated in his constituency when the Laurier government was turned out in 1911, but he came back to enter the contest for the national Liberal leadership in 1919 when he was seventy-one years old. Like so many finance ministers since then, he almost made it. Mackenzie King beat him by 476 votes to 438 on the third ballot. Charles Dunning gave up the premiership of Saskatchewan in 1926 with the hope of becoming Prime Minister, but he was appointed Finance Minister in King governments in 1929 and 1930 and then from 1935 to 1939. Looking after the country's finances in the depression took its toll. He resigned from the cabinet in September, 1939, his health destroyed and his dream shattered. He was only fifty-four. James L. Ilsley, the sober-faced Nova Scotia lawyer who was Finance Minister in the King government during World War II, was considered to have the inside track to take over from King when he retired, but King went on and on and outlasted Ilsley, who became Chief Justice of Nova Scotia. A favourite to crack the jinx was Douglas C. Abbott, who served as Finance Minister for about two years under King and almost six under St. Laurent. He was easily one of Canada's most popular parliamentarians despite the portfolio, and also a mentor to young John Turner before he entered politics. Abbott was being groomed by St. Laurent and the party for the prime ministership when he decided he'd had enough of politics and accepted an appointment to the Supreme Court in 1954.

The list goes on. There was Walter E. Harris, who succeeded Abbott in the finance post and was touted as the man to take over from St. Laurent when he retired. He lost credibility in the turbulent pipeline debate of 1956 and was personally defeated in the Diefenbaker surge of 1957. Diefenbaker's Finance Minister, Donald M. Fleming, contested his party's leadership three times, but never came close. The Coyne Affair of 1961 and an economic crisis the next year ruined his last try at the September, 1967, convention. And Mitchell Sharp, who hoped to succeed Pearson in 1968, saw his image tarnished by budget deficits, tight money, rising inflation, and the government's dramatic defeat on a money bill during the leadership race.

Turner has a keen sense of history, particularly of the Liberal Party, and he realized all of this in late November, 1971, when rumours started circulating in cabinet of another shuffle, in which he would be offered Finance.

"I was home in Vancouver briefly at that time," Turner recalls, "and Frank Ross asked me to take him for a drive. We went across the Lions Gate Bridge and out towards Howe Sound on the North Shore – that lovely drive up there – and I was telling him, 'You know, there is a little scuttlebutt around that I may be fingered for Finance?' And he said, 'For God's sake, avoid that. That's a grave-yard.' So I said, 'Well, I may have no alternative. If the Prime Minister of the day asks you to do a job – you do the job.' And the Old Man shook his head and told me again it was a graveyard. That was the last time I saw him because he died about two weeks later, and apart from telling me politics in general was a 'mug's game' that was the only advice he gave me in his life."

Trudeau called Turner to his office in January, 1972, and offered him the Finance portfolio. "I put it to Turner, who had done an outstanding job in Justice, that there was an equally difficult task that had to be done," Trudeau said at the time. "I told him we needed someone who likes to succeed in whatever he undertakes. I knew he was a very able and not an unambitious man. He thought it over a couple of days and said he'd be happy to do it."

In fact, there was a little more to the discussion than that. Before his acceptance Turner set out certain conditions to ensure his relative independence of authority in the post. Paul Hellyer, by now a columnist for the *Toronto Sun*, commented later:

> There is no doubt that Turner would like to be Prime Minister. There is equally no doubt that Trudeau will do everything in his power to prevent it from happening. Whether the difference between them is primarily ideological, as against pure power politics, is anyone's guess. The fact remains that the antipathy between the two men is enormous.
>
> It was no surprise then, when the PM appointed Turner as Finance Minister – the historic burial ground of future PMs.
>
> Turner had made the mistake of letting the Prime Minister know that he didn't think much of the way the country was being run. A few weeks later Trudeau reminded him of the conversation and offered Turner the opportunity to show how it should be done.
>
> There is no escape from that kind of proposition. To refuse the job would give his detractors in the Prime Minister's office the opportunity to leak to the press that he was all bluff. To take the job involved the risk of being tagged with economic chaos and uncertainty.

The economy was becoming a mess. Inflation was running at about 5 per cent and unemployment at 6.4 per cent. Both were horrendous statistics at the time. The deficit, on a national accounts basis, was about $600 million, and Canadian business was bitterly upset and uncertain because of massive tax reforms undertaken by Turner's predecessor, Edgar Benson. The government had clamped down severely on the economy in 1969 and early 1970 in an attempt to "wrestle inflation to the ground," then had been forced off its deflationary course by a heavy influx of foreign funds, which led to the unpegging of the dollar. The tight money policies had caused unemployment, which was bound to get worse in the winter, yet Trudeau and his advisers were afraid of stimulating demand, the traditional way of reducing unemployment, because that would create further inflation. The American Domestic International Sales Corporation (DISC) program, which was to permit U.S. export companies to set up subsidiaries eligible for tax benefits under U.S. law, was hanging like a sword over the Canadian economy. But on the positive side, money was pouring into the government's coffers as a result of inflation.

Turner was sworn in at Government House at 6 p.m. on Friday, January 28, and within half an hour he was on the phone to Simon Reisman, the Deputy Finance Minister, who was at a conference at the Seigniory Club in Montebello, fifty miles away. He wanted a briefing on the federal-provincial conference of finance ministers, which was to begin in Jasper, Alberta, in three days. Reisman, who was one of Ottawa's most senior mandarins, suggested a briefing on the plane trip west on Sunday night, but Turner said, "No. Now." So Reisman's role in the Montebello conference ended abruptly and he hurried back to the capital to advise his new minister. In fact, Trudeau had suggested publicly it might be better to postpone the Jasper conference because the new Finance Minister would not be ready, but that was not Turner's style. By nine o'clock Friday evening Reisman and two other senior officials were at Turner's Rockcliffe home and they debated the federal stand at Jasper into the morning hours. A new man was running the Finance Department and it was not the Deputy Minister. But Turner's attitude and his ability to absorb masses of intricate information impressed Reisman, and the two men have been friends ever since.

Turner put on a credible performance at the Jasper conference, pledged in his first Commons speech as Finance Minister to make employment his top priority, and began a series of almost non-stop meetings with corporate executives from many parts of the country and with labour leaders and consumer groups. As a result of these meetings he became convinced that the essential economic weakness

154

in the Canadian economy lay within the business community and was caused by a lack of confidence in itself, in government, and in the immediate future.

He was also convinced that emergency government make-work programs were almost worse than useless and that the real answer to the unemployment problem was an expansion of secondary industry. He told a meeting of the Canadian Club in Toronto:

> The only realistic solution for matching the tremendous increase in the labour force, which will continue at the present rate for the next three or four years, is greater growth in the economy. It is that growth that will create jobs. I mean growth in the private sector. I mean jobs, not temporary jobs. I mean jobs that last and satisfy. I believe we have to look to the expansion of secondary industry and the commitment of the private sector to find us those jobs. When I took on this job some of my friends told me business didn't trust this government. If that is so, I want to restore the working relationship between business and government.

He said Canadian industrial policy must emphasize the development and give high priority to creating jobs in the goods-producing industries and that "emphasis must be on the growth industries, the high-technology industries, the knowledge industries of the future, the ones that present possibilities of spin-offs. My number one priority will be jobs," he said, "a job for every Canadian who is looking for work. No economy is working as well as it should be if there are men and women seeking work who cannot find it."

Turner was a free enterpriser who had been known to remark that "greed makes the world go round," and his philosophies clashed tremendously with the musings of his master in the Prime Minister's office. "Perhaps more jobs is not the first thing we want in the long run," Trudeau had suggested in a contemporary interview. "Perhaps it's more wealth with more leisure and less jobs, less hours of work for less people." And in another interview in Victoriaville, Quebec, Trudeau had suggested that "the most sacred law is that a man who lives in society should be able to enjoy his own possibilities to the maximum, but work is perhaps not the way to do it . . . . The aim of man in society is not to work, it is to realize his own potential to the maximum." The difference between the two men on the need for secondary goods manufacturing was even more brutal. Trudeau felt the country might "skip secondary manufacturing altogether and have a hugely developed service sector. It would be based on the primary industries, and would serve the consumers through production of arts and all kinds of leisure services."

If Bay Street and Canadian business were to judge the argument, Turner won easily. Labour leaders at their unaccustomed meetings with a Finance Minister ("I hammered them around for a while, and then they hammered me around for a while," said Turner) were not unimpressed, and the press, in general, began to praise Turner's pragmatism and performance. Douglas Fisher, the former NDP politician, wrote in the April, 1972, issue of *Executive* magazine:

> Soon after Mr. Turner came to Ottawa it became usual (though not in any pattern) that he and I should argue and banter, sometimes seriously, several times a year. These talks plus normal observation, first as a fellow MP and then as a journalist, have made me both fond of John Turner and more respectful of his abilities than is the case with my radical friends and most of my colleagues of the media. It seems fair to declare my liking when I write about Mr. Turner because it does colour my judgements.
>
> The two exceptional qualities I have noted in John Turner – his quick mind; his well-informed mind – have been obscured to many by two curses of prejudices which prate that he is overambitious and a lightweight. These prejudices have been helped along in the past five or six years by what I call the old Princess Margaret caper and the silver spoon story.
>
> The dances as a young blade with the visiting virginal Princess and the tycoonery of his stepfather, the late Frank Ross, did not hurt his early political surge; nor did his Arrow-ad looks and their aura of social graces and wealth. But what was handsome in the early sixties is dead, supplanted by the shaggier, acne-scarred machismo of the newer male. . . .
>
> A quick mind, "a fast study" can bluff a wide contemporary knowledge, particularly if well-briefed by aides and a few intimates who range the forefronts of the current modes in ideas and topics. John Turner is both eclectic and much dependent on word-of-mouth information picked up in innumerable chats. He wears no mask of the brooder. While he never hints that he is really deeply philosophical, he is one of the best-read public men I know. It is rare to find a politician so without barriers or the sparring preliminaries to direct exchange of opinion and information. Often men have told me that "Turner is too glib." The fact is that he talks well, discursively. But he listens too, and with patience. These qualities, even manners, are unremarkable except in contrast to his unique alacrity. As one senior mandarin, a neighbor of mine, said after Turner

became his minister: "He's quicker than Trudeau; in fact he's almost as quick as Jack Pickersgill." There could be no higher encomium; this from a man who loathed what he thought Turner was before he worked for him.

Turner brought down his first budget on May 8, 1972, only three months after his appointment as Finance Minister and at a time of intense election speculation. He had almost $1 billion to spread around because of a gross national product rising at a healthy real value of over 6 per cent and the influx of tax revenues resulting from inflation. At the same time, the economy was being danger-ously distorted by the inflation and high unemployment. In the circumstances tax cuts could have been expected, but this was a different pre-election budget. It contained no goodies at all for the mass of the voters. Instead, its main measures indexed old-age and veterans' pensions to the cost of living and promised a steep re-duction in corporate income tax from 49 per cent to 40 per cent and a quick two-year depreciation write-off for machinery and equipment used in manufacturing or processing, both to take effect in January, 1973.

It was an unusual budget in other ways as well. Turner wrote much of it himself so that it read in many sections more like a human document than the usual, impersonal statement of fiscal facts and figures. His delivery of it in the Commons reeked of his own impatient personality and political style. It was not a pre-election-type budget partly because Trudeau had not consulted with Turner on his ideas about election dates, so Turner had simply gone ahead with his own ideas on his own initiative.

Its reception throughout the country was unusually good. The *Ottawa Journal* enthused editorially:

Mr. Turner is now trying to do what many Canadians have been urging upon the Trudeau Government for years: to build into the private sector of the economy the incentives for the growth on which the basic prosperity of the country, the job making capacity, ultimately rest. The budget is a shrewd po-litical document. Its basic philosophy can offend only doctri-naire socialists. There are no crude pre-election bribes, though the thought of trying to recapture some business support for the Liberals must have at least flitted through the government's collective mind. No one is going to do anything but welcome the modest assistance to old age pensioners and to war veter-ans. . . .However, Canada needs more than shrewd political documents. This moderate and reasoned budget will not in itself restore the confidence that has been seeping away from Mr. Trudeau's leadership of a motley cabinet.

And the *Montreal Gazette* proclaimed in an editorial typical of most newspaper reaction across the country:

His first budget makes clear that John Turner is his own man. For all the relief it confers, nicely balanced between individuals and corporations, it is not, in the political sense, a sunshine budget. Nor does it follow slavishly the lines so vigorously established in the budgets of his predecessor. In his own close calculation of what is needed and what can be afforded, he has managed to be both compassionate and sensibly pragmatic.

Business was, of course, delighted with the promised hefty corporate tax cut and relations with the government improved. But these tax proposals eventually were to become the basis of a successful campaign by NDP leader David Lewis against "corporate welfare bums." The employment situation worsened to 7.2 per cent in September and inflation continued to rise. So when Trudeau called the election for October 30, the Liberals were in trouble. Then the Prime Minister campaigned poorly, preaching vaguely like a Philosopher King under the slogan "The Land Is Strong" but making no firm future commitments. Trudeau said:

This is not a fight against anyone. It is a dialogue with the people. The election is an event during which the people are asked to think of Canada as a whole and on the political party that can best reflect the interests of the whole country. . . . Other parties may be running against us, trying to catch up . . . we are not running against them. We are trying to discuss Canada with Canadians. There are no spectacular choices in a country like Canada.

Turner didn't like the timing of the election. It would have been more favourable in June, shortly after his popular budget. And he didn't like the slogan. When a student at the University of Winnipeg suggested the slogan should be "The Land Is Gone," Turner replied: "It wasn't my idea. In fact I have used it only once on the whole campaign to see if I could get it out without breaking up." But he campaigned fiercely in defence of the government's economic record, constantly reiterating that it had firmly rejected wage and price controls as a means of controlling living costs. He also stoutly defended Trudeau as the leader's image faded. "The election issue is leadership," Turner said in Vancouver, "and that brings us to Pierre Trudeau. We don't have to compare him to the ideal. We don't have to compare him to the Almighty. We just have to compare him to the alternatives. . . . He has made politics more relevant to more Canadians than any other leader in the history of this country, and I believe he's still the one man who can lead us into the mid-seventies." But it didn't work. The election was a disaster for the Liberals. Robert Stanfield's Progressive Conservatives won 107 seats and the Liberals 109. The NDP held a decisive balance of power with 31 seats. Even Turner's vast plurality of nearly 17,000 in Ottawa-Carleton was cut in half.

The election, however, did serve to show a vast difference in attitude between Trudeau and Turner, one emotionally obsessed by the Quebec question, the other more calmly concerned with the country as a whole. Arthur Blakely wrote in the *Montreal Gazette* of January 11, 1973:

> Within the limits imposed by discretion and the venerable principle of cabinet solidarity, the Minister of Finance, John Turner, goes his own gait with surprising frequence and on some of the issues that count.
>
> He doesn't place his independence on parade.
>
> Turner's no cabinet rebel by any stretch of the imagination, leaking tidings of this lost battle and that to friends in the media.
>
> At 43, he's among the more youthful parliamentarians. He is certainly a young Minister of Finance.
>
> But he is no tyro. He is a wily political veteran who has been in Parliament for more than a decade. He's too shrewd to be trapped in an internal revolt.
>
> Yet he has a way, for all that, of making his point.
>
> On Monday, Prime Minister Trudeau took the Commons to the very edge of the abyss by resurrecting the theory (which had once left him unimpressed) that the setback his government suffered in the last election was attributable to an anti-French backlash in English Canada.
>
> He accused the Conservatives of having tried, successfully, to "divide Canada" by racist appeals in the election.
>
> What Conservatives?
>
> Well, there were some. In fact, there were "quite a few." Indeed, there were "many."
>
> He named none, though challenged repeatedly to do so. But he excluded no one, not even Conservative Leader Stanfield, though he had at first seemed to exempt him from the charge.
>
> The next day Turner offered an interesting preamble to a speech dealing, in the main, with weighty economic matters.

"The last election did result in, I suppose from our side, an unfortunate polarization of votes and I want to suggest, in a certain respect, an unfortunate polarization of votes as reflected in this House of Commons," he said.

"I think it is not necessarily an unhappy circumstance, but not a circumstance to be wished for by any member of the House of whatever political persuasion, culture or linguistic attribution, that so many members having their mother tongue the French language, sit on your right.

"I think that places a special burden on every member of the House of both languages in order that anything we say here enhances the unity of the country.

"I do not believe that any political party has a monopoly on national unity."

He didn't say that the prime minister had, in his opinion, been wrong. He didn't say that he disagreed with him. Turner didn't, in fact, even refer to the fact that Trudeau had spoken.

But he made a point, very pointedly, just the same.

And not for the first time.

In the shaky, minority circumstances, Canada's Twenty-ninth Parliament did almost nothing in the first fifteen weeks following the general election except survive. It survived blunders that saw the unemployment insurance costs soar to almost uncontrollable proportions, but at the first threat of NDP opposition it shelved a thorough reform of the system. It proposed, then shelved, a new law on foreign ownership and then it shelved a request for parliamentary approval of its actions in sending a peacekeeping force to Vietnam. It retreated whenever the opposition said boo. And the United States didn't help much by devaluing its dollar 10 per cent.

Turner had to bring down a budget on February 19 that the Conservatives could support and that also dealt with the corporate tax cuts and fast write-offs to which he was personally committed and which had died on the order paper when the previous Parliament was dissolved. These were absolute anathema to the NDP. In addition, he had to consider it an election budget with some measures popular to the public because the government could fall at any time. Turner was walking in a political, fiscal, and monetary minefield. Eric Malling wrote in *The Toronto Star*:

The budget Monday is crucial for Turner's career. If it's a success he will be a hero in the Party, but at the same time he will have propped up the Trudeau government and moved a leadership convention further away. If he fails, if the Party's defeated in the House and does badly at the polls, he might get a crack at the leadership but would probably be blamed for the debacle. Still, if there were a Liberal leadership contest tomorrow to replace Pierre Trudeau, most people at the heart of the party expect Turner would take it in a breeze.

The budget was a political masterpiece. It stole, almost holus bolus, a Stanfield plan for the indexing of income tax to the cost of living, which many Liberals had been ridiculing. It declared that the Trudeau government remained committed to the business tax concessions and fast write-offs, but that they would be dealt with in separate resolutions later on. It reduced income taxes 5 per cent and eliminated 750,000 lower-income Canadians from the tax rolls altogether. It increased old-age pensions across the board to $100 a month and abolished sales tax on children's clothing and candy bars and pop in an effort to control prices. As Turner read the budget speech, New Democrat Stanley Knowles presented David Lewis with a congratulatory flower, and at the point when Turner claimed credit for the tax indexation, the Tories cried, "Author, Author," while Stanfield rose to take a mocking bow. It was a raucous evening and even Trudeau got into the spirit of things, shouting at Stanfield: "Look out, we may even steal your underwear." But it worked. The NDP was neutralized. The Conservatives were sewn up. The people were pleased.

The budget also inspired Bruce Hutchison, the great old pro of political journalism, to write one of his Hercule Poirot pieces in the *Victoria Daily Times*, under the headline, "The Case of the Two John Turners."

As always when it is in trouble, the Canadian government summoned the famous European detective, M. Hercule Poirot. Even he, who has solved so many crimes, was baffled by the mystery of the two John Turners or, as the case is now called, The Grand Impersonation.

"Eh bien, I arrive by private plane in Ottawa," M. Poirot told me confidentially, "and there I witness a ghastly spectacle. M. Trudeau is prostrate, the cabinet in tears, the Conservatives laughing hysterically. What has gone wrong?

"I study the documents and at first I can hardly believe them. But the record is perfectly clear. In October, 1972, M. Turner has denounced the Conservative financial policies as a design for the bankruptcy of the nation. In February, 1973, his budget adopts all these mad schemes as his own original idea.

"In their childish professional cynicism the journalists agree that M. Turner has changed his mind merely because the government suffered certain minor losses in an election and now depends on the votes of the socialist party. This is what

161

you would expect from ignorant journalists but it does not deceive me for a moment.

"Mais, non. I realize at once that such an explanation is too obvious, too simple and naive. M. Turner is not the sort of man to worry about politics and votes. For him they are bagatelle. To suppose that he will be influenced by the threats of M. Lewis – that, of course, is absurd. I dismiss it from my thoughts and put the little gray cells to work.

"Alors, in a flash the whole affair is as clear to me as daylight – the real M. Turner did not make those speeches in October. Another man made them, a brilliant imposter, masquerading as the Minister of Finance."

Later, the inspector second-guesses himself and thinks that perhaps John Turner did make the October speeches, that the budget-bearing Turner is a clever Hollywood impersonator. Fingerprints he gets prove him right, but just as he is about to fly off in search of the real Turner he is stopped!

"In an embarrassed whisper, M. Trudeau says that I must abandon the search in the supreme interests of the nation . . . .

"It is regrettable, he agrees, that the real M. Turner has disappeared but he can be spared. His impersonator is doing much better work in the treasury. The actor from Hollywood has reduced the taxes, stimulated the economy, cured unemployment and saved Canada from ruin."

Hutchison concluded his satire by speculating on the fate of the real John Turner:

"But where is the real M. Turner? Doubtless toiling in the salt mine or sweltering in the jungle. No more will be heard of him, poor devil. The horror of his fate saddens me and even M. Trudeau suffers a brief depression. And yet, as he says, what does it matter after all? M. Turner has gone but the national economy is safe, the GNP is growing and the government endures. That thought must comfort and compensate M. Turner wherever he is. En verité, all is well with Canada."

Less satirical editorial comment across the country was almost unanimously enthusiastic. "The budget brought down by Finance Minister Turner on Monday evening in all likelihood eliminated any immediate threat to the Trudeau government," said the *Winnipeg Tribune*. "The budget was so skilfully contrived and so disarmingly presented that passage through the House, while there may be some stormy and noisy moments, may almost be taken for granted." The *Windsor Star* enthused:

> Apart from Robert Stanfield it would be hard to find a Canadian who isn't a winner from some part of Finance Minister John Turner's budget. Mr. Turner combined a bit of daring with his something-for-everyone budgeting, and ended up with a political and economic masterpiece. The Liberal government scores both ways: it is highly unlikely that it will be defeated in the House on such a widely appealing economic package, and even if the government does fall, it has an excellent campaign document in the budget. By keeping the concessions to business left over from last May's budget – the so-called "corporate ripoffs" – outside Monday's budget, Mr. Turner has made it difficult for NDP leader David Lewis to withhold his party's approval . . . .

Both Stanfield and Lewis supported and even praised the budget and the shaky minority government remained in power. But Turner was still determined to implement the corporate tax cuts. David Lewis was just as determined to defeat them. It was obvious that whenever Turner decided to fulfil his personal commitment to Canadian businessmen the House would come tumbling down.

16

The Budget-maker

By early March, 1973, John Turner was in deep trouble. He was still determined to implement his promised corporate tax cuts, but support from most of his cabinet colleagues was either lukewarm or non-existent. Most of the cabinet members were desperate to avoid an election and were concocting devious schemes to stay in power. A main cabinet plan was to not treat a defeat on the corporate tax issue as a vote of non-confidence. Then, the proponents of this scheme argued, the Tories would have to move non-confidence against the government and if the pattern of the session prevailed they'd fail to have it passed by the Commons. The government would survive as it did when defeated on a money bill in similar circumstances during the 1968 Liberal leadership convention. The New Democrats, who wanted to keep the government in power, had to have the corporation tax proposal packaged with personal tax improvements so they could vote for the package on second reading – approval in principle. Then eventually they could remain honest to their principles by opposing the corporation tax section later in committee. This would at least extend the government's life.

But Turner would have none of this sort of thing. He argued in cabinet that if a government were to be defeated on a key budget proposal, the people were likely to treat it as a matter of confidence whether the cabinet and its allies did or not. He warned that questions of credibility were involved and insisted he wouldn't allow any political manoeuvrings that would destroy his own standing.

In the middle of this cabinet argument Turner had to go to Paris for a Finance Ministers' conference dealing with the international currency crisis, and a vicious wave of anti-Turner leakages from cabinet circles swirled through the press gallery as soon as he left the country. According to W.A. Wilson, the *Montreal Star* columnist and probably the most respected chronicler of the era:

164

Anyone who would listen was told that the Finance Minister was: A, being unreasonable; B, caught up in the grip of his own pride in a most unpolitical way; C, caught up in the grip of his creations; D, caught up in the grip of his ambition; E, involved in an anti-Trudeau power play. The proper course, it was freely explained, was for the Finance Minister to get his feet back on the ground.

Then he would recognize that as long as his own party supported him nothing would be lost if the corporation tax proposals were defeated. He was not, after all, responsible for the composition of the new Parliament. And along with this the various pipelines contained a further tidbit: The Liberal party would never forgive Mr. Turner if he embarrassed the Prime Minister at this crucial point in party affairs and there were people, so it was said, who saw through Mr. Turner's warnings that in some circumstances he would have to resign. These warnings were not really aimed at protecting his own position. They were part of a crude power play to force an election, oust the Prime Minister and take over.

Wilson argued that there were basic flaws to all of this intrigue against Turner, mainly that he was too shrewd a politician not to know that an English-speaking minister who tried an anti-Trudeau play at that stage would split the party wide open, would never be forgiven by the Quebec wing, and would create more English-speaking enemies than he could ever handle. Wilson said:

The other great flaw in all the scheming that has been touted about is that its various proponents do not take seriously the point that Mr. Turner has warned is central: the issue of credibility. It may be that the public would not react badly if the government lost its corporation tax proposals and, after the Tories lost a subsequent non-confidence motion, stayed on. It may be – but it is highly improbable. The more likely development given the intensive coverage and the all-out political attack that would follow, is that a government that tried clinging to office in this devious way would be discredited.

The vicious leakages suddenly stopped when Turner returned to Canada. He stuck to his position, risking further breaks with the cabinet by proclaiming in a speech to the Canadian Club in Toronto that the corporate tax cuts were only a first step in a new industrial policy aimed at providing jobs in the medium and long term. "What is at stake is not the welfare of corporations and their shareholders. At stake is the welfare of every Canadian," he said. Then he added:

"In view of what is at stake, I would think that any member of any party in Parliament would have serious reservations about putting partisan interest ahead of national interest. We just can't afford to play politics with Canada's future."

But Turner was playing with the life of the government and his cabinet colleagues let him know it. Stories that he had threatened to resign the Finance portfolio circulated again on Parliament Hill. Anthony Westell wrote in *The Toronto Star* in March, 1973:

> Some commentators are suggesting that Trudeau will accept defeat in the tax concessions, take Turner's resignation, find himself a new Finance Minister and continue in power. But that surely is nonsense. The budget proposals are the policy not just of the Finance Minister, but the government. And the budget speech went to great lengths to make clear that tax concessions to business are an essential part of the whole economic strategy. It is politically inconceivable, in any event, that Trudeau could simply shrug off Turner, the number two man in his cabinet and the heir apparent to the Liberal leadership. The Liberal Party would be cruelly split by such a crisis within the cabinet and in no shape to fight the election which its opponents would rush to force upon it.

None of the commentators, however, counted on Turner's ingenuity in this affair. Nor did the Conservative and NDP politicians. In mid-March of 1973, Tory leader Stanfield, under pressure from his business-oriented caucus, decided to support the tax cut, but only for one year. This still left the Liberals and especially Turner the choice of facing defeat in the Commons or retreating on what they had billed as an economic principle. But Turner turned the tables on the Tories by presenting the corporate tax cuts as part of a package containing the proposed popular tax relief: a 5 per cent reduction in personal income taxes, an increase in personal exemptions, and the Stanfield-inspired provision to adjust tax brackets according to the cost of living. Thus he manoeuvred the Tories into the position of either supporting the tax measures or courting much unpopularity among voters and businessmen.

But that was not all. Stanfield's stated objection to the corporate tax cuts had been that he did not want them to become a permanent part of the tax system. Turner met this condition in an unusual way. He built into the legislation a section allowing Parliament to review the cuts after April 1, 1974, on a motion by any sixty members. The embarrassing hooker here was that the sixty members would obviously have to be Conservatives, or Conservatives allied with New Democrats, because there was little chance the Liberals would call for such a review. And the Conservatives who moved such a motion would risk alienating business supporters by disrupting a tax climate to which they would have then become accustomed. It was very clever and it was variously described as sharp, tricky, Machiavellian, and Pickersgillian. Geoffrey Stevens wrote in the *Globe and Mail*:

John Turner is, and has been for several years, one of the most accomplished politicians in Canada. One need not agree with everything he stands for to acknowledge that the Finance Minister is attractive, forceful, intelligent, and articulate (in both languages). He is a politician with instinct, style and appeal all his own.

But Mr. Turner proved this week he is more than just another rising young (44 next week) politician; he demonstrated that he possesses the quintessential quality that sustained Lester Pearson through five nerve-wracking years as Prime Minister – a highly developed sense of political self-preservation.

The proof came on Tuesday when Mr. Turner performed a dazzling backward somersault with the introduction of his long-awaited Ways and Means motions on income tax changes for 1973 and 1974. The gymnastics came on the issue of the corporate income tax reductions which Mr. Turner had promised away back on May 8, 1972, but had never got around to bringing before Parliament.

Mr. Turner's credibility and perhaps even his survival in the finance portfolio – not to mention the survival of the minority Liberal Government – were riding on the issue. . . .

Sad as it is to report, not everyone in Ottawa applauded Mr. Turner's performance. Some found him devious, even Machiavellian. Some were so unkind as to dig out his earlier utterings and to suggest he had compromised his credibility or principles. Some thought he had surrendered to the Conservatives.

It's not so. What Mr. Turner has done is demonstrate his mastery of the first rule of politics: Principles are fine if you can afford them, but survival is what the game is all about.

The tax cuts were given approval in principle on June 30, with little debate and only the NDP voting against them. Turner had won. The government had survived. And the Finance Minister was a hero again among his cabinet colleagues. He even won grudging respect from some prominent Tories. "Of course, he'll be head of the Liberal party some day," said Brian Mulroney, chairman of the

Quebec wing of the Conservative Party. "I don't know of anybody in that party who has his qualifications."

Business profits boomed following the tax cuts (up 37 per cent in 1973) and so did business expansion and employment, particularly in the manufacturing industry, but then the energy crisis began to take effect on the world's economies and food prices rose sharply in Canada, causing Agriculture Minister Eugene Whelan to suggest that Canadians who felt they could no longer afford high-priced milk should drink wine instead. He said studies had shown that Canadians had an iron deficiency in their diet and wine had a high iron content. Inflation reached a constant 11 per cent. John Turner blamed OPEC, soaring international inflation, and increasing international interest rates, and insisted that Canada, as a major trading nation, had no way to insulate itself from these external forces. He claimed also that Canada was doing much better in controlling inflation than most other industrial countries and he urged restraint. But the government continued to remain in power only at the whim of the NDP, which constantly demanded more social spending. And the first real signs began to emerge of Turner losing control of his portfolio to Trudeau and cabinet colleagues who were anxious to spend in order to survive.

Turner's February budget had gone a long way toward appeasing the NDP with some inflationary provisions, but now Minister of Health and Welfare Marc Lalonde was advocating massive new outlays on a guaranteed annual income and other cabinet ministers were threatening to exceed their estimates by large amounts and, hence, to turn a national accounts surplus of $387 million into a deficit.

"I was not being backed up by the government on spending," Turner says now. "We were fighting a rearguard action. Trudeau and Michael Pitfield had set up this cabinet committee system and we had Simon Reisman in one committee, Tommy Shoyama in another, Jack Young in another. The Deputy Minister and all of our assistant deputy ministers were covering these different committees and trying to kick five or six balls down the field at the same time. There were guys in those committees with new spending over here and new spending over there. We didn't have enough thumbs to put in the dyke. We were being overruled all the time. But we did manage to stop Lalonde's guaranteed income."

Turner announced a new economy campaign, designed to whip Ottawa's big-time spenders into line, at a press conference on August 2, stating that the government's fiscal policy remained expansionary in general terms but that "I have told my colleagues that we have to choose. Everybody is not going to have his own expenditure program accepted in full. They will have to choose their priorities." He intimated that only high-priority programs would be approved for spending purposes in the first place and even approved expenditures might be pared. He was tough and his economy campaign was hailed by the media as the most formidable anti-inflation weapon the government had yet brandished. But when Trudeau announced another set of anti-inflation measures a few weeks later, he failed even to mention the Turner move. Arthur Blakely reported sarcastically in the *Montreal Gazette*:

> There are several possible explanations for this oversight. Gossip has it that Mr. Trudeau and Mr. Turner aren't exactly the closest, most amiable of cabinet associates. In such circumstances, it would at least be understandable that the Prime Minister might find it difficult to dwell on one aspect of the war against inflation which might tend to focus public attention on Mr. Turner. It is equally possible that the Prime Minister has, for tactical reasons, decided to keep back tidings of Mr. Turner's penny-pinching activities, for the time being, as reserve ammunition. It is within the realm of possibility that Mr. Trudeau has never heard of Mr. Turner's economy campaign or that, if he did, it made so little impression that it has since slipped from his mind.

In any event, the government failed to take any notice of its Finance Minister's attempts to stop the spending. It tripled family allowances and sweetened the social security system in other areas. The easy-spending LIP and Opportunities for Youth programs were kept in place. Trudeau announced massive increases in consumer subsidies designed to offset increases in the prices of bread and milk. Total federal spending continued at an unprecedented high rate and Canada started down the road to large budgetary deficits.

Still the NDP was not appeased. At a secret caucus on March 20, 1974, all but three of its thirty-one members voted to defeat the government as soon as possible. David Lewis made the key speech. Then Turner delivered a speech in Winnipeg on April 26 strongly defending corporate profits as necessary for the health of the economy. This speech enraged Lewis and he countered with four "non-negotiable demands": an excess profits tax; a two-price commodity system; a prices review board; and 6 per cent housing mortgages. Turner brought down his third budget on May 7, and purposefully snubbed his nose at the NDP. In a budget he described as "fiscally responsible," he reduced taxes for people on low incomes, eliminated sales tax on clothing and footwear, and predicted a modest deficit. But he made no more than a cheeky gesture to the socialists by imposing a one-year, 10 per cent surcharge on some major corporations such as banks, financial institutions, and big realtors. By exempting manufacturers, processors, and small businesses from the surcharge, he stuck to his philosophy that manufacturing profits were crucial to industrial expansion and employment growth. The long and costly Liberal attempt to remain in power was over. Next day, for only the third time since Confederation – and the first time over a budget – the House fell. The traditional flurry of thrown paper littered the Commons. Trudeau called the election for Monday, July 8.

Turner's fight on the corporation tax issue was the most crucial of his career as Finance Minister. When combined with his left-wing reform attitudes in the Justice and Consumer Affairs portfolios, it completed a picture of a consummate believer in the free enterprise system, providing it was tempered with social security measures for the less fortunate in the sort of selfish and aggressive society that free enterprise encourages. He still insists that the cut in corporation taxes he had tried to introduce since 1972 worked extremely well and points to results of a government survey of business intentions released in April, 1974, that showed the measures probably led to an estimated $2.3 billion of new investment in 1972-75, almost half of this generated in 1974 and 77 per cent of it spent on machinery and equipment. In terms of direct impact on employment, the survey indicated that more than 94,000 new jobs were created in manufacturing and processing over the same four-year period and that 62,000 of these jobs were directly attributable to the tax measures in 1974 and 1975. And in this period, the Canadian economy did better than that of the United States.

On the eve of a visit by Prime Minister Trudeau to Washington early in December, 1974, the *Wall Street Journal* editorialized:

Mr. Ford should quiz Mr. Trudeau on the remarkable things his government has been doing with the Canadian economy. While Washington is immersed in doom and gloom over the shape of our economy, Ottawa's only problem is how to minimize the impact of U.S. stagflation on the Canadian scene. It's not doing badly. Unemployment actually declined last month to 5.4 per cent. Consumer confidence is high, real personal incomes are rising, and although the inflation rate is almost as high as ours, there is real economic growth on top of it. What is the key to Canada's success? The one possibility we would like American liberals to contemplate is Mr. Trudeau's bold gamble two years ago, inspired by Finance Minister John Turner, to slash the corporate tax rate from forty-nine per cent to forty per cent. The leftwing New Democratic Party screamed 'ripoff' and the Conservative Party grumbled about an inflationary effect. But once it was pushed through, Canada became a magnet for outside capital even as it generated it internally. Successive surveys of capital spending plans showed jumps from nine per cent to thirteen per cent to twenty per cent.

In contrast with the previous election, Trudeau campaigned enthusiastically for the election of July 8, 1974, spending most of his time on the hustings attacking Robert Stanfield's plan for a ninety-day freeze on prices and incomes so that Stanfield, the frontrunner at the start of the campaign, found himself constantly defending his anti-inflation program and never really able to launch an offensive attack on the Liberals' record on the economy. Turner was as tough as Trudeau in his attack on the wage and price control plan, claiming, as he had consistently in the Commons, that controls would do considerably more harm than good by reducing the supply of goods to the consumer, thus aggravating inflationary pressures, and that they would be useless in controlling food prices anyway because they were caused by worldwide shortages and the fact that farmers were at last getting a fair return for their product. At the grassroots level Turner would tell people who complained about high prices: "You know what the Tories would do, man? They'd freeze prices way up here. . . ." The hand would shoot skyward. "And wages, man? Way down here." The other hand would drop to knee level.

Trudeau and Turner campaigned skilfully together on this major issue and the Liberals won a surprising victory. Their strength in the House rose to 141, giving them a comfortable majority while the Conservatives declined to ninety-five and the NDP dropped disastrously to sixteen. (There were also eleven Social Credit members and one independent). Even NDP leader David Lewis lost his seat. In Ottawa-Carleton, Turner increased his plurality by almost 3,000 votes, although he had been confronted by the skilful, well-financed campaign of Conservative Bill Neville.

He wanted to get out of Finance. He had stipulated to Trudeau that he would carry the job only through the election but had no intention of continuing afterwards. It was a long time since he had reluctantly accepted the portfolio in the first place on grounds that, "Well, sometimes you have to swing for the fences." And he had held it for two and a half difficult years in which all of the economies of the West had been in turmoil and decline, but Canada's had performed comparatively well. He felt he had paid his dues. He had tiptoed through the graveyard and he had survived. He had also been highly successful on the global financial scene, travelling frequently to Europe and Washington, where he argued consistently that free-trade policies throughout the world were "absolutely critical," and where he made personal friends with many world leaders, from West German Chancellor Helmut Schmidt and France's President Valery Giscard d'Estaing to U.S. Secretaries of the Treasury George Schultz and William Simon. Later he was to be elected chairman of the International Monetary Fund's twenty-nation committee on economic policy, one of the most important international posts ever accorded to a Canadian. But now, after the election of July 8, 1974, he'd had enough. External Affairs would have been nice, or perhaps Transport. Yet, when Trudeau shuffled the cabinet exactly a month after the election, Turner was still Finance Minister. Allan MacEachen was given External, replacing Mitchell Sharp, and Jean Marchand remained as Transport Minister. Victor Mackie reported in the *Winnipeg Free Press*:

> John Turner has never been one to back off from a fight. He likes competitive politics, just as he likes competitive sports, so he agreed to continue as Finance Minister. He may well regret that decision. It could be that the Prime Minister left him no choice. After all, the Prime Minister had logic on his side and Mr. Trudeau is a great man for logic. He could point out to Mr. Turner that it was on his budget that the minority government came a cropper; therefore the Finance Minister owed it to the government to bring a revised budget before the new Parliament. And Mr. Turner would never back away from a challenge. Obviously, Mr. Trudeau was counting on this when he proposed that the Finance Minister carry on. What other portfolios could he offer that the Finance Minister would consider equally challenging?

All of the world's economies were challenging then. Members of the Organization for Economic Co-operation and Development recorded an average real growth rate of 6.3 per cent in 1973, but the growth rate for these industrial countries was close to zero in 1974 because of the oil crisis. The current account balance of the OECD group as a whole changed from a surplus of $2 billion in 1973 to a deficit of $40 billion in 1974. There was much slower growth throughout the world, as well as more protracted inflation and deeper imbalances of payments. And Turner was deeply involved in all of this as chairman of the IMF's interim committee on economic policy. He and Canada played a major role in trying to maintain some form of stability in the world's chaotic economic affairs.

"That IMF experience was a fabulous one," Turner recalls now.

172

"As chairman I had the confidence of the major powers and I had the confidence of the Third World as well. And this was good for Canada because we were right at the centre of things. We had to ease the IMF through the 1974-1975 oil crisis when the price of oil went up considerably and there was this tremendous movement of money to the Middle East countries. There was quite a dislocation of the liquidity position of the various other countries and all of a sudden the major industrial countries were running up tremendous deficits to pay for oil. There was a remarkable surplus building up in the Middle East which eventually got up to the $150-billion range, which was a lot of money and we had to somehow recycle that money back into the system.

"My role was to get the IMF into a position to aid and facilitate a lot of the recycling of those petrodollars," Turner explains. "On one particular trip in the spring of 1975, Geills and I went over to Iran, Kuwait, and Saudi Arabia for the IMF to get some recycled money and I ended up in Iran, and Geills had brought the Empress of Iran a beautiful Eskimo parka, a white one with embroidered red and blue birds on the back, because we knew she loved skiing at St. Moritz, and I've heard she still wears that parka. So we got along well. And I had lunch alone in the palace with the Shah. That was a $2-billion lunch. I put it to him what the problem was and I said we needed some good will from the petrodollar countries. So he signalled to some guy to come up and bring a chequebook and he signed a cheque for $2 billion and handed it to me right there at the lunch table. That was a good lunch and the $2 billion was used to re-lend to countries that needed it. I did the same thing in Kuwait and Saudi Arabia. And I met the kings and princes in their big tents and persuaded those fellows to start loosening up the money and get it back into circulation. But they didn't actually hand me a cheque on the spot.

"Now in all of that convulsion Canada played a very important part because I was the chairman and we were so well reinforced," Turner says. "Our Department of Finance really was as good as anything in the world in those days. Deputy Minister Simon Reisman had built up a tremendous department and I felt comfortable in there because I had the bullets to shoot. I mean we were very well intellectually prepared and Canada had never before had such influence internationally as we had in that slot. It was also helpful to us bilaterally because of the good relations we built up with the U.S. Federal Reserve and the American Treasury and the Department of Finance in Britain and France and so on. That's the way it works. You prove useful multilaterally and you can benefit from it bilaterally."

173

Turner points out that the IMF has become concerned about Canada's deficit in the years that have passed since then, particularly because the country's indebtedness to foreigners is in the range of $70 billion to $75 billion. "We're better able to service that debt than a Brazil or Argentina or Mexico but our foreign debt is now up there in that range," he says. "So that if we don't get our house in order we risk some serious international problems. I think the world situation is very fragile. Every half point or point the interest rate goes up adds hundreds of millions of debt servicing costs to many countries. So I think we have a very fragile situation and I think it's going to have to be renegotiated by putting a cap on interest rates or lengthening out the repayment of principal. Obviously there's going to have to be some give by the lenders and some give by the borrowers. It's going to have to be handled with a lot of common sense and a lot of cool because that debt hanging over the international markets is in the back of everybody's mind when they make decisions on capital flows and investments and it's having a negative effect on world confidence and therefore on world expansion and world investment and thereby on world employment.

"The Canadian government, Canadian banking, Canadian business both large and small have been all caught up in this and all have made mistakes; what worries me for the future is that a lot of people who got badly burned, big and small, will never have the same confidence to take a risk again and we may have to wait for another half generation of entrepreneurs to come along and another generation of managers to come along. And that is why I say we have to restore confidence in our country. I think we have been so scarred by what happened in those three years from 1972 to 1975 that it's going to take some psychological boost to persuade the country to invest and take chances again.

"I also learned in those years that we are totally interdependent economically in the world," Turner says. "Nobody is isolated. Not even the Americans can run an independent economic policy anymore. In the circumstances, we have to consolidate our position in our largest market – the United States, which takes 70 per cent of everything we sell abroad. I think we've got to see what we can do with Europe, which is in a very protectionist mood. We must continue to try to penetrate there. But the great thrust should be in the Pacific. And this is what western Canada is waiting for. They think that we have been acting as an Atlantic nation for too long. And we're not just an Atlantic nation. We're an Arctic nation and we're a Pacific nation. Now I think our thrust in terms of trade and tariffs and marketing ought to be heavily into Southeast Asia."

Canada was caught up in all of this international economic upheaval in the mid-seventies when Turner was Finance Minister, although not as badly as most industrial countries were. Canadian industry was holding its own and planning to expand rapidly, but in the overall economy the growth rate dropped to about 4 per cent. Inflation was running at about 11.5 per cent and unemployment was increasing. Housing starts dropped drastically, hurting domestic sales of lumber, steel, and appliances. The Bank of Canada interest rate reached 9.25 per cent, sending mortgage rates soaring, and the trade surplus fell by more than half in the first nine months of 1974. The value of the Canadian dollar dropped. And new union contracts were averaging 14.5 per cent, well ahead of the inflation rate, creating concerns of new waves of inflation as business increased prices to cover the higher wage costs. Turner warned a meeting of provincial premiers: "We are walking along a tightrope backwards."

Turner set out across the country in August and September of 1974, holding exploratory talks to see if organized labour, business, and industry would accept a system of voluntary restraints to limit increases in wages, salaries, prices, and profits. He warned leaders in all of these sectors that failure to reach agreement in the common interest could cause inflation to soar out of control, and this would be followed by a rapid spread of strikes and other economic strife. Organized labour was the main stumbling block to the success of such a scheme, but Turner seemed to be well on the way to achieving its co-operation. Arthur Blakely reported in the *Montreal Gazette* of September 11, 1974:

> Canadian Labor Congress President Joe Morris confirmed in a telephone interview in St. John's, Newfoundland, that he had discussed Canada's economic problems with Turner at a luncheon meeting "within the last two weeks."
>
> He said the discussions had been general in nature and far ranging. Morris said he had reiterated to Turner the CLC's flat opposition to price-wage controls as a possible solution, with the argument that such a solution was too simplistic and that it would place a disproportionately heavy share of the load on Canadian workers.
>
> Morris said Turner had discussed the possibility of holding conferences at which governments, labour, business and industry would be represented to discuss possible solutions to Canada's economic ills. . . .
>
> ". . . I told him that we have always been prepared to meet with government and industry and to discuss all aspects of the

problem and if we were able to come up with some solution which would be in the national interest we would be prepared to consider it."

Representatives of industry and business have expressed a cautious interest in Turner's initiative. Organized labour has been regarded as the possible stumbling block because of the CLC's hard line against price-wage restraints, freezes and controls in the recent election campaign.

But Turner felt he was not being backed by the Prime Minister in his attempts to negotiate voluntary restraints. "We might have had those voluntary controls but the Prime Minister would not commit," he says now. "We would have had that. I was bitterly disappointed because I thought we had an incomes control situation, which would have started putting a cap on inflation. So I wasn't being backed up by the Prime Minister in that, and I wasn't being backed up by the Prime Minister on spending control." Turner was also infuriated by an attempt by the Prime Minister's Office to establish an advisory body on economic policy, headed by Jack Austin, which would have further undermined the authority of the Finance Department. He resisted this move promptly, bluntly, and effectively by threatening to resign.

With the world economy in this fragile and precarious state, and the Canadian economy in its worst crisis in forty years, Turner brought down a budget on November 18, 1974, in which he gambled that he could moderate inflation without slowing the economy. Despite the tough times, his budget was expansionary. He promised an 8 per cent income tax cut, reduced the sales tax on building materials to make an average house $650 cheaper to build, introduced a $1,000 tax exemption in interest income, provided $100 million of tax cuts on transportation equipment, and extended fast tax write-offs of machinery and equipment costs. His main aim was to restore the purchasing power of Canadians while avoiding an increase in unemployment. But to do this he had to swing the budgetary balance from a small surplus of $275 million in 1974-75 to a whopping projected deficit of $1.55-billion in 1975-76. Then, in June of 1975, he introduced another budget, taking into account the worsening world recession and the continued pressure of inflation. "We are now faced with a dilemma," he admitted. "If we follow more expansionary policies at this time we run the risk of making inflation worse. If, on the other hand, we follow contradictory policies, we risk worsening unemployment." His solution was to do very little except cut back on government spending, raise income tax slightly on the upper-income groups, put a new 10 per cent tax on gasoline, while again offering some incentives to business expansion. The result was to increase the projected national accounts deficit to $3.8 billion, a huge amount at the time but tiny in comparison with a deficit a decade later of about $30 billion.

In Turner's term in Finance, the graveyard was more grim and gloomy than usual, but he managed not to tumble clumsily into any deep grave, as he had as an altar boy in New Brunswick, and he personally escaped most of its political horrors. According to the *Bank of Canada Review*, which uses calendar-year rather than fiscal-year statistics, a national accounts deficit of $556 million in 1972 changed to a surplus of $387 million in 1973, a surplus of $1.1 billion in 1974 and a deficit of $3.8 billion in 1975. The four-year average deficit during Turner's time as Finance Minister was $719 million.

17

From Cabinet to Bay Street

By early summer of 1975 John Turner was frustrated, concerned, and unhappy. He had reluctantly accepted the Finance portfolio almost four years previously and in a time of economic crisis because it was a challenge, and only on condition he could try to sort out the mess his way and without interference. But it hadn't worked out like that. As early as the summer of 1974, when Trudeau had first failed to back him on government spending restraints, he had thought of resigning and joining a law firm in Vancouver. Then an attempt by Trudeau and Clerk of the Privy Council Michael Pitfield to set up an advisory body on economic policy in the Prime Minister's Office and thus undermine Turner's authority had angered him. He met with Trudeau and gave him a choice between the group and his resignation. "It was well known that I didn't like the collegial style of government that Pitfield was introducing to try to cripple major departments and make the PMO and Privy Council Office the strong agencies of government," Turner says now. "I didn't like that at all." Turner won his point and the group was not formed.

Turner also believed he had negotiated with business and labour a method of voluntary wage and price controls to dampen the surging inflation that was central to the problems of the economy, but he had failed to win the support from Trudeau that was essential to clinch the deal. And his respected Deputy Minister, Simon Reisman, had resigned in the spring of 1975, years before the age of retirement, making it clear that he didn't like what was going on.

"For a while new programs were coming in so fast we felt like a pair of goalies trying to bat them away," Reisman said at the time. "Sure, a lot went by. But we won the big one – the social welfare legislation that Marc Lalonde and his deputy (Al Johnson) were pushing. That was a multimillion-dollar program and we really went to the trenches on that one." In a summation of the early

Trudeau years, Reisman said: "In the 1960's and early 1970's we went ahead at breakneck speed – new hospital programs, education programs, a new Unemployment Insurance Act, just about everything you could think of. We did it faster than the country, the economy, could absorb. We're discovering that now. But the politics were such that these programs were seen to be good and essential. If one had a history of spending decisions, you'd find that the decision to spend is always, invariably, made before the decision on how it could be financed. You spend first, then figure out how to pay for it. But this is always a balancing act. The government wanted the programs but cabinet didn't want the high taxes that should have accompanied them. At Finance we wanted to stay away from high taxes; a heavy tax system is devastating on personal creativity and individual effort."

When Reisman resigned on March 31, 1975, after twenty-nine years of public service, gossip denigrating his abilities began to spread through the corridors of power and Turner did an unusual thing for a cabinet minister. In an attempt to straighten the record he wrote an article for the *Ottawa Journal*, entitled "In Defense of a Deputy Minister." Turner wrote:

> From my experience in the subtle craft of government, I have formed the opinion that a good Deputy Minister must possess at least three virtues. He must, first of all, be competent in administration and in the general field he supervises. He must, in a word, know what he is talking about and be able to muster or initiate action. Secondly, he should possess a spirit of political awareness in a non-partisan way. He ought to be able to warn his minister of the dangers or pitfalls of the various options which he puts before his minister. Finally, he must be loyal – but in the wider sense – supporting not only policy but also his minister in personal terms; and not only publicly but in the corridors and on the cocktail circuit. Simon Reisman has these qualities in abundance. He has been more than a good Deputy Minister. He has been a great public servant. In almost 10 years in government, I have known no one better. . . .

Turner was being loyal to his friend. He was also unsubtly insisting that the economic policies of Trudeau and others in the PMO were wrong, while those he and Reisman had been trying to implement were right.

"I was damned annoyed with Pitfield and whoever was knocking my guy," Turner says, "so I wrote this three-column defence, and that really rocked Ottawa because it brought out the fact that there was something going on. Reisman was fighting against the additional expenditures and we couldn't get any support from Pitfield or the Prime Minister. They were trying to surround the department. And Reisman just didn't want to work for the government any more."

As the summer of 1975 approached, the two different men in the country's two most powerful positions differed more and more on economic philosophy. Turner was a free enterpriser. Trudeau was convinced that the free-market system wasn't working and that a new system, a "new society," would have to be imposed on Canada. He was obsessed by the economic theories of John Kenneth Galbraith, which envisaged what the Harvard economist called "the new socialism" – a combination of public ownership and permanent controls by government over corporations and unions strong enough to manipulate their own wages and prices. Essentially, Galbraith subscribed to the egalitarian concepts of the economic and political system in which the gross national product is heavily taxed to remove profit from those who achieve and distribute some of it to those who do not. Turner did not disagree with this principle of wealth redistribution but was concerned about how much social security could be supported by Canada's existing GNP. The difference was a matter of degree, but it was a serious difference. The egalitarian society envisaged by Galbraith and enthusiastically endorsed by Trudeau and his advisers does not accept that there is some limit to the level of social services that can be supported by the country's productive capacity. Turner believed there had to be limits, and also that the limit had been passed as far as the Canadian economy was concerned. He believed in balanced budgets whenever possible and that any higher taxes to pay for more social services would be counter-productive. Instead, he argued, the tax load on the most productive elements of society should be reduced to encourage their enterprise and thus expand the economy to a stage where more egalitarianism was affordable.

The two men were holidaying in Jamaica, by coincidence, early in 1975 and they went out with their wives to dinner several times. "We got along fine," Turner says. "He was a difficult guy to handle, but Margaret and Geills got along fine. And on the way back in the plane here he was reading Galbraith's *Economics and the Public Purpose*. I said to him, 'That book is getting you and me into trouble.' And I knew he was talking with Galbraith and Galbraith was giving him all this stuff, and I said, 'That book is flawed. That's not the way our economy works.' But whatever I said didn't seem to make any difference to him." Turner was also miffed by the way Trudeau handled his personal economy. Trudeau had made no attempt to pay for the dinners in Jamaica and Turner had had to pick up all of the tabs, one of them for $250.

So Turner was browned off, not because of any one thing but a cumulation of them. He was left with three choices. He could continue to present and try to defend fiscal and government policies with which he strongly disagreed; he could openly challenge the Prime Minister's leadership, gather his supporters, split the party, and eventually force a leadership convention; or he could resign. He was also heavily in debt. Entertainment and keeping up appearances was helping take all of his cabinet minister's salary of $54,600 and there was a mortgage of $50,000 on his Rockcliffe home. His children were growing and he wanted to give them an education similar to his own. "During that summer I came to the conclusion that I had served about as well as I could serve and that it was about time for me to look after my personal affairs," he says. "I'd spent almost fourteen years in there. I'd been ten years in the government. I just didn't feel like it any more. My heart wasn't in it." To defend policies he disagreed with would have been dishonourable, to challenge the Prime Minister publicly would have been disloyal. He decided to offer Trudeau his resignation.

As he walked across Parliament Hill from his office in the West Block to Trudeau's East Block office on September 10, 1975, Turner hoped that Trudeau would help find a way to settle their differences in a friendly, possibly even paternalistic talk and then persuade him to remain in government, perhaps in External Affairs or Transport. But he didn't really understand Trudeau and never has. They were two such different men. In his book published in 1978, Trudeau's biographer, George Radwanski, wrote of Trudeau:

> In Trudeau's case the greatest weakness is in the human-relations aspect of political leadership.
> It is here that his sensitivity, his self-discipline and his pursuit of his own freedom combine to cause him serious difficulty. Sensitive, he protects himself by holding himself at arm's length, behind a barrier of apparent coldness. Having disciplined himself to be immune from most forms of criticism or praise, he cannot understand why others are not similarly indifferent.
> Mitchell Sharp, Trudeau's former External Affairs Minister, says: "One of Trudeau's serious faults is his lack of sensitivity to human relations. He has never been able to generate a feeling among his followers that any individual is important to him, except for close personal friends like Jean Marchand and Gerard Pelletier. He doesn't have any skill in human relations. He told me once: 'I find the most difficult part of this job is dealing with people.'
> "He's a man who inspires but who seems to lack warmth in

his personal relations. I've heard this from so many people. They're here, they're gone, with never any appreciation expressed. . . ."

But Turner is a handshaking, backslapping extrovert, a sentimental man who keeps his many friends, lets them know he appreciates them, and goes out of his way to genuinely praise their successes and worry about their illnesses and family affairs. As he entered Trudeau's office to resign he expected Trudeau would try to talk him out of it. But Trudeau was just not that sort of man and it didn't work out that way. Radwanski wrote in his biography:

> Even within the sphere of political activity, Trudeau refuses to employ the conventional artifices of leadership. He won't make any minister feel specially important, won't express gratitude, and won't ask anyone to remain in office as a favour or a duty.
> "I think it's a flaw in my character, quite frankly," he says. "When I see the pleasure I could give people by saying, 'Jeez, you've been doing a good job,' you know, and I don't do it . . . there's something wrong. I guess in a sense it's a different code of behaviour. It seems to me when you're on a team and you're doing a good job, if you're kept on the team that's the proof that you're doing a good job. But it probably would be nice if one expressed it."

The two men talked for almost an hour about their differences and Trudeau, characteristically, didn't try to make Turner feel important or express any gratitude or tell him he'd been doing a good job. It was only in the last ten minutes that Turner's future was discussed and Trudeau made no attempt to convince him to remain in government. "Well," he said, "if you've made up your mind, I respect your decision. What are you going to do?" Turner said he didn't know and Trudeau asked him if he'd like to be a senator or a judge. Turner stormed angrily out of Trudeau's office, feeling insulted and betrayed.

"I guess I didn't handle that very well," Trudeau later told an associate. And Turner says now: "The guy is a Cartesian logician and I'm an empiric guy. I'm an Ango-Saxon. I'm not for codes and all that. I'm for working it out. I can't speculate, but if Mr. Pearson had been in a similar circumstance I would still have been in government."

Turner's resignation from the cabinet split the Liberal Party, creating one of its worst crises. Members were naturally shocked by the angry departure of the heir apparent and its political consequences. But there was more to it than that. Turner had represented the pragmatic liberalism of King, St. Laurent, Pearson, and Howe, while Trudeau, the party interloper, embodied his own brand of "new liberalism," which had little to do with the past. Now the party was torn between tradition and Trudeau.

Turner sat in the back benches until February 12, 1976, while Trudeau took to the airwaves to insist the free-market system was not working, proclaim Galbraithian theories, and perform a remarkable political somersault by introducing the stringent wage and price controls advocated by Opposition Leader Stanfield, which he had campaigned so strongly and successfully against in the election campaign. Turner did not publicly explain the reasons for his resignation from the cabinet. He said practically nothing at all in the Commons, but in his letter of resignation from Parliament and later at a final press conference in his office in the West Block he took a few indirect swipes at Trudeau. "I have enjoyed every moment in Parliament," he wrote in the resignation letter. "I shall miss the companionship of the House and the honor of sitting amongst the most distinguished assembly in the country." This was a dig at Trudeau, who had frequently criticized Parliament and expressed indifference to it. And in another indirect swipe at the Prime Minister, who was being attacked for making major policy speeches outside the House, Turner insisted that he had made all of his major speeches in Parliament.

A few days after Turner resigned from the Commons, W.A. Wilson wrote in his syndicated column:

> John Turner is a man of stature on the Canadian political scene, with considerable international standing, yet no effort was made to dissuade him from leaving the cabinet nor, after that, from resigning his seat in the House of Commons.
>
> The Turner affair, indeed, has been handled as if the Liberal party and the government were both so bursting with talent that the departure of one of its most important figures was of little consequence.
>
> The reality, of course, is far from that.
>
> Mr. Turner's resignation (from the Finance portfolio) in September produced far greater shock waves than anyone, he himself included, foresaw. There was a clearly discernible wave of public sympathy and support for him and a corresponding feeling of antagonism towards the government he had just left. It was a highly unusual reaction to the resignation of a minister, even an important and popular one.

There is little real doubt that one of the main reasons why this country now lives under a price and incomes control policy is to be found in these shockwaves after Mr. Turner's resignation. Ironically, when he himself canvassed his ministerial colleagues and the Liberal caucus on the subject before his June budget he found no support for such a policy. Nor was it discernible then in the country. In effect, Mr. Turner's resignation and the unusual reaction to it made the policy of controls possible. . . .

Mr. Turner's departure from the cabinet and the House of Commons is not the only example of this government's indifference to the loss of valuable men. Unnecessary resignations from the upper levels of the bureaucracy have also taken place, at cost to the country. . . .

Men like these have gone and others will probably follow in a slow, costly trickle. There is little to be gained now, though, by dwelling on the losses that already have taken place. There are some other aspects of Mr. Turner's departure.

Mr. Turner's international standing is probably higher than that of any other Canadian since L.B. Pearson. One of his last callers while he was still an MP was the ambassador of a European country. After Christmas he vacationed in Jamaica with the Secretary of the U.S. Treasury, William Simon. While he was there the Finance Ministers of France, Belgium and Germany came to call on him. Henry Kissinger came to dinner. . . .

But from within the cabinet and in some sections of the party there was also criticism that was to follow Turner for years to come: that he had quit when the going got tough and let the party down at a time he was needed most.

Turner had many lucrative offers in the private sector and finally accepted a partnership in the growing Toronto law firm of McMillan, Binch at a salary estimated at about $200,000.

His departure from Ottawa was emotional. He was popular not only in the Commons but in the community where he had gone to school and where he represented a suburban riding, and he did not like leaving the city. At an Ottawa Rough Rider football game shortly before he left, 22,000 people stood and cheered him as he entered the stadium, bringing tears to his eyes. ("They wouldn't have done that for Trudeau," he says.) And there were many farewell parties.

Eddie McCabe, the tough little sportswriter who used to fight with Turner at St. Pat's College and became his friend, attended one of the posher dinner parties, packed with senators, judges, lawyers, MPs, and sports figures, at the Louis Neuf restaurant in Hull and reported in the *Ottawa Journal* that,

> While the farewells were in their last stages, the unseasonal rainstorm broke and the heavens lit up with sheets of lightning . . . most unusual at this time of year . . . and a phenomenon we can't pin to the departure of any other man . . . save one. And, of course, for St. Pat's boys, it's sacrilegious even to think such things. But then again if you're Irish, and superstitious at all . . . well . . . Now, I've been at gatherings of less sophisticated lads who, on such theatrical evidence, would have prostrated themselves immediately. Of course, I wouldn't even suggest such a thing. Still, have you ever seen lightning at this time of year? And the timing was exquisite. Hurry back John!

Turner took out a large bank loan to buy a nice older house for about $265,000 on Russell Hill Road in Toronto's classy Forest Hill area. The house had a large, private backyard, where Geills loved to weed and garden, and it was close to tennis courts where Turner played frequently with his sons. And offers of directorships on company boards flowed quickly to him. He became a member of the board of Canada's largest private corporation, Canadian Pacific, and one of its most profitable, Seagrams. He became also a director of Sandoz Canada, subsidiary of a Swiss-owned pharmaceutical firm; Bechtel Canada, a megaproject engineering company; Holt Renfrew, the retailers; MacMillan Bloedel, the British Columbia forestry giant; Credit Foncier, a Quebec trust company; Marathon Realty, CP's real estate arm; and Massey-Ferguson, the financially troubled farm equipment firm. He joined the boards of two relatively small mutual funds, Canadian Fund in New York and Canadian Investors Fund in Montreal. Each of the board memberships paid him about $12,000 a year plus up to $800 a day and expenses for each meeting. He mingled on these boards with the elite of Canadian business, for instance, Adam Zimmerman of Noranda Mines and MacMillan Bloedel, who is a Progressive Conservative and maintains that "the only thing wrong with Turner is that he's in the wrong party," Conrad Black of the Argus Corporation, Charles Bronfman of Seagrams, and Hal Jackman of Victoria and Grey Trust, who says he likes Turner because they both smoke the same six-dollar cigars. (In fact, Turner insists he only smokes six-dollar cigars when Jackman or a client gives him one. At other times he smokes a plebeian House of Lords. But he does like his cigar and constantly chomps on one in private.)

His business took him around the world, frequently to Australia, where his old Oxford friendship with Malcolm Fraser, who was then Prime Minister, didn't do any harm; to the Caribbean, where he is still a member of the bar and there are more old friends; to Europe, where his Oxford track-and-field friend Chris Chataway now represents a big London bank, and they often did business together. Old friends in the royal family occasionally called for a bit of advice. His network of friends in the U.S. also helped. For instance, George Schultz, the U.S. Secretary of State, and Turner liked each other when they were both representing their governments at the International Monetary Fund. Schultz was instrumental in having Turner appointed to the board of the huge Bechtel company, whose alumni also include Defence Secretary Caspar Weinberger, U.S. Deputy Secretary of Energy Kenneth Davis, and Philip Habib, the special Mideast emissary for President Ronald Reagan. He dealt with McMillan, Binch's expanding business in Japan and Latin America.

So Turner prospered. He made some good personal investments and one bad one. He guaranteed a bank loan to start a film company, CFI Investments Inc., which went bankrupt, and personally lost about $35,000. He was also on the board of Infinitum Growth Fund Inc., a venture-capital firm using government incentives to invest in risky businesses. Three of the seven businesses Infinitum invested in either were liquidated or went into receivership and the company ran up a deficit of $2.99 million in 1983. But the other four companies proved to have good prospects so that Infinitum survived and began to return to the black in 1984. "We had a venture-capital company and usually only one in five initiatives succeeds in that type of company," Turner says. "That's why Ontario subsidizes the shares 30 per cent to encourage people to invest in a small business development corporation like Infinitum, which helps high-risk companies trying to get off the ground. I lost dough in the film company but I didn't lose any money on Infinitum. And that thing's coming back. You know in eighty-one, eighty-two, and eighty-three, there were thousands of small businesses going broke across the country. So when I say in public speeches that I'm talking small business – you win and you lose, and I know this – I get applause. I've been there and they know I've been there. And nobody publicizes the companies I've been in that have been big successes and I don't want to talk about them. But I've been involved not only as an adviser to big business but as an adviser to small business. We have a lot of small business clients in this firm and I've been out there myself. Frankly, the few small business setbacks I've had are a plus. I understand the situation. I've been there."

Turner was involved in many multimillion dollar deals in his period on Bay Street. His connection with the huge, $11.5-billion-a-year, privately owned and operated Bechtel Group Inc. of San Francisco was particularly important. He travelled the world as a director of the company, which has interests from California to the Kremlin and Australia and has played key roles in Canadian megaprojects ranging from the $14-billion James Bay hydroelectric scheme to the $2.3-billion Syncrude tar sands project and the now shelved $9-billion Alsands project.

But Turner's biggest personal satisfaction came from the rapid and highly successful expansion of McMillan, Binch. It was a comparatively small firm of twenty-seven lawyers when he arrived in 1976. By 1984 it had become one of Toronto's major law firms with ninety partners. Its offices had expanded from a single floor in the glittering Royal Bank Tower to fill three and a half floors. Its billings, mostly to blue-ribbon clients, rose from about $4 million a year to over $20 million. "My principal activity was building this firm, widening our business, strategizing our major clients and our major negotiations and our major deals and helping to sit in on our major cases," Turner says. He also conducted a few major cases himself, but usually on appeal because appeal dates are set and he was so busy his own calendar had to be set three to four months in advance.

He found time, despite this, to do some charitable work. He was on the board of York University and of the Collegium of St. Michael's College and the Toronto School of Theology. He worked for the Salvation Army and the Catholic Church. "I spent a lot of time as a citizen of this town, doing my commitments," he says.

His business acquaintances say he was one of the busiest and most successful men on Bay Street. "He was very well respected," says Conrad Black. "He's a good scout, you know. Anybody who meets him likes him and he was able to bring people together because he has such a great understanding of people. He knew which client would interact with another client on a personal basis and he was able to bring together a lot of deals in this way. He can do this with anybody. He'll be able to do it with business and labour and apparently almost did in his period as Finance Minister. When he first came into business an aura hung over him because he was so well regarded for his public record. Then we found him to be a man of conservatism and change at the same time and that he had a deep understanding of economics and the law and that there was nothing superficial about him. You know, McMillan, Binch wasn't doing very well when he arrived and he saved it. Now it's one of the country's most successful law firms. So he was just very good at what he was doing. And I don't know of anybody who actually dislikes him. In the next ten years politics in Canada is going to improve immensely because of the presence of two good men, Turner and Mulroney."

"He was as bright as a new pin," says Victor Rice, chairman and chief executive officer of Massey-Ferguson. "He came in when we were in trouble and he didn't rest until we were well on the way to recovery, so he did a great deal to help save us. He didn't exert any influence on government. I don't think he had any. He didn't say all that much at board meetings but when he did he summed up situations succinctly and his advice was solid. The difference between Turner and other directors was his understanding of nuances. He had a clear understanding of all the nuances involved in anything we were doing."

And Bill Daniel, president and chief executive officer of Shell Canada, who did business with Turner personally and took a close interest in his other Bay Street activities, says: "Turner's connection with the Bechtel company was particularly significant because Steve Bechtel, who runs the company, is recognized in business circles as the shrewdest judge of men in the world. And he chose Turner as one of his directors. And John was extremely well respected in Canadian business circles as well. He was very objective and sound. He thought through the logic of everything. There was nothing superficial about him. He was a deep thinker, able to grasp the essence of a matter and pull ideas together and then he was pragmatic. He also showed a great deal of interest in people and their affairs, a genuine interest. He cared about them as individuals. I went on a three-day fishing trip up the Restigouche River with Turner and Jack Nicklaus, the golfer, once. We spent the whole three days together in primitive circumstances and you get to know people best that way. I found out that Nicklaus was much more than a golfer and Turner was much more than a lawyer. Turner is a good man to be with, an interesting, highly intelligent man's man who loves the outdoors, cares about people, and is a particularly good family man. He also has a great sense of humour. You know, a lot of people come and go on Bay Street, but in the time he was there John Turner was highly successful and he really paid his dues."

But Turner still had the bug. He never really did get away from politics.

18

Private Citizen, Public Figure

Even within a month of leaving Ottawa, while he was still settling into the law practice, Turner was in politics again, making a speech to the Ontario Economic Council. He wanted to get something off his chest and he did. Before this audience of economic experts he castigated the federal government's failure to control its spending, urged an early end to wage and price controls, complained that unemployment insurance and other benefits may be undermining the work ethic, and called for less government interference so that market forces would have a better chance to work.

Almost everything he said was in direct contrast to the policies of the Trudeau government. He was particularly critical of Trudeau's adoption of the Galbraithian philosophy that the free-market system was defunct and that more government intervention in the economy was necessary. The government, he suggested, was "trying to cover up the economy's boils with pancake make-up." Turner said:

Suddenly, everything seems to have come unstuck. We have an inflationary bias. Economic policy has created a floor under expenditures. An expanding money supply has validated the demands of the powerful. There have been chronic government deficits. We have blunted the downside risks (through social welfare). But nothing comes without a price. Now we are paying for it. The failure of governments to specify their priorities has intensified this bias. Political commitments have overloaded our economy. New public programs have at times been introduced without regard to our ability to carry them. There has been a failure to examine existing programs in terms of their efficiency or effectiveness or without concern for whether they are still relevant and necessary. Clearly some federal-provincial programs are out of control. I mean the open-ended programs of medicare, hospitalization and post-secondary education. These programs are essential. But they can be redesigned so that the costs do not continue to rise at a rate well above that of the gross national product. There should be a moratorium on new programs. No hiring of additional public servants until the economy catches up.

The hard-hitting speech made the main reasons for his resignation obvious. He argued for a better control of the money supply and a tighter fiscal policy to stop the escalation of federal expenditures, but not, he said, at a cost to the weak, the needy, and the powerless, and he gave a half-hearted endorsement of wage and price controls because of a "desperate need" for more discipline in wages and prices:

Now that controls are in place, they must be made to work. In my view they would have been more likely to succeed had they been preceded by a freeze and applied across the board rather than selectively. . . . Controls are neither a final nor a permanent solution. They are not a panacea, neither politically nor economically. I think it essential that Canadians understand that controls cannot replace fiscal and monetary policy. They will not work unless expenditures are brought under control and the increases in the money supply are gradually limited so that it accommodates only the real growth in the economy.

Thus his position on controls was much closer to that of Opposition Leader Stanfield's than it was to Trudeau's.

Then, in a direct attack on Trudeau's personal economic philosophy, he added:

I do not believe that the existing economic system, with all its limitations and strengths, is falling apart. What kind of economic system do we have? Is it essentially a market system? Is it dominated by a few large corporations and unions that do not respond to market forces? Galbraith states that the market system is now defunct. I do not agree . . . . Nobody has convinced me there is an alternative system that would work better, while preserving the economic and political freedom we now enjoy. I do not, of course, reject modifications. I believe we should have a market economy where individual effort is rewarded and where people are free to pursue their goals within the social and legal framework. I believe there is a role for state enterprise when public objectives are inconsistent with private profitability and a natural monopoly is involved. But in my view, when in doubt, let the private sector continue to function.

It was certainly not a speech aimed at winning popularity with the Liberal Party establishment he had just left and it didn't, but it countered the vague condemnation that he had "quit the party when the going got tough." It was obvious he had left the cabinet because he disagreed fundamentally and almost completely with the way it was running the economy. He had no other honourable choice.

According to the polls at the time, many others shared this or some other disagreement with the government. The Liberal Party's popularity dropped drastically, and when Trudeau called a by-election to fill Turner's vacant seat in Ottawa-Carleton in October, 1976, the Liberal candidate was crushed. Not only did Tory Jean Pigott overcome Turner's 11,000-vote plurality in 1974, she piled up a huge 15,000-vote plurality of her own over Turner's would-be Liberal successor, Henri Rocque. The Liberals had held the seat for ninety-four years, losing it the last time in 1882 when the main issue was Sir John A. Macdonald's tariff policy. This time the main issue was bilingualism, and as new Conservative Party Leader Joe Clark gloated over the victory and a similar, simultaneous rout of the Liberals in St. John's West, Newfoundland, Trudeau admitted his grave disappointment and stated that, "Obviously, the voters were trying to convey a message to the government and the government will try to respond."

Later in 1976 and throughout 1977, in the period when the country was shuddering under the effect of the victory of René Lévesque's separatist Parti Québécois in Quebec, Turner went on a quiet but consistent campaign across the country, speaking mostly at Canadian Clubs and to professional organizations. He preached a formula for national unity, criticized the government's economic philosophies, particularly the Galbraithian theories, advocated a redistribution of powers to the provinces, denigrated Trudeau's system of government by committee and centralization of power in the PMO and PCO, opposed the Trudeau plan for unilateral repatriation of the Constitution, made proposals to offset western alienation, and stated that the issue of bilingualism had been blown out of proportion. His speeches in this period, when he was his own man, unencumbered by party discipline or the pressures of an election or leadership campaign, give a good indication of the manner of the man himself and the way he would try to direct the country as Prime Minister.

In one "off-the-record" speech to the influential, private Primrose Club in Toronto, shortly after the Parti Québécois victory, Turner caused controversy by stating: "It's not enough to say we will not negotiate Confederation, and that Canada is one and indivisible. We must show Quebecers their membership in Confederation is essential." His remarks were interpreted as a blast at Trudeau's earlier affirmation that Confederation was not negotiable and Canada was indivisible. And *The Toronto Star*, which sneaked a reporter into the meeting, headlined: "Turner hammers PM: hasn't done enough to rescue Quebec." Turner insisted this report was substantially inaccurate, mainly because he hadn't mentioned Trudeau by name. But his theme was the same in subsequent speeches. One to the Canadian Club of Vancouver, in March, 1977, covered most of his concerns about Quebec and the future of Confederation. He said in part:

Canada is a country in deep political and economic trouble. We need spokesmen, both in and out of politics, to speak for her with compassion and understanding, but also with realism, offering Canadians new directions and new goals. We need to rise above our current cacophony of special pleading, above the babel of special interests. We need voices to join the great debate for our country.

November 15 [the Quebec election] has meant that, whatever happens, our country will never be the same again. It will not be the same in political or even constitutional terms. Change in our national structures is now inevitable. We must do some urgent rethinking about our constitution. I don't think that the status quo is any longer a realistic option. Not only has the current federal arrangement become less and less acceptable to Quebec, but I don't believe it is any longer acceptable to western Canada.

If not the status quo, then what? We can start from the proposition that we do not accept the separatist option of Quebec as an independent nation. I don't believe most Quebecers want this. I don't believe the rest of us do, despite a little grumbling here and there. If it happens it will be by default and not by conscious choice. It would be a confession of failure and the end of our national dream.

I agree with those who have already said that political independence for Quebec, but under some kind of economic union with the rest of Canada, is not an option either. How can one conceive of an independent Quebec with one-quarter of Canada's population and one-fifth of our economy having a veto against the rest of Canada over fiscal policy, monetary policy, energy policy, and commercial policy? Would the rest of the country accept this? No way. We would be back to the type of paralysis that prompted our confederation in the first place.

I believe, however, that we do have a valid option – the option of decentralizing or at least rearranging our administration and even our constitution. I have held this view – and expressed it publicly – for over ten years. I believe we must contemplate giving more powers and responsibilities, not solely to Quebec under some form of special status, but to all the provinces. I believe that the time has come for some broadening and sharing of power in both political and economic terms. I believe that the time is here for contemplating a degree of decentralization in our country that will reflect our new reality.

I agree with the Prime Minister that Canada in many respects is already highly decentralized. But that is the nature of the compromise we made in 1867. I also agree with Mr. Trudeau that no amount of decentralization will satisfy Mr. Lévesque or other committed members of his party. But surely the point is to reach over them to the mainstream of opinion in Quebec. I believe that most Quebecers would like a new deal, but within Confederation, just as I believe that most westerners would like a new deal, but within Confederation.

What direction should negotiations take? First of all, we should recognize that national unity is not a one-dimensional issue. Excessive emphasis has been placed on bilingualism as the sole prerequisite to national unity. This is difficult to swallow, particularly in western Canada where acceptance of two languages means rewriting history, where issues of resource ownership, transportation, and tariff structure are perceived to be equally important.

Bilingualism is not the total answer even to the aspirations of French Canada. If I had been born a French Canadian I would have insisted on equal access to my federal government in my own language. And that is now the law. But that wouldn't have been enough. I would have never felt completely comfortable as a French-speaking Canadian if I did not have enough scope in the constitution of the country to fulfil myself, not only as an individual human being, but also as a member of a distinct cultural society. This would have meant for me that I would want to feel secure in my own language, under my own civil law, with my own culture and within my own collective psychology – on my home ground known as the province of

Quebec – the only piece of geography on the face of the globe where I find myself among my own kind in a majority.

It would have meant that in terms of my own culture, my ability to communicate, my ability to fulfil myself in economic terms, I could do so as a Canadian within a constitutional fabric flexible enough to give me as a Quebecer enough living room.

Well, I was born English-speaking, but I don't think I'm talking in a vacuum. I can understand (if I don't always agree with all the details) the thrust towards a better equilibrium in our constitution. This urge is not unique to Quebec. I have heard the same arguments emanating from British Columbia and Nova Scotia, Alberta and Newfoundland.

Any reworking of confederation would have to treat all regions of the country equally. It would have to reflect the collective needs of French Canadians as a community or society. It would have to ensure equality of language rights in Quebec and in Canada as a whole. It would have to recognize a greater measure of equality of economic opportunity for Atlantic Canada. It would also have to satisfy the grievances of western Canada.

There are some items which are essential to nationhood and to the vitality of a modern state. These would include fiscal and monetary policy, international and interprovincial trade and commerce, foreign affairs, defence, and sufficient revenue to ensure a minimum equality of services and tax burdens in various parts of the country. Most of the rest is surely negotiable and could be largely left to the provinces: culture, communications, health, welfare, resource policy, housing, urban policy, agriculture, even some aspects of immigration.

I am acutely aware of the feeling that has been building up here, over the last fifteen years, that the concerns and goals of western Canada have been left off the list of national priorities . . . that, in political and economic terms, decisions have been made by people living in the Montreal-Toronto-Ottawa triangle, and that the western perspective has been ignored or bypassed. But more than that, westerners resent the hoarding of power, both public and private, in eastern office towers and cabinet rooms.

I said in Toronto to the Canadian Club some five months ago that Ontario has been the main beneficiary of confederation, and has prospered under a common market stretching from sea to sea. Now is the time for some re-dispersal of power and economic advantage. The people of Ontario will accept any new arrangement that preserves and enhances the unity of Canada.

The battle for the minds and hearts of French Canadians will be fought in Quebec, but the tangible encouragement they receive from the rest of the country is intensely vital. The unity of this country is too important to be left only to the politicians. The negotiation will have to be done by those elected to public office, but it will be the public opinion across Canada that will determine the scope and success of that negotiation.

As a nation, Canada is not a product of logic, nor economics, nor even geography. Only history explains us. Canada was a hesitant historical compromise between two cultural strains and diverse economic regions. We wove the threads of parliamentary tradition and territorial federalism into a consensus called the British North America Act. As a country we are a creation more of hope than of reality. The "Canadian Identity" is almost impossible to define. Whether we have been fashioned by the vastness and remoteness of our land and water, by the composite of our varied heritage, or by our resistance to American "manifest destiny," we are a unique and distinctly separate people on this continent.

And, as others judge us, we have been a happy people, a fortunate nation, blessed with abundant resources and free from the ravages that have scarred so many other places.

I cannot admit that we have lost the will to stay together as the most favoured cluster of men and women on the face of the globe. There comes a time in a nation's history when that will must be proclaimed. Now is the time. I hope none of you will remain silent in the days ahead.

His economic policies were summed up in a speech to the annual conference of the Canadian Institute of Chartered Accountants in Bermuda in September, 1977, and they showed that he was consistent in the belief expressed in his budgets as Finance Minister – that the key to solving Canada's economic woes lay mainly in encouragement of the private sector:

Our prime purpose must be to restore incentive for productive investment, corporate liquidity and business confidence. Until controls are lifted or phased out and it is clear what latitude the government will allow for the private sector, confidence will not be restored. Canada is now caught in the reality of market forces. We are going to need three to five years to re-establish our former position in the world – if we start now. Our costs will have to be brought in line with our competitors'. Our productivity will have to be raised, and here both new capital investment and better labour relations are crucial. Corporate liquidity will have to be further restored by way of higher margins of real rates of return which reflect the impact of inflation on traditional accounting. Government expenditures must be even further restrained at all levels. Any stimulus to the economy should favour investment over consumption . . . .

Our manufacturing industries are under growing pressure. We are less and less competitive on a unit cost basis, and in terms of productivity. A growing energy shortage and rising energy costs will make them even more vulnerable. Uncertain labour relations in the post-control world will be troublesome. Weak capital investment will hurt their productivity and competitiveness even more, as will a continued uncertain political climate. Competition will become more severe. Third World countries will invade more and more of our traditional markets, including our own domestic market, with cheaper manufactured goods. Their favourable labour rates will enable them to under-price us. Some of our industries will have difficulty in repelling that competition. Canada will have no alternative but to look to new post-industrial techniques and systems as a compensation for losses in standard and traditional manufacturing. We should be exploring now how we can do better in new industries involving electronics, communications, space, the oceans, plastics, petrochemicals and so on. Unless we switch our emphasis to this type of enterprise we will not find the new jobs to make up for the ones we are going to lose in basic manufacturing.

Turner made several speeches in this period charging also that Canadians were being denied real democracy because of government secrecy and, again, he appeared to be directing his criticism at Trudeau, who had made "participatory democracy" the main theme of his first election campaign in 1968. "A few years ago, we heard the phrase 'participatory democracy,'" Turner told the Canadian Bar Association in Winnipeg in August, 1976. "These were favourite Ottawa buzzwords. But there is no way a citizen can participate unless he knows the facts and reasons upon which policy is based. Governments often complain that citizens do not understand what they are doing. Politicians feel that the remedy is in more ministerial speeches, news releases and even Information Canada. That doesn't work. The only cure is the facts . . . produce the facts and you restore public confidence. But in Canada there is no legal right to know. Nor is there a legal duty on the government to inform. On the contrary, secrecy is sanctified by the Official Secrets Act and the civil servant's oath of office and secrecy." (An Information Act guaranteeing citizens access to some government information was eventually passed by the Trudeau government in 1983 and John Grace, Turner's close friend and best man at his wedding, was appointed Privacy Commissioner to administer the Act.)

Turner's political activity in this period was consistent enough to cause *The Toronto Star*'s satirical columnist, Gary Lautens, to write:

> Former Finance Minister John Turner is stepping up his campaign to be a private citizen.
>
> Ever since he left the Trudeau cabinet, Mr. Turner has been denying any interest in becoming Prime Minister of this country. It has become almost a crusade.
>
> Just a week or two ago, for example, he spoke to the Canadian Club in Toronto and told reporters at his umpteenth press conference: "I am not a political commentator any more."
>
> Nobody was convinced.
>
> "Why is it people don't believe Mr. Turner when he tells them he's a private citizen and not involved in politics?" I asked one of my Ottawa contacts.
>
> "It beats me, too," was the reply. "By my count Mr. Turner has given 215 interviews, delivered 37 major speeches, and appeared on TV a dozen times to emphasize he's just a private citizen like anyone else. And still Canadians believe he wants to be Prime Minister."
>
> "It isn't easy to stop a rumour once it gets started," I agreed. "What can Mr. Turner do to convince voters from Victoria to St. John's he's just a private citizen and doesn't want their X next voting day?"
>
> "He may be forced to make a cross-country tour and go to every hamlet, city and farm to get his message across," my informant confided.
>
> "If he shakes enough hands, signs enough autographs, and appears on enough podiums and open-line shows, Mr. Turner could hope he'll make a dent in the popular belief he's just waiting in the wings to take over the Liberal Party and the government of Canada."
>
> "Sounds like a high price to pay for a man who only wants to be a private citizen," I commented.

"Not if you want to be an ordinary Joe so badly you can almost taste it," my contact responded.

"Ever since he was a child, John Turner has had only one dream – to grow up and be a private citizen. And now, apparently, thousands of Canadians want to dash his hopes and make him Prime Minister."

"It doesn't seem fair," I admitted. "Why doesn't he just refuse to give major addresses, hide whenever a newspaper photographer wants to take his picture and put it on page one, and take his telephone off the hook?"

"Mr. Turner wouldn't last a year as a private citizen if he did that," my informant advised.

"It's only by discussing his lack of interest in becoming Prime Minister almost daily with the media that he's managed to stay a private citizen this long.

"If anything, Mr. Turner may have to step up his campaign in the months ahead to remain a private citizen."

"How?" I wanted to know.

"By putting up billboards, mailing out literature, and buying full-page ads in the newspaper to stress his lack of interest in Prime Minister Trudeau's job."

"I hate to be a spoilsport," I commented, "but does Mr. Turner realize all this publicity could backfire and put him in the very place he doesn't want to be – 24 Sussex Drive?"

"I'm sure the thought hasn't even crossed Mr. Turner's mind," my informant said. "Maybe someone should warn him."

In fact, after his initial flurry of speeches, in which he highlighted the vast differences between his own philosophy and that of the government, Turner went back to his business at McMillan, Binch and genuinely tried to keep out of politics. It was difficult at times. He consistently declined interviews but the media continued to regard him as the heir apparent to the prime ministership and made occasional mentions of his regular lunches at table number 23 at Winston's in Toronto (although he frequently lunched elsewhere as well), his board memberships, and his progress in the business world. Books and magazines of the era continued to mention him prominently as the possible saviour of the Liberal Party, and people continued to approach him on the streets of the cities where his work took him, or on the Toronto subway on the way to the office, to shake his hand and wish him well. For some mysterious reason he was not forgotten across the country. In June, 1978, a poll of women in the Moncton area, conducted by the *Moncton Transcript*, voted him the "sexiest man in Canada" although he had then been living in relative obscurity for almost three years. Francis Fox, the former Solicitor-General, was second and Pierre Trudeau third.

Turner suffered one apparently serious lapse, however. In September, 1978, "newsletters" of a highly political nature bearing his name and that of William A. Macdonald, the other senior partner at McMillan, Binch, were revealed by *The Toronto Star* along with the claim that the firm was charging a fee for the "newsletters" of about $15,000 a year to some of the country's biggest tycoons and companies. Several of the letters were strongly critical of some of Trudeau's cabinet ministers, particularly Finance Minister Jean Chretien ("The minister's optimism is leaving him with a growing credibility gap"), and Turner subsequently wrote a letter to Chretien and the other ministers, which they described as "both an apology and an explanation."

"I've always believed that modern law is what I call 'total package' law – total strategy," Turner says now in explanation of the newsletters. "And we've done a lot of things at McMillan, Binch for clients where the problem has not only been legal, but involved in taxation, accounting, engineering, the environment, image, and public relations. And for a particular client with a particular problem we'd contract out all of the expertise beneath us and give him a total package. We're far ahead of the country on that. As a result a lot of our clients wanted specific advice on what was happening in Ottawa, or in Quebec City, or in Queen's Park, or Victoria or Edmonton, and we'd give it to them. And they weren't newsletters, they were responses to specific problems. The one I regret was the one that mentioned Chretien and some other cabinet ministers by name. Personally I didn't write it, but as with cabinet solidarity you have to take collective responsibility for what your firm does. I telephoned and wrote those gentlemen and apologized for that. So there was no newsletter. What we did was respond in a confidential way to clients wanting to know the picture, and McMillan, Binch still does that."

Then in 1979, while Turner was concentrating on this type of "total package" law with enormous success and trying almost desperately to keep out of the public eye, the entire Canadian political scene dramatically changed. Trudeau called an election for May 22 and the Liberal Party was soundly defeated by the Conservatives led by Joe Clark, who had replaced Robert Stanfield. The Conservatives held 136 seats to the Liberals' 114 and the NDP's 26, while the Social Creditistes held six. Consequently, there was tremendous party pressure on Trudeau to resign.

Even before the election a poll by Peter Regenstreif had shown that if Turner had replaced Trudeau as Liberal leader, the Liberals would have a five-percentage-point lead in popular support over the Conservatives led by Joe Clark. The poll, taken in December, 1978, showed the Conservatives 10 per cent ahead of the Liberals when no leadership names were mentioned. But with Turner as the Liberal leader it showed the Liberals to be well in front with 44 per cent of the popular vote and 39 per cent for the Conservatives. In other words, the Liberals would probably have won the election with Turner as leader.

But Trudeau insisted he would not resign and that he would fight his way through a leadership convention in order to oppose any challenger who rejected his concept of a strong central government. He was obviously referring to Turner and when asked by reporters if he would accept a leadership push by his former Finance Minister, Trudeau thought for a moment and bluntly replied: "Turner, no."

Then, in November, Trudeau attended a Liberal convention and fund-raising dinner in Toronto. He had seldom felt so miserable. Dental surgery had twisted his mouth. It hurt him to smile and even to speak. But for four days he made speeches, chatted with party members, and socialized as best he could. The word he heard from the rank-and-file Liberals made him even more miserable. Val Sears wrote in *The Toronto Star*:

> It was then, for long hours alone in his modest two-bedroom suite at the Harbourfront Hotel that Trudeau came to his final, irrevocable decision: To hell with it. He would quit.
>
> It was a decision he had been coming to all summer. There were days when he thought he might carry on, at least through the fall session of the House of Commons and then make up his mind. He did not really want to quit – he did not like the idea of John Turner, his one-time Finance Minister who resigned in an hour of need, inheriting the party.
>
> The work that began his eleven-year reign as Prime Minister was not finished. Quebec would hold a referendum in the spring that would help decide whether Canada would, in Trudeau's thinking, survive. He wanted to lead the federalist forces against separatism.
>
> But events had closed in on him. The executive council of the party was meeting this weekend and wanted some indication from him of his plans.
>
> His flaky wife had moved into a house ten-minutes' walk from his Rockcliffe home and God knows what mischief she had in store. He had been told, over and over, that the west was lost as long as he was leader of the party.
>
> And he had been assured that Turner had an organization

pretty well in place for the leadership convention. The more time Turner's rivals had to prepare their teams, the more likely Turner could be beaten. He could not afford a last-minute decision that looked as though resignation had been forced on him and gave Turner the edge.

So Trudeau went back to Ottawa and sat in the gloomy study of Stornoway on the night of November 21, called a few close friends to tell them of his decision, and wrote his resignation by hand in French and English. Next day in his office the man most Canadians regarded as cold and remote broke down in tears as he told one of his first visitors: "It's all over . . . ."

Almost immediately the madness began again. Within days of Trudeau's announcement, Vancouver lawyer Keith Mitchell, John deB. Payne, the Montreal publicist, and Toronto lawyers David Smith and Jerry Grafstein were meeting in Toronto to try to start a campaign for Turner. Others jumped to the phones to line up Turner support. These included Heather Peterson, who had been second-in-command of the party's Ontario campaign the previous May; Irene Robinson, a long-time party worker; Norman MacLeod, the party's Ontario president; and MacLeod's two predecessors, Jeffrey King and Bruce Laird. But Turner himself remained aloof from them and the press. Donald Macdonald, who had replaced Turner as Finance Minister when he resigned in September, 1975, implemented the wage and price controls, then resigned himself in September, 1977, to follow Turner into a prosperous Toronto law practice, was also a strong favourite for the succession and Trudeau's obvious choice. Others agonized about their chances, including former Finance Minister Jean Chretien, Health Minister Monique Begin, former Solicitor-General Francis Fox, former Treasury Board President Robert Andras, Agriculture Minister Eugene Whelan, and backbenchers Lloyd Axworthy (Winnipeg-Fort Garry) and Herb Gray (Windsor West). Chretien was regarded as a particularly important player, whose support to either Turner or Macdonald would be crucial if he decided not to run himself. However, although there was strong pressure on the powerful and popular politician from Shawinigan to run, he was not personally enthusiastic. "I have no commitment with destiny," Chretien said. "I never wanted to be Prime Minister. I'm a realist and I will assess my position very seriously." Whelan indicated the main reason for his possible candidacy would be to oppose Turner. "I can't support him," Whelan said, "not after the kicking he gave us. You don't expect that kind of kicking from a Liberal."

The undeclared race was really between the two Toronto lawyers,

201

both former Finance Ministers, both out of politics for several years and friends who respected each other and had lunched together at Toronto's York Club the day after Trudeau's announcement in a meeting arranged some time in advance. But Turner, regarded as the anti-establishment candidate, had some obstacles to overcome. Geoffrey Stevens wrote in the *Globe and Mail* of November 27, 1979:

> If he [Turner] wants to be leader he will have to start early and run hard to prevent the party establishment from locking up the leadership for Donald Macdonald long before the convention opens in Winnipeg on March 28.
>
> There are at least five major obstacles to his candidacy. First, the opposition of the retiring leader, Pierre Trudeau, who has made no secret of his desire to keep Mr. Turner from the leadership and whose encouragement of Mr. Macdonald has been less than subtle. Second, Mr. Macdonald's strong support in the Parliamentary caucus. Third, the influence of senior figures (including Senator Keith Davey and James Coutts, Mr. Trudeau's chief of staff) who will try to swing the party to Mr. Macdonald. Fourth, the perceived ability (how real it is remains to be seen) of Marc Lalonde, Mr. Trudeau's right arm in Quebec, to deliver Quebec delegates to Mr. Macdonald. Fifth, resentment over Mr. Turner's resignation from the cabinet and Parliament four years ago.

Turner had at least one other serious obstacle. His wife, Geills, was not at all anxious for him to return to the turmoil and insecurity of politics while the children were still young, their education in its early stages, and the family's financial security as yet unsettled. Turner also liked Donald Macdonald and regarded him as a suitable man to lead the country. Thus he was relieved of the sense of duty imbued in him by his mother. And he also had an intuition of the type essential to successful, surviving politicians. He wasn't quite sure that Trudeau had really resigned; there was the chance he would come back if he saw that the former Finance Minister who had disagreed so strongly with his policies had the best chance for the succession. So Turner talked with close friends, including John deB. Payne, and he also sought theological advice on the balance between family and civic responsibilities from Father Harold Conway, who had taught him at St. Pat's in Ottawa. Then, on December 10, three weeks after Trudeau announced his intention to resign, Turner called a press conference in Toronto. He said:

> Four years ago when I resigned from the government and

later from my seat in the House of Commons, of which I was a member for over thirteen years, I decided that I was leaving public life for good. In the intervening years nothing has happened to change my mind, despite speculation by the media that I was contemplating a return to politics. During the past three weeks I have heard from many friends, both inside and outside the Liberal Party, urging me to seek the leadership. I felt that I was bound to listen to what they had to say. I have considered carefully everything they have said to me. I am grateful to them for their encouragement and concern. After deepest reflection, I have not changed my mind. I do not intend to seek the leadership of the Liberal Party. . . .

People who considered ambition to be Turner's main driving force were surprised and the media was astounded. "Imagine," headlined the *Ottawa Journal*, "He wasn't interested!" But Turner had conceded to a friend shortly before the Trudeau announcement that the flame of desire for the party leadership – and the Prime Minister's office – which used to burn steadily in him, "now only flickers once in a while." And one of the cabinet ministers closest to him summed up: "The numbers were there, but the flame wasn't."

Then the political scene again changed abruptly. On December 13, a budget presented by Finance Minister John Crosbie was defeated in the House by a vote of 139-133 and Joe Clark's Conservative government fell after less than nine months in power and eight weeks in Parliament. An extraordinary few days followed.

December 14: Clark went to Government House to ask Governor General Edward Schreyer for dissolution. The Liberals were thrown into an election with no leader. Pierre Trudeau told the Liberals he didn't want to be leader again but would return if they really wanted him. Some of the party establishment did, but many others wanted Macdonald. Others also suggested drafting John Turner, who had dropped out of the race earlier in the week. After twelve hectic hours and many meetings, those who wanted Trudeau to resume the party leadership won over those who wanted Macdonald as leader. But there were several conditions on Trudeau's renewed leadership, including a decline in power among his aides. Also, Trudeau must run as a team player, not a solo star. Trudeau asked for time to think.

December 15: While Trudeau was making up his mind he was contacted by Macdonald supporters, who tried to dissuade him from returning to the leadership. Trudeau was noncommittal.

December 16: Trudeau arrived back in Ottawa from a weekend in Quebec and aides showed him a private opinion poll that indicated the party could win an election with him as leader. Trudeau asked for more time to consider.

December 17: Liberal cabinet ministers André Ouellet and Jeanne Sauvé began a movement to draft John Turner as party leader. Robert Kaplan, the member for York Centre, and Edward Lumley, the MP for Stormont-Dundas, planned to fly to Toronto to persuade Turner to accept the draft. Turner heard of the draft movement and tried to discourage it. In the evening Trudeau phoned Macdonald and asked him if he had decided to run should the leadership post remain vacant. "I told him that I would stand at a January 18 convention. He also asked me if I would be a candidate for the House if he stayed on and I said I wouldn't," Macdonald remembers. Trudeau told Macdonald he had been receiving a lot of advice about his future and wanted to take a walk to think about it. He did not tip his hand about what he intended to do and Macdonald began preparations for a news conference the next day to announce he would run.

December 18: In the morning word began to filter from Trudeau's office to Liberal MPs and reporters that he would not run. The Draft Turner movement immediately took off again. André Ouellet phoned a key Turner friend in Toronto and reported there was strong support in caucus for Turner. He was told the message would be passed along. Then word of the renewed Turner draft reached Trudeau's office. It is not clear whether Trudeau had already decided to stay on, but if he was wavering, the Turner news may have been the deciding factor. Trudeau called Macdonald to tell him what was coming, putting an end to his hopes for the Liberal leadership. Half an hour later Trudeau told a news conference he intended to stay on.

Trudeau led the Liberal Party to victory in the February 18, 1980, election, winning 147 seats to the Conservatives 103 and the NDP's 32. And Turner continued in his law practice. He would not have accepted a draft for the leadership anyway. He had made a decision that the family had to come first. Turner is also a great believer in the theory that leaders are chosen for specific times, conceding even that Trudeau was the right man in the right place to deal with many of the issues confronting the country during much of his long period in power. But that time in late 1979 and early 1980, Turner believed, was not his time and he was relieved that it wasn't. He thought then that his time had passed forever, that now he would never be Prime Minister.

In the next few years he appeared at some Liberal Party conventions and made a few, mostly private, speeches, some still strongly critical of the Trudeau style of government and its handling of the economy. Polls still showed he was a power in the land likely to do better in an election against Joe Clark than Trudeau, and he still missed the House of Commons. But the fire wasn't there anymore. The Canadian economy was in a mess while his own life in Toronto was comfortable and interesting. The hair was silver now, the athlete's body no longer tireless, and the brashness of the young politician drowned long ago in experience. Even the driving influence of a remarkable mother, now lying mindless in a nursing home, was beginning to fade, and the ego that helped push him in the 1968 leadership race was tempered with concern and even fear for the responsibilities of leadership in a country that had become more restless and a world that was more dangerous.

19

"My Time Is Now"

Turner was nervous. People who knew him in his track and field days said he was always nervous before a big race, like a young colt prancing and fussing behind the starting gate, and he was like that now in March, 1984, in his lawyer's office high in Toronto's Royal Bank building. He had a good idea that Trudeau was about to resign, finally, although he was never certain what "that unpredictable Trudeau" would do, and he was genuinely puzzled about the way power still clung to him. The phone rang constantly with pressures for him to run again for the Liberal Party leadership, and he would ask close friends almost pathetically: "Why me?"

This was not the same as the 1968 leadership contest, when the ego was strong and politics fun. Then, sixteen years ago, the active mind was finely tuned to the country and its power centre, the youthful body was fitter. And, after all, there had only been a chance at the top job then. Now, if he chose to go for it, that job appeared to be a virtual certainty, and its responsibilities were onerous.

"It's ridiculous," he would say in casual chats in the plush but fairly small office at McMillan, Binch. "I've made maybe eight real speeches in the last eight years. I've been out of politics. I really did mean to quit forever." Then he would pace the grey carpet, contemplate for a while, and pronounce: "I was good in the House, you know, but that was a long time ago and it might be different now. Do you think I can handle the House now?" And friends would reply: "You'll be all right, John. Nothing has changed all that much. You'll be better than Mulroney."

"Well, I don't understand it," Turner would say, still pacing the office. "You know, it's a terrible thing, a terrible responsibility. And it doesn't make sense. People have an image of me that may not be right. I'm older now and hopefully I'm wiser. But I'm not the blue-eyed boy of the image anymore. And Geills is not too keen, you know, and there'll be criticism and I have to drag my family into all that. Why me?"

"Maybe it's because it's your duty," the friends would say. "Maybe it's just that your time has come and therefore you must do it. Maybe you do know the country better than anybody and the people feel that. Maybe it's magic. Maybe greatness is being thrust upon you and that's the best way to achieve it. But most of all," they would say, "you've got to run because you can win."

"But why me?" Turner would repeat. "You know it's a terrible thing." Then he would calm down and become contemplative, and once while in this mood he said: "You know, this time the country is different, the problems facing the country are different. In 1968 we were on top of the world. We had come through Expo – and this is why a man like Trudeau captured the imagination. But right now the country knows we're in trouble. There is a lot of anxiety out there, you know. People are concerned about their jobs. Youth is concerned. I mean, there are 700,000 kids out there coming out of school who can't find anything. So we've gone through some traumatizing years and the mood of the country is serious out there. They are concerned about jobs; they are concerned about growth; they are concerned about the prosperity of the country; they are concerned about the educational system; they are concerned that we had better get down to business. You know, there is a very serious tone out there. The problems are far more difficult to solve than they were in 1968."

Father Conway, his old teacher at St. Pat's, dropped by the law office for a chat and Turner told him: "I've got a lot of pressure on me, Father. What the hell should I do?" And this time the old priest didn't hesitate. "Go, John, go," he said. He talked with his sister Brenda and she reminded him of their mother's edict: "Strive for excellence. Don't be ambitious for money. Don't be ambitious for power. But you've got brains and talent. Use them. Whatever you do, don't waste your talents."

Geills and the family were again the major consideration in the decision and Turner did not tell his wife he would run until the second week of a vacation in Jamaica, where they had gone to talk about the possibility shortly before Trudeau's resignation announcement on February 29. They decided to relax for the first week and not discuss the matter at all. Then, in the second week, the phone rang. It was John Payne from Toronto telling Turner that Trudeau had resigned. "Have you talked with Geills about the possibilities?" Payne asked. "No, not yet," Turner replied. "Well, for God's sake you had better talk to her now," said Payne. Turner didn't have to. Geills had heard the phone conversation. She knew what was going on and she asked her husband if he was going to run.

Geills Turner is a formidable woman in her own right and much prettier than some of her photographs show. She was an excellent basketball player in her youth, captain of sports at Balmoral Hall School in Winnipeg, and gymnastic champion of Manitoba, and she is a canoeist of consequence, sharing and perhaps even exceeding her husband's love of the rough and lonely wilderness. She was clever academically and successful in her career as a computer specialist, and in recent years she has become a skilled photographer after a four-year full-time course in graphic art at Ryerson Polytechnical Institute. She is much travelled, well-read, intelligent, charming, and curious. She would like to have another career of her own, probably in photography, but possibly in partnership with another woman in a small business. She is not entranced by the glitter of public life at the top level and the interesting people involved. She has already experienced that and paid her dues as hostess and confidante and adviser in politics and she understands the exercise of power and what it can do to people. She likes her freedom and privacy also and fears that a Prime Minister's wife can lose both; that when she travels officially in future, either as Canada's First Lady or as the wife of the Opposition Leader, she will be stuck under the chandeliers in the isolation of embassy opulence and security, unable to take her cluster of cameras and personal curiosity into the world's dusty back alleys where the real people are, with the real faces that make the best photographic portraits. She went on a previously planned trip to China, doing just that, in the first weeks of Turner's campaign for the leadership.

There is also a great love and respect shared between Geills and John Turner, as there has to be in a marriage that has lasted twenty-one years, particularly a marriage of mixed religions, and there is an intense pride in the children noticeable in both sets of clear blue parental eyes when they talk about them. Elizabeth, now twenty, a brilliant student and one-time possibility for the Canadian downhill ski team, is studying history, economics, and literature at Stanford University in California and is fluent in French and German; Michael, eighteen, has been elected head steward – head boy – by his peers at Upper Canada College; David, sixteen, is an outgoing, thoughtful, popular boy, also a student at Upper Canada, who follows politics closely and is likely to come home and proclaim, "Whoops, Dad had another bad day today"; and Andrew, twelve, is a skilled soccer player and promising athlete. He won the junior 400-metre, 800-metre, and 1,500-metre championships at Upper

Canada in 1984, competing against boys two years older, just as his father had at other schools (but now his father was upset because he thought the boy was running in too many races).

Geills Turner had played a major role in her husband's decision not to run for the leadership when Trudeau first resigned briefly in 1979. The children were younger then and the Toronto law practice was only beginning to bring the family some financial security. The family had to take top priority and Turner agreed with her. But this time on the beach at Jamaica she did not object so strongly. She was, after all, a bit of a political groupie who had worked hard for candidate Turner in his first 1962 campaign in Montreal, when she hardly knew him and he was a political nobody. She had revelled in the excitement, drama, and rivalry of the 1968 leadership campaign and convention, and she had performed like a trouper even though she was eight months pregnant. So now she told her husband he must do what he thought he should do and she would support him as always, but that he must "be his own man." By the middle of the leadership campaign, Geills Turner was representing her husband at meetings he couldn't attend in the Yukon, the Northwest Territories, and New Brunswick. She was often at her husband's side and even appeared to be enjoying herself.

John deB. Payne, sixty-seven years old, the owlish, affable Montrealer who made the phone call to Jamaica, has been Turner's alter ego for the more than two decades since they first met at the Liberal Party's 1960 Kingston Conference. There Payne found Turner to be "an extremely attractive young guy, very impatient with his ambition, but a reformer, a guy who really liked people and cared for them."

Payne was originally a CBC producer who helped start the English-language network in Quebec, then an executive with the Hudson's Bay Company in Winnipeg, an executive assistant to Prime Minister Lester Pearson, and now a political analyst and consultant on labour matters in Montreal. He and Turner have been in touch at least once a week and sometimes three times a week ever since the 1960 conference. He is a little to the left of Turner politically, particularly in his sometimes highly critical attitude to banks and big corporations, but in general they think as one and they are as close as friends can be.

Both were fatherless. Payne's father was killed in World War I, a few months after he was conceived, but he says Turner missed having a father more than he did. "You have to start with the premise that John is very much his own man, but he has always searched for a father figure," Payne says. "It shows in the respect he has for certain older men, for Bill Bennett [the former assistant to C.D. Howe and president of the Iron Ore Company of Canada], for Frank Ross, for Diefenbaker, Pearson, and some of the archbishops. Pearson was perhaps the closest. I mean, I respect some of those men, but John has a reverence for them. They are all still 'Sir' or 'Mr.' to him. I think John missed having a father more than I did. I haven't had that capacity of John's to become a friend of older men. Still, the fact that we were fatherless might help us think the same way. We have exactly the same political instincts. Sometimes you just can't tell the difference between us. And we both work so quickly together. You know, in twenty-five years you come to know each other so well.''

When Turner nervously left his office at McMillan, Binch on the afternoon of March 15 to announce in Ottawa next day that he would run for the party leadership, he was carrying a speech written mostly by his friend, John deB. Payne. And as soon as Turner's back vanished into the thirty-eighth-floor elevator, Payne, the publicist and political analyst, settled himself comfortably behind his friend's desk at McMillan, Binch, under the portrait of Laurier, chatting with Turner's secretaries as if he'd been there all his life. He was perfectly at home. He was, after all, the alter ego.

In the previous few months, when there appeared to be a possibility that Trudeau would resign, Payne and a few others had been meeting regularly in a room at the Royal York Hotel to discuss Turner's options and try to plan the beginnings of a campaign if he decided to run. The group included John Swift, a Vancouver laywer and former executive assistant to Turner, Rick Alway, warden of Hart House at the University of Toronto, Irene Robinson, a one-time candidate and popular party worker, and Bill Lee, possibly the most astute political organizer in the country. But they were all under strict instructions from Turner not to start anything or do anything.

"He was determined that Trudeau and the Trudeau people would never be able to say he was lusting for the job," Payne says. "He wouldn't allow a single thing to be done. He wouldn't talk to Geills and he didn't decide to run until after he'd talked with her in Jamaica. So we had a standing start and we had the kind of messy operation that is synonymous with a standing start. There really was no Club of 195 working in the background to make John Prime Minister. It might have been there once but now it was a myth. Before March 16, when John announced he would run, I asked John Swift to come up with the 195 names and he could produce only twenty-three. Then, suddenly, after March 16 there were 695 club members and we didn't know what to do with them all.''

The mess was monumental. Strong attempts had been made by

many members of the party establishment to convince Turner he should be ready because, after all, the organization of his main rival, Jean Chretien, had been operating quietly and efficiently behind the scenes for almost two years. But Turner had refused to make any political move at all. Herb Gray, the party's Ontario political boss, made one such attempt, for instance, at a secret breakfast meeting with Turner at the Harbour Castle Hilton in Toronto late in November. But Turner told him he was a private citizen who intended to carry on with his law practice and do nothing at all political until Trudeau decided to quit, at which time he would consider his options. Hank Karpus, the head of the large Toronto advertising company, Ronalds-Reynolds, helped arrange the secret Turner-Gray meeting with Frank Felkai, a former executive assistant to Gray. Karpus said that "Turner had to come from Ground Zero. The big myth of it all being wound up like a mainspring ready to go into orbit just wasn't so." And Shaun Sullivan, a Vancouver member of the Club of 195, remarked: "The assumption was that we had a great organization. You know, ten years in the waiting, slick, professional, perfect. So what happens? Nothing, that's what! Just a mad goddamn scramble."

When Turner did decide to run about a week before his March 16 public announcement, Heather Peterson, forty-two, wife of Toronto MP Jim Peterson and sister-in-law of Ontario Liberal Leader David Peterson, was recruited as campaign manager, while Bill Lee, who is a baseball nut, flew off with his wife to Florida to watch spring training, as they do every year. Lee is fifty-nine now, although still boyish looking, and is highly successful in his Ottawa consultancy business. He did not need or want the grind of another campaign.

Peterson is bright, personable, and politically astute, but she had never run a national campaign and when it finally got under way she found herself surrounded by former executive assistants who thought they could run campaigns and by committees that couldn't come to decisions. One of the committees made a politically unwise decision to use American rather than Canadian computers, at much greater expense, simply because they considered the American product must be better because it was American. Another committee couldn't decide on campaign colours so it employed Angus Reid and Associates, the Winnipeg polling company, to do a "focus research study" at a cost of $12,000. Reid's group was asked to send people into the streets of all major Canadian cities, holding up colour cards and asking people their reaction to them, a process that would take at least several weeks. More than 2,000 volunteers called to offer their services in the first few days of the campaign, and nobody knew what to do with them. Turner was out on the campaign trail, unaware of this mess, until a number of old-pro politicians, among them Senator Alasdair Graham of Nova Scotia, told him as gently as possible what was going on. So late one night in Regina he called Bill Lee in Florida and pleaded: "Please come back, Bill. I need you."

Bill Lee is a Hamilton boy who joined the Air Force in World War II and flew with the RAF Ferry Command to India, Australia, Africa, and a lot of other places. When he was discharged he went to the University of Toronto for a while but was offered a permanent commission in the RCAF and went back to a military career. He was appointed public relations officer for the Transport Command at Trenton but he knew absolutely nothing about public relations. So he went to the headquarters of the Canadian Broadcasting Corporation in Toronto in his flying officer's uniform and asked to see whomever the head man was. It was Harry Boyle, who listened to the young man's problems and agreed to give him some instruction. (Harry Boyle now works for Lee at his Ottawa public relations company.) Then Lee went to *The Toronto Star* and asked the managing editor, Borden Spears, how he should go about his job. Spears was so impressed by this initiative he not only agreed to help – he had a reporter write a story about the interesting young airman.

Lee became a good public relations person. He was sent to Europe as head of public relations with Canada's NATO air division, then was appointed director of public relations for the entire Air Force. Promotions came quickly for him so that he became the youngest group captain in the service and he met many politicians on overseas trips, including a young MP named Paul Hellyer, who visited Europe with a delegation concerned about crashes of T-30 (Tomcat) training planes. Lee didn't think there was anything wrong with the Tomcats and to prove it he offered to take all members of the delegation for a flight in one, but only Hellyer, who had been a leading aircraftsman in the war, and an elderly lady senator were brave enough to accept. Hellyer enjoyed the flight and Lee's direct style of public relations, so when he became Defence Minister in 1963 almost the first thing he did was to convince Lee to leave the Air Force and become his executive assistant. Subsequently, throughout the sixties Hellyer and "Leaky Bill" Lee became the most impressive team on Parliament Hill, and Lee became by far the most active and powerful executive assistant, popular with the press for his frankness and honesty, but often the centre of political controversy as Opposition members complained about the power exerted by a non-elected military man in the affairs of the Defence Department.

Lee organized Hellyer's unsuccessful leadership campaign in 1968, which was generally regarded as the best-run campaign, and then after Trudeau won and called a snap election he received a call from Marc Lalonde. "Look," Lee remembers Lalonde saying, "we've got a problem. We won the leadership on charisma and now we're into an election and we don't have any policy. I understand you've got policies. Can you put together a platform?"

"Hell," Lee says now, "we had lots of policies. You name it, we had it. So I just put together all the Hellyer stuff and away we went on the Trudeau campaign."

Lee was appointed policy adviser on the Trudeau campaign and then when it ran into trouble from amateur organization ("Trudeau was as mad as hell," says Lee), he was also appointed campaign tour manager in a move that put many noses on the original Trudeau team out of joint. He ran the tour smoothly, as usual, except for one bitter argument with the young cabinet minister, John Turner. Turner called him one day at the Constellation Hotel in Toronto and said he wanted to see Trudeau, but the Prime Minister was having his usual afternoon nap and had given instructions to Lee not to disturb him and to take care of any problems that arose while he was asleep. Lee recalls Turner insisting, "I've got to talk to him. I'm a cabinet minister. Wake him up." And he says he replied, "John, you might be a cabinet minister but I'm not waking him up. You tell me what the problem is and I'll make the decision and Trudeau will back me. There's no way I'll wake him up." There was quite a battle of wills, Lee remembers now, but later, when the tour reached Ottawa, Turner approached him quietly and said, "Hey, Bill, I'm sorry about that. You were right, you know." The two men have been close friends ever since.

Lee did not want to come back when Turner called him in Sarasota, Florida. His wife was dead against it. He was comparatively rich now and he'd paid his political dues. And spring training wasn't over on the baseball fields. "But," says John Payne, "Bill Lee is a war horse, and he heard the gong." Lee took the first flight back to Toronto. He insisted that he work for no pay and he saved the Turner campaign.

The first thing Lee did was call Angus Reid and cancel the contract for the focus study on campaign colours. Then he called Hank Karpus and had all of the colours under consideration lined up on the wall and floor of his office. Lee studied the colour cards for a few minutes and said, "We'll have that one and that one," choosing the yellow and red that were to become the campaign colours. He chose the colours because he liked them. Then he cancelled the order for the American computers and ordered Canadian equipment. Lee was in charge and it was that way throughout the rest of the campaign.

In the beginning, however, there was also trouble with the candidate. At his Ottawa press conference announcing his candidacy he was asked about his attitude to the federal government's intention to ask the Supreme Court to settle the question of language rights in Manitoba, where the legislature had been brought to a halt by the Opposition Conservatives who refused to let a vote be held on the government's bills to extend French-language services and entrench rights for Franco-Manitobans in the Constitution. Turner said he thought the issue was "a provincial initiative, and that the solution will have to be provincial. I hope that it would be resolved by a political process, not the legal process," but he added that he supported the "spirit" of a House of Commons resolution supporting the Manitoba government.

Turner's statement was consistent with his position when he piloted the Official Languages Bill through the Commons, but it was in direct conflict with the current attitude of the Trudeau government and caused great controversy in central Canada. Turner subsequently issued a four-page "clarification," stating his belief that minority rights must, if abused, be remedied by the judicial system and that the federal government had the duty at times to intervene. It was a little embarrassing but not entirely uncalculated. Turner's apparently moderate attitude to language rights won him considerable support in western Canada, where people were angry at attempts by the Trudeau government to have the French language "rammed down our throats."

And Turner had trouble handling the media. He knew before he decided to run that the media would be different, a group of younger, ambitious, aggressive men and women trained in the Trudeau era when the name of the game was to be adversary. They were people of the thrusting microphone and the fleeting thirty-second TV clip who didn't know him, who dealt with each story as if it was their last, and then when they found they had lost their contacts went into public relations or government jobs. Except for a few, this new breed had no experience of any Prime Minister except Trudeau, who disliked and distrusted them. Turner knew there would be no more long and friendly discussions over hamburgers at the Belvedere Hotel or in the West Block office with the Bill Wilsons, the Tony Westells, the Val Sears, the John Grays, and the Rae Corellis of the more casual Pearson era, in which a man could speak his mind, a reporter was expected to be fair, and there were unwritten rules to be kept. But he was still not ready for a thrusted microphone in an elevator at a Montreal hotel and a question about Quebec's controversial language law: "What's your position on Bill 101?" "I agree with it in principle . . ." Slam. The elevator door closes in mid-sentence. Someone has half a story on a thirty-second clip. And when he chatted casually with some of the old hands at the back of the campaign bus as he used to in the old days, the young ones were there, too. They didn't know the old rules and they broke an embarrassing story stating he'd resigned in 1975 because Trudeau had failed to back him on voluntary wage and price controls.

"In the bus, for God's sake," Turner said later. "And Tom Walkom of the *Globe and Mail* said he was going to file it, so Val [Sears] had to cover for *The Star* and so did Bill Casey for the CBC. I don't blame Val or Casey. Those guys are all right. But that Walkom! This *Globe and Mail*, you know! I've never had a thing broken in a bus in my life. And I wasn't talking about resignation there. We were talking about wage and price controls and then we got back to voluntary controls and I said, 'We might have had those voluntary controls but the Prime Minister would not commit.' And then, of course, you saw that the labour leaders, Joe Morris, Bill Mahoney, and Stan Little, backed me up. I mean, I'm sorry it came out but, goddamn it, we would have had that thing."

The story was denied by Trudeau, distressed Turner, and was another setback in the early stages of the campaign. "He [Trudeau] just waited for that occasion to dump on me," Turner said. "I mean, that was an extraordinary thing, and now I'm just delighted that the labour leaders came along and backed me up. I called Trudeau and, in restrospect, I shouldn't have because it made it look like an apology. And I wasn't apologizing. I just said to him that I was not talking about my resignation conversation with him. That was the only reason I called him and I did not retract what I said about his failing to back me on voluntary controls. And he said, 'That's not the way it was.' And I said, 'Mr. Prime Minister, that was the way it was.' And he said, 'Well, I'm going to issue a statement,' and I said, 'Well, issue a statement, but I'll consider the matter closed.' And he said, 'So will I after the statement.' Of course, he went out of his way in that statement, you know. But the labour guys backed me up. I liked what Joe and Mahoney said. You know, 'After Turner left there was never a close relationship with labour.' And that's what I'm saying now. I can get these guys together. I don't care whether they're supposedly for the NDP. I mean, in a human way they know what's wrong with the country and they want to make it work. I believe in that, you know."

But after the first few weeks and these few gaffes Turner regained his confidence. He began to run smoothly and hard as he had after the nervous starts in the sprints of his youth. The old drunken major who had trained him then had long gone to his pauper's grave but now the group captain had taken his place. Bill Lee taught him to coast through the press scrums by saying absolutely nothing. He encouraged him to relax with reports of increasing delegate support, particularly from the party establishment. They knew he could win the race as long as he ran confidently and didn't stumble. But they also knew it would not be a walkover. The champion had first to shake off a strong challenge from a tough, awkward-looking runner from Shawinigan, Quebec, who was popular with the crowd.

20

Mr. Prime Minister

Dalton Camp, the columnist and former Conservative Party president, once remarked that Jean Chretien "looks like the driver of the getaway car." Chretien has a crooked grin, caused by infantile paralysis in his youth, and a nose flattened from frequent fistfights outside the poolroom next to his family's tarpaper house in the rundown part of Shawinigan, Quebec. He was the eighteenth of nineteen children and the eighth of the nine who survived infancy and is about as opposite in appearance, style, and background as anyone could be to the handsome, patrician John Turner. Chretien's father was a worker at the local paper mill and also a Liberal organizer, and young Jean worked hard and long in the mill and in local politics until he found enough money to study law at Laval University and then win the federal election in the riding of Saint-Maurice-Lafleche in 1963.

He couldn't speak a word of English when he arrived in Ottawa and there were many who said he didn't speak much proper French either, but he was appointed Minister without Portfolio in 1967 in the same shuffle that made Turner the Registrar General and brought Pierre Trudeau into the cabinet as Justice Minister. And he subsequently handled seven senior ministries with administrative skill and personal popularity. Chretien, fifty, has always portrayed himself as a lovable "pea souper" and a populist underdog, although his daughter, France, married André Desmarais, son of Paul Desmarais, the powerful boss of Quebec's rich Power Corporation, so that his corporate connections were good and there was much money and a smoothly oiled organization behind him when he announced his candidacy for the leadership on March 20, four days after Turner.

Chretien was uncertain about whether he should run. The party establishment was not backing him. He had the support of only forty-four MPs, five senators, and three cabinet ministers. Most of the rest were in Turner's camp, including Labour Minister André

217

Ouellet, the party's powerful Quebec organizer who had been a key player in the Draft Turner movement of 1979 and now controlled many Quebec delegates, and Transport Minister Lloyd Axworthy from Winnipeg, who controlled many western delegates. Chretien also knew he would have to break the party's tradition of alternation because it was an English Canadian's turn in the top spot. But Turner's apparent mistake on the Manitoba language issue, his own pride in the achievements of the Trudeau era, and his streetfighting instincts helped convince him he just might win. So he made a belated but typically flamboyant entry into the race, cheered on by a busload of supporters who had set out from Shawinigan at six in the morning to be present for the announcement in Ottawa. He became the defender during the campaign of the record of the Trudeau government. He was the faithful and popular prince, claiming his right to proper succession to the vacant throne to counter the challenge of the usurper returning after eight years in exile. And he had the apparent though unspoken support of the King.

There were five others in the race, but none were given much chance. Economic Development Minister Donald Johnston, forty-seven, an intelligent, likable, though uncharismatic right-wing English Quebecer, was first to declare on March 8, seeking a head start to overcome the fact that he was not widely known and had no national base. He was followed by Justice Minister Mark Mac-Guigan, fifty-three, a left-wing humanist, who, it was said, had more university degrees than delegates although he had been working on the leadership race for almost two years before he declared his candidacy in Edmonton on March 12. John Roberts, fifty, the leftist Employment and Immigration Minister, entered the race two days later, proclaiming he was a reformer representing the "new Liberalism," despite his having been a firm backer of Trudeau government policies. Then, after the frontrunners Turner and Chretien declared, Indian Affairs Minister John Munro, fifty-three, jumped in on March 21 with a message that the party must not move to the right, and Agriculture Minister Eugene Whelan, fifty-nine, was last to enter on April 12, wearing his green stetson as a trademark and declaring he was the world's best-known politician, although he had no real power base in Canada.

The way Canada chooses its leaders had changed. When Walter Gordon called Lester Pearson three days before the January, 1958, Liberal leadership convention and asked who his campaign manager was, Pearson replied: "I don't have one."

"Meet the train at 7 a.m," Gordon said. "I'll be on it and I'll do the job for you. And bring along your list of delegates."

"I don't have a list of delegates," Pearson protested.

Gordon suggested he get the list from his headquarters, but Pearson said he didn't have any headquarters either, and when Gordon asked who was raising money for him, he replied: "No one." Gordon booked a suite in the Chateau Laurier as headquarters and wrote a personal cheque for $3,000 and that was the entire cost of the campaign. Nevertheless, Pearson won on the first ballot over Paul Martin, whose ostentation in greeting delegates as they arrived at the railway station was frowned upon.

In contrast, in 1968 there had been the excitement of Trudeaumania, intense and sophisticated organization, computerized delegate lists, the cross-country circus by eight high-profile candidates to woo delegates in slow, little, borrowed aircraft – all the hoopla of an American-style political convention and costs that amounted to $128,000 for candidate John Turner and up to $200,000 for some of the others.

Now, in 1984, the Liberal Party put a limit of $1.6 million on each candidate's costs and some of them came close to spending that huge amount. Toward the end of the 1984 leadership campaign Turner's costs were estimated at about $1.2 million. Chretien's were expected to be at least the same or even more. Some of the "pack candidates" trailing far behind the leaders with little chance of winning spent well over $500,000 on highly organized campaigns that threatened to throw them into deep personal debt.

One candidate emerged from this pack. Donald Johnston, the man with no charisma who is actually convivial and charming in private, began to look human when he appeared at candidates' meetings with a black eye received in a tennis match. He attracted delegates also with a series of firm policy statements that were not always in line with those of the government. Johnston was hampered by a reputation as a far right-winger and his attempts to alter that image were reminiscent of those of the late Robert Winters, who almost defeated Pierre Trudeau in 1968 and who used to say: "Tell me where the centre is, and I'll tell you where I stand." But Johnston's policies were not new. Many of them were carbon copies of policies propounded by the youthful John Turner in the 1968 leadership campaign and in subsequent cabinet posts. They included a transfer of power from the Prime Minister and cabinet to the House of Commons, recognition of the regional diversities of the provinces, encouragement of new high-technology industries, development of small business by tax incentives as a key to creating permanent jobs, freer trade, and more control over free-spending bureaucrats. Johnston also proposed a guaranteed annual income, which Turner had once flirted with and dropped, and the sale of many Crown corporations.

219

The polls showed, however, that the real fight was always between the two frontrunners, Turner and Chretien; that neither Johnston nor any of the others in the pack had enough third-place support to sneak through the middle and win or even become kingmaker at a close convention. They also showed that Chretien was closing on Turner as the campaign progressed. But there was not as much excitement and uncertainty as there had been in 1968. The candidates spent much time away from the Commons, but the majority government was in no danger of losing a vote, as it did then.

The selection of the 3,437 delegates was in general orderly and fair. There were no scandals as in the Tory leadership campaign won by Brian Mulroney the year before, when party meetings were stacked with alcoholics and nine-year-olds, although some anonymous organizing of "instant Liberals," particularly among ethnic groups, produced a few strange moments and odd results.

The main exchanges took place at five all-candidates' meetings in major cities and they resulted mainly in polite and friendly expressions of their differences despite many often veiled references to frontrunner Turner's resignation from the Commons and his Bay Street image. The country, said Chretien continuously, needed a man from Main Street, not Bay Street, and he stressed his own faithful and uninterrupted service to the Liberal cause. The self-styled *petit gars* from Shawinigan delivered much the same speech throughout the campaign, a passionate and eloquent appeal to the heart, full of patriotic sentiment, humour aimed mainly at himself, and commitment to the policies of the past. He insisted that minority language rights were a national responsibility, that Canada needed a strong central government, and that attempts to cut the deficit of about $30 billion would cause too much suffering in the current economic circumstances.

Turner, on the other hand, promised to cut the deficit by 50 per cent in seven years and create jobs by restoring national confidence so that business and consumers would be willing to invest and spend again. He proposed tax reform for small and medium-sized businesses and plans to help workers retrain to meet technological change. He also urged freer trade and greater co-operation with the provinces, and he vowed to build a truly national party by particularly catering to western needs and aspirations. Turner took what he called "the high road," refusing to criticize other candidates and claiming he intended to fight Tories, not Grits.

He was nervous and rusty at first, after his eight years away from politics, but gradually his speeches improved and as he talked with the delegates, remembering names, clutching each hand and staring straight in the eyes, making each man or woman feel that for at least that moment they were the most important person on earth to him, the old feeling he had described in his political youth returned – that "walking into a roomful of people was like stepping into a warm bath." He began at last to enjoy himself, and, more importantly, he began to look like the winner he was supposed to be in the first place. And being a winner was what the leadership campaign was mainly about.

The Liberal Party is as much about power and patronage as it is about policies. An election against the Tories, revitalized by the leadership of Brian Mulroney, had to be held within a few months. In the circumstances, Turner seemed to have the race won when several public polls late in the campaign showed that there was a better chance of winning with him than there was with the more popular Chretien. These polls coincided with his own, taken by Angus Reid and Associates, which showed that by far the most important consideration of delegates was who could win an election (followed by who could make the party truly national again). So Turner gained confidence. But he could still make a mistake at the convention in Ottawa on June 13 to 16.

Ottawa had changed since 1968. Where there had been only a few hotels, now there were more than thirty. For a good meal then a politician, deputy minister, or journalist on expenses had to cross the river to Madame Burger's or the Chateau Neuf in Hull. Now there were classy restaurants on almost every corner packed every lunchtime with apparently prosperous civil servants and secretaries. In 1984 there seemed to be a security guard for almost every patron at the National Art Gallery and the son or daughter of a political power broker in almost every minister's office, solving at least to some extent the country's unemployment problem. The business of government had burgeoned enormously since the last Liberal leadership convention and now the capital was a big, neat, and opulent city.

The buildup to this convention was more sumptuous, too. There were candidates' marquees in the downtown parks and empty parking lots serving seafood, barbecued steaks, hot jazz, and rock and roll; candidates' faces smiling from huge posters in yards and on street corners; placard-waving demonstrations everywhere, noisy and colourful and about as spontaneous as a prostitute's kiss. Only the hockey rink at the Civic Centre was the same as sixteen years before, hot and stuffy and packed with serious delegates, the smell of power in them as they questioned the candidates in workshops concerned mainly this time with youth and women's issues.

The rear-runners had to catch up in these workshops and some seemed to do well, but so did Turner and Chretien, with the

221

Shawinigan streetfighter obviously winning sympathy and some votes in his role as the popular underdog. By Thursday quite a few pundits were predicting Chretien would win on a second or third ballot. The excitement intensified. Now it all depended, everybody said, on the final speeches on the Friday night, on whether Chretien could win the hearts of the delegates with his passion, while Turner lost their votes with a poor presentation.

First, however, on the Thursday evening about 10,000 delegates, party supporters, and journalists packed the arena for a nationally televised tribute to Canada's fifteenth Prime Minister, Pierre Trudeau. (Joe Clark was briefly the sixteenth.) "Our hopes are high, our faith in the people is great, our dreams for this beautiful country will never die," said Trudeau, speaking without notes. He mentioned the major achievements of his long reign, notably the Constitution, the Charter of Rights, the defeat of separatism in the Quebec referendum, the institution of federal bilingualism, the promotion of women to high office, and the advancement of minorities in public life. Jamming his thumbs into his belt in his famous gunslinger pose, he described Liberalism as "not so much a program or a series of policies, it's an approach to politics, it's a belief in people." He proclaimed that Liberals "confront the powerful, confound the secure, and challenge the conventional," and he described the past fifteen to twenty years in Canada as "the period of the adolescence of our country, our coming of age." It was an eloquent speech and it brought tears to the eyes of many in the audience. The party presented him with a painting by Toronto artist Charles Pachter. Then, with typical panache, as he left the stage Canada's fifteenth Prime Minister performed a pirouette.

John Turner worked long and hard on his final speech, writing it himself from suggestions made by advisers and putting the final touches to it in the sunny backyard of his Toronto home the previous weekend. Bill Lee was particularly concerned about the speech and had reason to be. He had written a speech for Paul Hellyer's final appearance at the 1968 convention and so had Bill Neville, then executive assistant to Judy LaMarsh. Lee believed both were good, but Neville's was better and he wanted Hellyer to go with the Neville version that was full of humanity as well as policy statements. But instead Hellyer delivered a speech written mainly by Toronto tax lawyer William Macdonald, who was later to be the other main partner at McMillan, Binch with John Turner. It was an interesting economic treatise, but it was a terrible speech and it cost Hellyer at least 100 votes and possibly the prime ministership. So Lee advised Turner to be his own man and write his own speech. But he worried more than most about it.

Turner, who can occasionally make what he calls "a real barn-stormer," decided to play this speech safely. He had run consistently after a shaky start and was in front. He had not stopped to eat an orange as those older boys had in the well-remembered cross-country race he won at Ashbury College years ago. And he would not change stride now near the finish, as Hellyer had done so disastrously. So he put a speech together that was not much more than a summation of those he had made in the campaign. Turner was second-last speaker, to be followed by Chretien. The big crowd had received the other candidates' efforts politely, like mildly interested ringsiders watching the preliminaries in anticipation of the main event, although Johnston was given a rousing ovation.

Then, as Turner mounted the stage, the arena erupted in waving banners and a parade of provincial flags, a subtle dig at Trudeau's central Canadianism. He seemed confident. He spoke well without a single nervous throat-clearing that sometimes mars his presentation. The speech was not nearly as good as the one on the same stage in similar circumstances sixteen years earlier when the young politician had insisted that "I'm not bidding now for your consideration at some vague convention in 1984 when I've mellowed a bit. My time is now, and now is no time for mellow men."

But Turner had mellowed a bit since then. Now he looked and sounded like a leader and that was what was needed. He began by praising Trudeau. "No Canadian deserves more credit today than the Prime Minister in his search for peace," Turner said. "I have said on several occasions, but never face to face with him, that he has surely been the most remarkable Canadian of his generation." Trudeau, in his front-row-centre seat, smiled fleetingly and nodded at Turner. Then Turner launched vaguely and safely into his plans for the econ-omy – "no easy solutions, no quick fixes, but whatever we do, however we do it, it will never be done at the expense of the unemployed, the poor, the aged, the sick, or the disabled" – and into an attack on Conservative leader Brian Mulroney and his party: "We won't let the Conservatives sweet talk Canadians by painting over the old-style Tory principles of privilege and preference for the few. They don't fool me – they don't fool you – and they won't fool the Canadian people." The delegates stood and cheered and the sea of red-and-yellow banners waved.

Chretien followed and also took no chances. He read from a text, which caused him to lose some of his usual passion, and he, too, made much the same speech as he had throughout the campaign, stressing that he was "proud to be part of the Liberal record," and taking some veiled potshots at Turner, promising, "I will not move this great party to the right," and insisting, "We are selecting a leader, not a chief

223

executive officer." Most pundits ruled the speech match a draw, but Turner really won because he was in front and he hadn't lost any ground.

Bill Lee was busy in the backrooms. He had calculated that Chretien would have to have 1,250 of the 3,437 votes on the first ballot to have a chance of winning on the second. He visited the top organizers of all of the other campaigns or they came to him. Two key organizers of the John Roberts campaign, Bruce Ogilvie and David Hurle, met with him at the Four Seasons Hotel two nights before the vote and indicated a large number of their young delegates would go to Turner if Roberts himself decided to support Chretien on the second ballot. Whelan's organizer, Greg Ashley, phoned two days before the convention and said he'd like to talk. Lee sent a car to bring him to the Turner headquarters on Sparks Street and they had a preliminary conversation. Next day Ashley showed up at the headquarters unannounced and promised he would deliver sixty Whelan votes to Turner. Isabel Finnerty, Munro's longtime personal aide, promised she would deliver a majority of Munro supporters on the second ballot, even if Munro supported Chretien. Bruce Laird and Jim McDonald, of the MacGuigan campaign, made a similar promise, and Alex Macdonald, an executive assistant to Edmonton Mayor Laurence Decore, who was a key backer of MacGuigan, phoned to say Decore could deliver thirty Alberta delegates to Turner but he'd like to meet with Turner first. The meeting was arranged for the Saturday morning in a trailer at the convention site, but then Macdonald phoned again and said a phone call from Turner would do. Turner made the phone call. The Johnston team was more solid, promising to stick with their man, and so were the Chretien organizers, although the talks with them were friendly.

Lee stressed in the backroom discussions that Turner was making no promises, no deals, but that after it was all over Turner would continue on the high road with no criticism of any of his rivals. He suggested that all of the organizations should show their campaign books, with names of their key organizers and recommendations on their abilities, to whomever won so that the winner could make use of them in an election, and he promised to hand over the Turner books if he lost.

After these discussions Lee counted up his figures. He knew it was unlikely Turner would win on the first ballot. There were 3,437 registered delegates so that the majority of votes needed to win was 1,719 and he figured that Turner had about 1,600 of them on the first ballot. His estimate of Chretien's strength was about 1,100 votes, with the others holding about 750 among them. If more than 500 votes for the other candidates didn't swing to Chretien on the second ballot, which Lee knew from his backroom talks wouldn't happen, then Turner would win. It could be close, however, if Johnston, who might possibly have 300 votes, decided to move to Chretien and was able to take all of his supporters with him, which was unlikely. But, even in that event, as long as Chretien didn't have those 1,250 votes on the first ballot, Turner would win on the second.

Late on the Friday night, Johnston and Chretien held a private meeting to discuss the possibility of a Stop Turner movement, but Johnston, confident that he was securely in third place following the good reception to his speech, refused to have any part of a deal. Decore met with MacGuigan, warning him he intended to desert after the first ballot and would take much support to Turner, and urged him to consider dropping out of the race. MacGuigan did not want to lose a $25,000 deposit by failing to contest the first ballot, but he knew then that his campaign was over and he promised that he, too, would eventually go to Turner.

The arena was muggy and the atmosphere tense when the delegates gathered to vote on the Saturday afternoon. Turner, in a dark grey suit and red tie, his silver hair shimmering under TV lights, sat with his family around him. Geills, who hadn't wanted him to run, fresh in a neat blue frock, was waving happily to the delegates, adding greatly to her husband's appeal. Bill Lee sat on Turner's right, busy with telephones, and then, suddenly, External Affairs Minister and Deputy Prime Minister Allan MacEachen appeared on his left. When he was an executive assistant to Mike Pearson, the canny Cape Bretoner had persuaded Turner to enter politics and run in the 1962 election. He had contested the 1968 leadership campaign against his protégé and remained neutral in this one. Now his surprise, last-minute gesture, stage-managed at the arena by Lee, gave the Turner forces a profound psychological boost. Laurence Decore moved to sit in the Turner box even before the first-ballot votes were counted, causing MacGuigan to scold him: "I understood that we were supposed to stick together until after the first-ballot results." Brenda Norris sat behind her brother almost unnoticed. Many journalists wondered aloud who the attractive woman was. She had come a long way with John, from London to the miner's home in Rossland, to the little walk-up apartment in Ottawa, then to the luxury of the Ross mansion in Vancouver's Point Grey, sharing with him the mystery of their father. She was excited and proud. But briefly, in the middle of all of the hoopla and excitement, she thought of their mother, ill with Alzheimer's disease, and she wept.

Chretien was at the other end of the arena, with Aline, his wife of twenty-seven years, at his side, surrounded by row after row of blue-and-white banners and singing and shouting supporters, batteries of television cameras watching his every expression. Jazz bands played on the floor and people wearing funny hats danced. Campaign workers carrying walkie-talkies hustled delegates; delegates hustled other delegates; and journalists hustled everybody looking for indications of the first-ballot result. "What a crazy way to pick the leader of a country," somebody remarked in the crush. "It's a lot more civilized than shooting people," somebody replied. "You're right, you know," the first man nodded. And then he picked up a discarded banner and began shouting, "Turner, Turner."

It was after 5 p.m., two and a half hours after the balloting began, before Party President Iona Campagnolo announced that the count was complete. The madness turned to a hush. She read the results alphabetically:

"Chretien, 1,067 . . ."

Bill Lee turned to Turner and said, "You've got it." Turner looked worried. "How do you know we've got it?" he asked. "Because I've got the commitments on the second ballot," Lee said. Turner said, "Oh?"

"Johnston, 278," Campagnolo shouted into the microphone. A good result. Then, "MacGuigan, 135 . . . Munro, 93 . . . Roberts, 185," disastrous for all of them. "Turner, 1,593," about what Lee had expected but still 125 votes short of a majority. Whelan trailed with 84 votes, enough to save his deposit.

The result cast a pall over the Chretien camp. The candidate's homely face fell, but only momentarily. The banners stopped waving briefly. "We fell 200 short," said Pat Lavalle, one of Chretien's key organizers. "I can't see any way we can do it."

Then Chretien began to smile and wave again. "Chretien never quits," he told a reporter. "It's not Mission Impossible. But it's a tough situation. And I love tough situations. And when I'm having a tough situation, here I go. I fight all the time."

In Turner's box, Bill Lee, the baseball nut, switched the TV monitor from the convention to the game between the Baltimore Orioles and the New York Yankees.

Mark MacGuigan moved to Turner's box. It took him five minutes to move through the crush of delegates and reporters but he brought most of his support with him and Bill Lee was elated. He raised two thumbs in the traditional Air Force style and gleefully began to pass out red-and-yellow Turner buttons to the arriving converted.

Eugene Whelan, Turner's most bitter opponent in the campaign, made a long trek to Chretien's box and Chretien hugged him so hard his famous green stetson fell off. But most of his supporters went to Turner. John Munro moved to Chretien's box while his key aide, Isabel Finnerty, went to Turner's, taking many Munro supporters with her. Then John Roberts, his eyes brimming with tears, also moved to Chretien, after releasing his delegates to vote how they pleased. Many of them went to Turner.

Now it was up to Donald Johnston. Chretien supporters gathered around his box, chanting, "Johnston, Johnston," but there was no response from Johnston supporters. Then Chretien himself walked across the aisle and pleaded: "I cannot win unless you come." Johnston gave him a friendly slap on the back but stayed where he was. He intended to go down fighting as John Turner had in 1968. Then it was all over for Chretien and he knew it. He returned to his section shouting "Let's go! Let's go!" but he knew it was useless and so did his supporters.

Iona Campagnolo announced the results of the second ballot at 8:31 p.m. "Chretien, 1,368 . . ." In the Turner box Bill Lee punched the air, but Turner continued to stare silently at the TV monitor in front of him. "Johnston, 192," a figure reminiscent of the vote Turner held to the end in 1968. "Turner, 1,862." There was a great roar and the arena erupted again with red-and-yellow banners. John Turner leapt to his feet and Geills embraced him. His sister Brenda kissed him gently. "That's from Mom," she said.

John Turner and Pierre Trudeau met on the stage where all of the candidates gathered. There was warmth in Trudeau's eyes as he saw Turner place an arm affectionately around the shoulders of his youngest son, Andrew, and for an instant there seemed to be at least the bond of fatherhood between the two different men. But when Campagnolo announced Trudeau to the crowd he did not speak. He remained at the back of the stage, smiling his wry smile. And when Turner invited him to join him at centre stage, possibly to perform the traditional raising of the victor's arm, Trudeau remained where he was.

Finally the arena was quiet. Brenda Norris picked her way through the piles of discarded placards to a telephone and called the Lady Minto Nursing Home on Saltspring Island to ask the nurses if her mother knew what had happened. The nurses said they had seated her all day in front of a television set tuned to the convention. All day long Phyllis Turner Ross had stared at the flickering screen as her golden boy became Canada's seventeenth Prime Minister. But the reality didn't occur to her. All she saw were images and she didn't understand them.

Acknowledgements

This book could not have been written, of course, without the help of John Turner and I am grateful for his trust and confidence in me as an objective reporter. I also appreciate his opening of his life, including personal aspects of it, to a journalist at the height of a leadership campaign. This took courage. Geills Turner was also charming, frank, and helpful, and Brenda Norris, Turner's sister, was most gracious in her co-operation, which provided many insights.

I am also indebted to many colleagues, mostly in the national press gallery, past and present, who are also friends. Some are quoted in the book – some more than others and some not at all. Some of those who are not quoted earned that distinction by being good reporters of facts rather than commentators on them. Some are now dead. I found in my research that my old friend Bill Wilson of the *Montreal Star* was the chronicler of record of the era and I used many of his reports for perspective and understanding. But there were many others: Martin Sullivan, Peter Newman, Christopher Young, Doug Fisher, Vic Mackie, John Walker, James Stewart, Charlie Lynch, Blair Fraser, Tony Westell, Geoff Stevens, Peter Thomson, Richard Gwyn, William Heine, Al Fotheringham, Bruce Hutchison, George Bain, Val Sears, Arthur Blakely, Gordon Pape, Rae Corelli, George Radwanski, John Gray, to name just a few and risk failure to mention others.

One of the great reporters, Ray Timson, now managing editor of *The Toronto Star*, arranged with publisher Beland Honderich for my leave of absence and I am grateful to both of them. My immediate editor at *The Star*, Geoff Chapman, encouraged the project with his usual friendly professionalism. I never did meet McClelland and Stewart editor Richard Tallman, who removes himself from harsh reality somewhere in the countryside, but he proved to be not only classy with commas and quotation marks but knowledgeable on facts. There may still be some errors in the book, but several are not there because of his carefulness.

Beverley Slopen, my literary agent, was much more than that. She not only knows how to bring the cheques in on time, but is a journalist herself and a knowledgeable political junkie. Even more important, she was fun to work with. And the book couldn't have been written without the help of two other women, Isobel Holder and Rusty Anderson, who were John Turner's secretaries at McMillan, Binch. Rusty in particular helped overcome many obstacles, arranged access to many people, found many old speeches and pictures, and managed to be highly efficient and very nice at the same time, which is a trick. She took a great interest in both her boss and the book, and the book is partly hers.

Index

Duplessis, Maurice, 68, 70, 71, 74
Dupuis, Yvon, 97

Edwards, Claude, 134
Elizabeth, Queen, 77
Elliott, Fraser, 69, 85
Everard, Tim, 60

Fairweather, Gordon, 134, 144
Felkai, Frank, 211
Fielding, William S., 152
Finnerty, Isabel, 224, 226
Fisher, Douglas, 100, 156
Fleming, Donald, 93, 152
Forbes, Bill, 60
Ford, Gerald, 170
Fortier, Yves, 16
Fox, Francis, 199, 201
Francis, Lloyd, 134
Fraser, Blair, 105
Fraser, Malcolm, 57, 60, 186
Frum, Barbara, 139

Gage, Walter, 50
Galbraith, John Kenneth, 180, 183, 190
Gibson, Gordon, 96
Gill, Diana, 65
Gillespie, Alastair, 64
Gillespie, Michael, 34
Giscard D'Estaing, Valery, 172
Goldsmith, Oliver, 142
Gordon, Donald, 39, 64
Gordon, Walter, 38, 39, 83, 90, 91, 102, 104, 110-112, 115, 117, 118, 123-125, 218, 219
Grace John, 42, 92, 197
Grafstein, Jerry, 16, 18, 25, 29, 201
Graham, Alasdair, 212
Gray, Herb, 89, 92, 201, 211
Gray, John, 214
Greene, Joe, 13, 15, 16, 19, 26-29, 100, 104
Gregory, Gladys, 33
Gregory, Howard, 33, 35
Gregory, Jim, 33, 34, 37
Gregory, Marcella, 33
Gregory, Mary Margaret [nee Macdonald], 33, 34
Gregory, Phyllis [see Phyllis Ross]

Habib, Philip, 186
Haggart, Ron, 52
Hahn, David, 89
Hall, Belle, 144
Hall, Emmett, 144
Hanley, Frank, 87, 88
Harkness, Douglas, 84
Harley, Harry, 90
Harris, Lawren, 48
Harris, Walter, 152

Harterre, Gertrude, 79
Hartt, Patrick, 145
Hawke, Bob, 58
Hayes, Dick, 16
Hees, George, 134
Hellyer, Ellen, 14
Hellyer, Paul, 13-15, 26, 28, 29, 128, 153, 212, 213, 222, 223
Henderson, Lloyd, 14, 28
Highley, Francis, 52
Horner, Jack, 134
Horsman, John, 64
Howard, Frank, 93
Howarth, Dorothy, 75
Howe, C.D., 44, 45, 53, 72, 82, 83, 183, 210
Hurle, David, 224
Hutchison, Bruce, 123, 124, 161, 162

Ilsley, James L., 152

Jackman, Hal, 185
Jewett, Pauline, 90
Johnson, Al, 178
Johnson, Daniel, 70-72
Johnston, Donald, 218, 219, 223-227
Jolliffe, Ted, 130

Kaplan, Robert, 204
Karpus, Hank, 211, 213
Keay, Fraser, 82
Keenleyside, Hugh, 38
Kelly, Fraser, 106
Kennedy, John, 115, 121
Kierans, Emmet, 84
Kierans, Eric, 13, 26, 28
Kilgour, David, 85
King, Jeffrey, 201
King, William Lyon Mackenzie, 30, 53, 72, 86, 151, 183
Kinley, H.B. Morris, 54-56
Kirkwood, David, 65
Kissinger, Henry, 184
Knowles, Stanley, 161

Laing, Arthur, 52, 89, 96, 99, 118
Laird, Bruce, 201, 224
Lalonde, Marc, 134, 168, 178, 202, 213
LaMarsh, Judy, 29, 92, 222
Lamontagne, Maurice, 97
Lang, Dan, 16
Lang, Otto, 64
Laporte, Pierre, 145, 146
Laskin, Bora, 145
Laurier, Sir Wilfrid, 17, 29, 33, 86, 152, 210
Lavalle, Pat, 226
Lee, Bill, 28, 29, 210-214, 216, 222, 224-227
Lesage, Jean, 72

Printed in Canada